In this book, Professors Erikson, Wright, and McIver argue that despite what many observers see as the relative inattentiveness to state-level issues by the U.S. voter, state policies are in fact highly responsive to state public opinion. The authors find that while individual states vary both in the ideological division of their electorates and in the ideological direction of state policies, there exists a strong connection between opinion and policy, with liberal states producing liberal policies and conservative states producing conservative policies.

The authors base their analysis on a comprehensive study of state-level opinion surveys and an examination of state policy from the 1930s onward as measured by a composite of state policies in areas such as welfare, Medicaid, education spending, and consumer affairs legislation. The authors also examine the major role of state political parties, which must balance the ideological preferences of the general electorate with the more extreme preferences of party activists. They show that state electorates respond to these balancing acts. By their collective preferences in terms of party identification, state electorates reward and punish state parties for their degree of representation. Historical state differences in relative Democratic or Republican strength largely reflect which party has been closer to most state voters.

STATEHOUSE DEMOCRACY

STATEHOUSE DEMOCRACY

Public opinion and policy in the American states

ROBERT S. ERIKSON

University of Houston

GERALD C. WRIGHT

Indiana University

JOHN P. McIVER

University of Colorado

Published by the Press Syndicate of the University of Cambridge
The Pitt Building, Trumpington Street, Cambridge CB2 1 RP
40 West 20th Street, New York, NY 10011-4211, USA
10 Stamford Road, Oakleigh, Melbourne 3166, Australia

First published 1993

Library of Congress Cataloging-in-Publication Data
Erikson, Robert S.
Statehouse democracy : public opinion and policy in the American
states / Robert S. Erikson, Gerald C. Wright, John P. McIver.

p.   cm.
Includes bibliographical references and index.
ISBN 0-521-41349-4. – ISBN 0-521-42405-4 (pbk.)
1. Public opinion – United States – States.   2. State governments –
United States.   I. Wright, Gerald C.   II. McIver, John P.
III. Title.
HN90.P8E76   1993
303.3'8 – dc20   93-7076
CIP

A catalog record for this book is available from the British Library.

ISBN 0-521-41349 4 hardback
ISBN 0-521-42405 4 paperback

Transferred to digital printing 2002

Contents

v

Preface

In recent years, citizens of many nations have struggled to establish democratic institutions where none had existed before. As political scientists, we can ask what justifies this passion for "democracy?" Part of the answer is easy: political freedom. Empirically as well as in theory, where democratic institutions prosper, people are freer to speak and act without fear of arbitrary intrusion from government authority. But freedom *from* government intrusion is not the sole justification for democratic government. In theory, the democratic ideal of popular sovereignty means that collectively, citizens can *actively* shape what their governments do. The relevant empirical question becomes whether, in practice, democratic institutions allow public opinion to influence government policies very much. Modern political science is still working on the answer to this important question.

This book addresses the question of democratic representation for one set of democratic governments: those of the 50 separate states of the United States. The Constitution of the United States reserves many government powers to the states. The policies that states enact are often described in terms of their ideological content as relatively liberal or relatively conservative. We use this ideological dimension to assess the correspondence between public opinion and policies across the states.

We began this project several years ago, from a sense that public opinion had been seriously neglected in the political science literature on state policymaking. As we assembled our statistical evidence, we found a pattern that was even stronger than our initial suspicions: State ideological preferences appeared to dominate all other variables as a cause of the ideological tilt of a state's policies. This result further stimulated us to seek an understanding of the mechanisms by which state electorates are able to generate policy mixes that reflect their ideological tastes.

The states as political communities and as centers of policymaking have not, in our opinion, received the research attention from the political science community that they deserve. Political scientists' collective fascination with politics in Washington, D.C., has had the unfortunate consequence of neglecting the politics in the state capitals. At a time when the states are increasingly the primary policy innovators and much of the attention in Washington is consumed with dealing with or avoiding the federal budget deficit, the states should be an important focus for policy analysis, as well as for testing more general theories of politics. We hope our research will contribute to a renewal of the interest in comparative state politics that flourished in the 1960s and 1970s.

This book, however, is about representation as much as it is about state politics. In this we see our work contributing to a revisionist view of the citizen in politics. Earlier work focusing on individual opinion formation and decisionmaking through the lens of the sample survey found the typical citizen sorely lacking in the requirements expected by the standards of democratic theory. The role of the citizen in democratic governance, however, is about the values and decisions of the mass public – of aggregates – not about individuals. Taking this macro-view of mass behavior and opinion yields a significantly more favorable view of the coherence and the importance of public opinion in the United States.

To estimate the ideological preferences of the American states required a massive data collection effort. Our measures of state ideological preferences are mostly based on the cumulative surveys of CBS News/*New York Times*. Kathleen A. Frankovic of CBS News Elections and Surveys Unit, and Warren Mitofsky, then at CBS News and now head of Voter Research and Surveys, deserve special thanks for collecting these data and for making the CBS/NYT polls accessible through the Interuniversity Consortium for Political and Social Research. John Benson of the Roper Center was helpful for guiding us through the Roper collection of Gallup polls. The contributions of several individuals were indispensable for the task of making sense of what in effect was a cumulative survey of over 170,000 individuals. We are grateful for the help and advice of a number of students, some of whom served as research assistants, others as interested readers and critical consumers of our data: Joseph Aistrup, Betinna Brickell, Robert Brown, Darren Davis, Thomas Carsey, Kisuk Cho, Robert Jackson, Mohan Penubarti, David Romero, and Jeanne Schaaf. The data collection would not have been possible without the financial support of the National Science Foundation (grants SES 83-10443, SES 83-10780, SES 86-09397 and SES 86-09562).

This project made use of far more data than simply the ideological preferences of the states. For providing the wealth of state-level data that made our statistical analysis possible, we owe thanks to many among the community of scholars who study the politics and the policies of the U.S.

Preface

states. For allowing us to ransack their survey of state legislators, we owe special thanks to Eric M. Uslaner and Ronald E. Weber; for allowing us similar privileges for their survey of national convention delegates, we owe special thanks to M. Kent Jennings and Warren E. Miller. For generously providing us with his unpublished estimates of AFDC and Medicaid state effort, we thank Russell Hanson.

Several colleagues have contributed by reading and critiquing our work. We especially thank Christine Barbour, Thomas R. Dye, James L. Gibson, Virginia H. Gray, Alexander Hicks, Robert Huckfeldt, Kathleen Knight, Jon Lorence, David L. Lowery, Donald Lutz, Michael B. MacKuen, Bruce I. Oppenheimer, Benjamin Page, Lee Sigelman, James A. Stimson, Ronald E. Weber, Frederick M. Wirt, and Christopher Wlezien.

Some of our analysis draws on the material appearing in earlier articles: Wright, Erikson, and McIver, "Measuring State Partisanship and Ideology with Survey Data," *Journal of Politics* 47 (May 1985): 469–89; Erikson, McIver, and Wright, "State Political Culture and Public Opinion, *American Political Science Review* 81 (September 1987): 797–813; Wright, Erikson, and McIver, "Public Opinion and Policy Liberalism in the American States," *American Journal of Political Science* 31 (November 1987): 980–1001; and Erikson, Wright, and McIver, "Political Parties, Public Opinion, and State Policy in the United States" *American Political Science Review* 83 (September 1989): 729–50. The research reported here is appreciably updated from these articles, incorporating measurement of state ideological preferences through 1988.

1

Democratic states?

Unless mass views have some place in the shaping of policy, all the talk about democracy is nonsense.

V. O. Key (1961, 7)

Popular control of public policy is a central tenet of democratic theory. Indeed, we often gauge the quality of democratic government by the responsiveness of public policymakers to the preferences of the mass public as well as by formal opportunities for, and the practice of, mass participation in political life. The potential mechanisms of democratic popular control can be stated briefly. In elections, citizens have the opportunity to choose from leaders who offer differing futures for government action. Once elected, political leaders have incentives to be responsive to public preferences. Elected politicians who offer policies that prove unpopular or unpleasant in their consequences can be replaced at the next election by other politicians who offer something different.

Of course, this picture describes only the democratic ideal. A cynic would describe the electoral process quite differently: Election campaigns sell candidates in a manner that allows little intrusion by serious issues. Once in office, winning candidates often ignore whatever issue positions they had espoused. Voters, who seem to expect little from their politicians, pay little attention anyway.

The actual performance of any electoral democracy probably falls between these extremes. Acknowledging the factors that impede effective democratic representation, we can ask to what degree does public opinion manage to influence government decisions? This is an empirical question, often noted as the central question of public opinion research (Key, 1961; Converse, 1975; Burstein, 1981; Kinder, 1983; Erikson, Luttbeg, and Tedin, 1991).

Ultimately, virtually all public opinion research bears on the question of popular control. The most directly related studies are those that examine the statistical relationship between public opinion and public policies on

I

specific issues, a task that is never easy (Weissberg, 1976; Monroe, 1979; Page and Shapiro, 1992). On balance, the somewhat ambiguous evidence suggests that the government does "what the people want in those instances where the public cares enough about an issue to make its wishes known" (Burstein, 1981, 295).

Almost all U.S. studies of the influence of public opinion focus on the national level. However, the ideal place to investigate the relationship between public opinion and public policy would seem to be the American states. With fifty separate state publics and fifty sets of state policies, the states provide an ideal laboratory for comparative research. Yet there has been little research on the opinion–policy linkage at the state level. The decisive inhibiting factor has been the lack of good survey-based measures of state-level public opinion.

This book attempts to fill this research gap. We develop new measures of state-level opinion. They are the liberal–conservative ideological and the partisan identifications of the state electorates. These new measures are based on an aggregation of 13 years' worth of CBS News/*New York Times* (CBS/NYT) national opinion surveys. The resulting data set has rather large state samples, often exceeding the size of most national survey samples. It provides the measures we need to explore the relationships between the ideological leanings of state publics and patterns of policies in the states.

THEORY AND EXPECTATIONS

We approach our exploration of the opinion–policy connection in the states guided by some conflicting expectations. One starting point is the elementary "democratic theory" of the sort developed by the economist Anthony Downs (1957) in his influential *An Economic Theory of Democracy*. Downs's model in turn draws on the work of an earlier economist, Harold Hotelling (1929).[1] In its basic form, the Downs model assumes that voter preferences can be arrayed on a single ideological continuum, from the political left to the political right, with citizens voting for the candidate closest to their own position on this ideological spectrum. The basic Downs model also assumes competition between two political parties or candidates for majority support. These assumptions drive the outcome: Parties and candidates converge toward the middle of the spectrum, with the winner being the candidate closest to the median voter. Since the winning program converges toward voter preference at the midpoint of the ideological continuum, the policy result renders an accurate representation of the composite position of the electorate as a whole.

---

1. Political scientists generally refer to the Downs model; economists often call it the Hotelling model.

Democratic states?

How accurate is this Downsian interpretation of elections? Economists and political scientists tend to divide on this question. Economists who write of politics and elections generally accept the Downs (or Hotelling) model free of empirical complications, as if nonideological (or nonissue) variables did not matter. At the extreme, the economists' view of the political world reduces to figuring out what the median voter wants, as if (in the words of Plotnick and Winters, 1985, 460) "the political process proceeds straightforwardly to translate the median voter's preferences into public policy."

Political scientists tend to be more skeptical about the degree of democratic representation. To political scientists, the Downs model often seems politically naive, particularly in its assumption of ideologically interested voters. Voting studies show, for example, that vote choices are motivated by variables like party identification and aspects of candidate attractiveness that often override any considerations of the candidates' issue positions or ideological proximity to the voter.[2]

Political scientists are also sensitive to the strong role of political parties, particularly the parties' policy-motivated activists (Schattschneider, 1942; Morehouse, 1981). Very real differences between the preferences of Republican and Democratic activists (including candidates) preclude candidate positions from converging in straightforward fashion to the position of the median voter. Accounting for nonconverging candidates is a challenge to analytic modelers (e.g., Wittman, 1990).

Despite problems of complexity, the elegance of the Downs model has influenced political science greatly as a paradigm for electoral research. Electoral researchers know that while voters do not always vote for the candidate closest to their views, voters are influenced by candidate ideology among many other factors. Electoral researchers also know that while political parties and candidates certainly care about winning, they also care about the policies they will enact if victorious. A Downsian process may push government policies toward the center but also into competition with many other political forces.[3]

---

2. Economists' and political scientists' differing visions of democracy in practice can best be seen in their varying paradigms of legislative representation. Following the influential research of Miller and Stokes (1963; see also Stokes and Miller, 1966), the general expectation within political science is that representative behavior only minimally reflects constituency preferences. Political scientists are inclined to resist evidence of strong congressional representation as implausible, given the public's lax attention. Economists have a different starting point: Assuming the median voter is electorally decisive, why do legislators so often engage in the risky behavior of "shirking," or seemingly voting against constituency preferences? For a sampling of recent contributions from economics, see Pelzman (1984), Nelson and Silberberg (1987), and Lott and Davis (1992).
3. When ideological voting (or "issue voting") is probabilistic rather than determinis-

Thus, the correctness of the Downs model is a matter of degree. For candidates, appealing to the political center is important but not always crucial. One can imagine an electoral system inhabited by voters so inattentive (or uninformed) regarding the ideological positions of candidates that elected politicians enact policies totally unburdened by the constraint of public opinion. One could also imagine the opposite, a system in which the electorate actually dictates the ideological tone of government policy making. From the standpoint of democratic theory, this latter outcome may be the more desirable. But we must ask, How much is required of the electorate and of elected officials for public control of the direction of government policy to become reality?

Judging solely from what we now know about the political readiness of the typical voter, there might appear little hope for much policy representation in any political arena, let alone the U.S. states. Thanks to the classic *The American Voter* (Campbell, Converse, Miller, and Stokes, 1960) and subsequent research on electoral behavior, we have convincing evidence that individual voters tend to be rather ignorant and indifferent about matters of ideology and public policy. We should keep in mind, however, that collective outcomes, including election results, can be driven by a relatively small number of actors, not just those who are "typical." Economists know this lesson well. When, for example, they forecast a response in the national economy to a change in the prime interest rate, they naturally do not assume that the typical U.S. consumer is closely monitoring the activities of the Federal Reserve Board. But they do assume that some small number of economic actors will watch and serve as the engine for general economic change. We believe the political analogy here is quite plausible. While we would not expect the typical U.S. voter to respond to the politicians' everyday political posturing or specific roll call votes, some important individuals do pay attention, with consequences that can extend to the ballot box. Moreover, just as the Federal Reserve Board will anticipate the economic response to their actions, so too will politicians gauge and anticipate the electoral response to their possible actions.

The question is, Where on the continuum of possibilities lies the truth about democratic accountability? We know a lot about individual voters and some things about politicians, and not all of it is favorable for representative democracy. As U.S. government is currently practiced, are policies guided by public preferences? A discerning reader of contemporary political science might think not. This negative conclusion would seem to

tic, the exact median voter result does not necessarily hold. For instance, if issue proximity is represented as the difference in the squared differences between the voter and each of two candidates (the common assumption), then the equilibrium result is the mean voter preference. See Enelow and Hinich (1984) and Erikson and Romero (1990).

be particularly compelling when the discussion centers not on matters of central concern to the U.S. public, but rather on the arcane world of state politics. Sheltered from the public limelight and constrained by limited resources on the one hand and federal requirements on the other, state-level policy making would seem to offer little leeway for innovation in response to public demands. Understandably, tracing the policy impact of public opinion has received low priority in state politics research.

STATES AS LABORATORIES

The role of public opinion has been largely neglected in the study of state politics. One way of seeing this is to note the disjuncture in the importance of public opinion in policy studies at the national versus the state levels. In national studies, public opinion (and its expression through the electoral process) is frequently of central concern in explaining the processes of policy development and change over time. Public opinion has a major explanatory role in historical studies of realignment (Burnham, 1970; Clubb, Flanigan, and Zingale, 1980), national policy change (Carmines and Stimson, 1989; Stimson, 1991; Page and Shapiro, 1992), and roll calls and policy making in Congress (Miller and Stokes, 1963; Schwarz, Fenmore, and Volgy, 1980; Sinclair, 1982; Wright, 1986; Brady, 1988) and of course, voting in presidential elections particularly through the very extensive use of National Elections Studies data. The pervasive attention to the connections between public preferences and the actions of government on the part of scholars of national politics is not in the least surprising. Whether we try to make sense of the observed government behavior or try to assess the democratic quality of policy making in the United States, we fully expect analysts to incorporate the public's preferences about policy and judgments of politicians in their explanations of politics.

In sharp contrast to this familiar attention to public opinion at the national level, state policy studies have proceeded with only passing attention to public opinion. A contributory reason surely is a prevailing scholarly viewpoint that because state politics is beyond the attention of most citizens most of the time, there is little reason to expect state policies to reflect public preferences. In fact, more reasons are usually offered for why public opinion is irrelevant than for why it is influential. Jack M. Treadway's review of the state policy literature dismisses the contribution of public opinion this way:

There is every reason to assume a lack of congruence between policy outputs and political opinion. First, given the lack of public information and interest among the public, there will be many issues for which no public opinion exists. Second, even if opinions exist they must be conveyed to policymakers. Since few citizens regularly contact their elected officials, it is quite possible that opinions will not be transmitted to the policymakers. . . . Third, even if policymakers hear from the public they may choose to ignore what they hear. Finally, because the public is generally uninformed about the policy attitudes and activities of their elected leaders, they may not be aware of how accurately their opinions are being reflected by policymakers. A lack of congruence between public opinion and public policy could be perpetuated by public ignorance that such a situation exits. It seems likely that would be more of a problem at the state level. (Treadway, 1985, 47)

Treadway's articulation, though unusually explicit, is consistent with the generally implicit assumptions of much of the state policy literature. In practice, explanations of patterns of policy in the states have incorporated an impressive range of variables, but only sporadically have public preferences been among them. From reading the state policy literature, one might conclude that policies generate mysteriously from a variety of state-level variables ranging from state affluence to the professionalism of the legislature. The idea that policy choices might be driven by electoral politics – so common in the national-level literature – is seldom articulated in literature on state policy.

This neglect of the potential opinion–policy connection in the state politics literature represents a missed opportunity. At the national level, effects of public opinion are often difficult to ascertain because the rate of opinion change on most issues is slow and often entangled with the flow of events and policy change itself (Page and Shapiro, 1992). The states, by contrast, offer real-world laboratories for the comparative study of all sorts of political processes (Jewell, 1982). Since the individual states encompass groups of citizens of widely varying political attitudes and values, scholars can use this variation to assess the responsiveness of state policies to citizen policy preferences. Additionally, the states offer an opportunity for the analysis of the impact of political structures on the opinion–policy representional process that cannot be done at the national level, where but a single set of unvarying institutions prohibits effective assessment of their effects on representation.

Comparative analysis of the U.S. states, therefore, offers great potential for research on public opinion–public policy linkages. However, this potential has not been exploited. The reasons, we have suggested, appear to be twofold: a lack of adequate data on the preferences of state electorates and problems of conceptualization concerning the policy processes in state studies.

Measuring state opinion

The central reason for ignoring public opinion in the states is a practical problem of inadequate data on state opinion. The explanation for this gap

6

in our data collection was identified by Richard Hofferbert in his summary of the state policy field:

A glance at the literature makes clear the difficulty of studying all the intricacies of individual citizens' political participation. If such "micro" data are to be the basis of comparative analysis at the aggregate (for example state) level, the problems of data collection alone (not to mention conceptual difficulties) are nearly astronomical. . . . To make equally accurate estimates about the residents of all fifty states, one would have to interview fifty times as many people as are included in the national sample. Neither the resources nor the motivation to do a sample survey of 75,000 people has yet risen to the task. (1972, 22–23)

Still, some scholars have seen the relationship between public opinion and state policy as sufficiently important to risk assessing the role of public opinion indirectly. Not surprisingly, surrogate measures of state opinion have their drawbacks; each rests on tenuous assumptions regarding the linkage between the intended attitudes and the measurable variables. We consider some examples.

One common substitute for direct measurement is the "simulation" of state opinion from the demographic characteristics of the state residents (Pool, Abelson, and Popkin, 1965; Weber and Shaffer, 1972; Weber et al., 1972). For instance, Weber and his associates (Weber and Shaffer, 1972; Weber et al., 1972) "simulated" state opinion on a variety of issues. Using a two-step process, they first used national opinion surveys to establish the opinions that were typical for groups of citizens defined by their combinations of social and economic characteristics. The simulation then consists of constructing a state opinion index that represents an average of the groups' opinions weighted by the sizes of the groups in the states' populations.

Weber et al. report strong relationships between simulated opinion and policy on two of the five issues they examined. Unfortunately the simulation technique suffers from two important problems. One problem is that "simulation" taps only the demographic sources of opinion and not those due to the state's political culture or the state's particular history. Second, these demographic sources of opinion may reflect the causal impact of the socioeconomic indicators themselves rather than the impact of public opinion (Seidman, 1975).

We can also mention other efforts. In a simpler procedure, Nice (1983) inferred state ideological preferences from the state two-party vote in the ideological Nixon–McGovern presidential election of 1972. Nice found strong and significant relationships between the McGovern vote and several indicators of state policy, most of which survived controls for standard demographic variables. Although Nice produced some of the strongest evidence of policy responding to public opinion, doubters may question whether the predictive power of presidential voting is due to ideology or something else.[4]

Finally, the dilemma of how to measure state opinion is made evident from Plotnick and Winters's (1985) analysis of state welfare policy. Needing measures of "voter preferences for redistribution," Plotnick and Winters chose per capita United Way contributions and charitable deductions on federal income tax returns as a percentage of adjusted gross income. These measures performed miserably in an otherwise satisfactory causal model explaining state welfare guarantees. As Plotnick and Winters explain, "Although this first effort at measuring voter sentiments at the state level and identifying its effects on policy is disappointing, it demonstrates the need for better measurement of this theoretically important variable" (1985, 469).

Armed only with weak, indirect, or dubious measures of state opinion, analysts who dare estimate the opinion–policy connection cannot easily be sure of their results. A poorer than expected correlation can be due to poor measurement. A strong correlation, on the other hand, can be challenged on the grounds that the surrogate measure of public opinion actually measures something else.

State socioeconomic variables

In lieu of the generally unmeasurable preferences of state electorates, state policy researchers have focused on variables that they could actually measure. The central preoccupation of the state policy literature has been an ongoing contest between "political" and "socioeconomic" variables as competing explanations of state policies. Socioeconomic (or "environmental") variables, by almost all accounts, are the winners of this contest. Such variables as state wealth, urbanism, and education appear to be the best predictors of state policy. These predictors work at the expense of certain political variables, such as voter participation, party competition, and the quality of legislative apportionment. With socioeconomic variables controlled, these political variables do not predict policy liberalism in the manner once hypothesized (Dawson and Robinson, 1963; Dye, 1966; Hofferbert, 1966, 1974).

Yet considerable uncertainty exists regarding what the socioeconomic indicators actually measure. An early and influential view is Dye's "economic development" interpretation (1966, 1979). Dye posited that the socioeconomic measures reflect the stages of economic development through which states evolve. As states become more developed, they also

---

4. The 1972 presidential vote has often been used as a surrogate for the ideological preferences of congressional districts. See, e.g., Schwarz and Fenmore (1977) and Erikson and Wright (1980).

adapt a predictable set of policies. But while the state's economic base and social needs matter, state politics does not.

Dye's analysis was widely interpreted to mean that the workings of the democratic political process are largely irrelevant to understanding state policy. But this verdict now seems premature. For instance, it may have been naive to assume that if "political" variables like party competition, voter turnout, and proper apportionment enhance popular control, they would always do so by stimulating liberal or pro-"have-not" policies. A better assumption would have been that these variables enhance the democratic process by facilitating the translation of the majority viewpoint into law, whether it is liberal or conservative (Godwin and Shepard, 1976; Uslaner, 1978; Plotnick and Winters, 1985).

More important for our purposes is the question of whether the predictive power of the socioeconomic variables reflects something more than the deterministic force of economic development. On this, the early literature expressed a certain ambivalence.[5] Some scholars have expressed the view that socioeconomic variables reflect the input of political "demands" (Jacob and Lipsky, 1968; Godwin and Shepard, 1976; Sigelman and Smith, 1980; Hayes and Stonecash, 1981). The difference between seeing socioeconomic variables as reflecting economic development and seeing them reflecting political demands may seem little more than a matter of semantics. But if we go one step further and substitute "public opinion" for political "demands," we can begin to see the importance of this distinction. We may then speculate that the predictive power of socioeconomic variables is due to the correlation of these variables with the unobserved variable of public opinion, which is actually a major determinant of state policy. Dye (1990, chap. 2) offers an interesting exposition of this new interpretation.

We have, then, two distinct views of what socioeconomic variables stand for. Seen as nonpolitical indicators of economic development, socioeconomic variables cause policy through some unspecified, but nonpolitical process. Elections, legislators, interest groups, and citizens play out their roles in a sideshow devoid of policy consequences. The implications

---

5. Consider a typical example from the literature of the 1960s and 1970s. From conducting a factor analysis on state socioeconomic characteristics, Hofferbert (1968) identified the two dominant dimensions as "industrialization" and "cultural enrichment." Labeling a factor as "cultural enrichment" would seem to imply that it taps citizens' values and preferences rather than economic determinism. However, labeling a socioeconomic composite as "opinion" or "values" requires a strong act of faith. It is difficult to give an unambiguous attitudinal interpretation to factors that are made up of indicators of wealth, ethnicity, and education. This uncertainty about what is measured is reflected in Hofferbert's subsequent analysis in which the cultural enrichment label is converted to an equally apt but perhaps safer choice of "affluence" (Sharkansky and Hofferbert, 1969; Hofferbert, 1974).

for meaningful democratic governance could hardly be more perverse. But when the same socioeconomic indicators are seen as measures of public opinion, the findings that socioeconomic variables "cause" policy yields a positive message about democracy in the U.S. states. High correlations between environmental measures and policy show that public demand is usually satisfied; state politics "works." In fact, in this view, low correlations between socioeconomic measures and policy would be evidence that state political institutions fail to translate public preferences into policy.

In summary, the role of state public opinion has not fared well in the comparative study of state policy. Much of the literature has emphasized the importance of socioeconomic variables. These variables are easily quantifiable and predictably potent, but their theoretical meaning continues to be unclear. Variables that are not readily measurable, like state public opinion, have received lesser recognition. Studies that do give state public opinion full attention are handicapped by severe problems of measurement.

THE PRESENT STUDY

Our thesis is that public opinion is of major importance for the determination of state policy. We will show that in terms of ideological direction, state policies tend to reflect the ideological sentiment of the state electorates. Moreover, we will show that party elites and two-party electoral politics, as these interact in the American states, are crucial elements in the linkage process. The progression of our argument can be seen in the following summary of the chapters to come.

Chapter 2 introduces our state opinion data. From pooling CBS News/*New York Times* surveys from 1976 to 1988, we obtain measures of state ideological identification and state partisan identification. Chapter 2 presents this data and describes the reliability and stability of the new measures of state opinion. Chapter 3 asks the question of where these differences in ideology and partisanship among the states come from. While some of the state-to-state differences in ideology and partisanship are attributable to differences in demography, we also find that state of residence has a large impact on citizens' liberalism–conservatism and partisanship even after state demographics are taken into proper account. States are active and meaningful political communities whose electorates have distinctive preferences; the states are not just collections of atomistic individuals whose opinions automatically flow from their personal socioeconomic characteristics.

Chapter 4 introduces our composite measure of state policy liberalism. This chapter shows that the ideological direction of state policy largely follows from the state citizens' mean ideological preference. Policy and opinion, in other words, are highly correlated. As part of this demonstration, Chapter 4 shows that the well-known correlations between socioeconomic variables and policy liberalism (previously discussed) actually reflect the effect of opinion on policy. To the extent that socioeconomic variables predict policy, they do so because they correlate with state opinion.

Chapter 5 shows how the ideological preferences of Democratic and Republican elites reflect the pull of their own "extreme" ideologies in one direction and the push of the electorate's ideological moderation in the other direction.

Chapter 6 presents our general model of the policy process in the states. It shows how state electorates control the ideological tone of state policy by rewarding the state parties closest to their own ideological views, and how party control does have policy effects, albeit in ways that are more complex than is commonly thought.

Chapter 7 examines the theory of state political culture developed by political scientist Daniel Elazar. We find rather strong evidence that Elazar's typology of state cultures distinguishes among states in terms of their representational processes.

Chapter 8 renews the focus on state elections by using Election Day exit poll data to assess the different ways states vote for president, U.S. senator, and governor. Here we find important interoffice differences in some patterns of electoral behavior. Our analysis includes factors from both the micro- and macrolevels to demonstrate an important relationship between state partisanship and state ideology that is completely missed at either level alone.

Chapter 9 examines the state representation process – from the 1930s to the present – by utilizing Gallup poll questions to create aggregate measures of state ideology and state partisanship.

Chapter 10 summarizes our findings in accounting for how apathetic and generally poorly informed state electorates are able to achieve remarkably high levels of popular control over a broad range of state policies. The process is anything but automatic; representation requires electoral competition and motivated party activists to achieve statehouse democracy.

2

Measuring state partisanship and ideology

When analysts classify the citizens of the various American states in terms of their political differences and similarities, the standards most often imposed are in terms of partisanship and ideology. One can generally classify a state's partisan tendencies with some assurance, since we can make inferences from state voting patterns and, in some instances, party registration. Classifying electorates on the basis of ideology is riskier for the reason that available indicators of ideology are at best indirect. Politically knowledgeable observers do commonly attribute liberal or conservative tendencies to state electorates. Among the factors that enter into these impressionistic judgments are the states' electoral affinities for liberal and conservative candidates, the ideological proclivities of their congressional delegations, and the general imprints of their unique political histories. Still, it is far from certain that state electorates' ideological reputations are deserved. It may be an unwarranted leap of democratic faith to attribute ideological motive to ideological consequences.

For our investigation of the public opinion–policy connection in the U.S. states, the most crucial challenge is the measurement of state-level public opinion. This chapter presents our measures of state-level ideological identification and partisan identification, from CBS/NYT polls. Our overall strategy is straightforward. We simply aggregate by state the responses to the 122 national CBS/NYT telephone polls for the period 1976–88. These polls are conducted on a continuous basis, maintain the same questions for party identification and ideology throughout the time period, and use a sampling design that serves our purposes very well.

Actually, CBS/NYT conducts three different types of surveys: general surveys representative of the full adult population, surveys of only registered voters (interviewees are screened for registration at the beginning of the interview), and Election Day polls of voters as they leave the voting booths. The first two are telephone interviews and employ identical sampling designs. The exit polls, which are quite different, include fewer states and are not used for our estimates of state partisanship and ideology. (We do, however, make occasional use of exit poll data apart from our main analysis.)

For our state estimates, we combined 122 CBS/NYT surveys. Of these, 113 are general population surveys, and 9 are registered voter polls. Respondents were asked about their party identification in all 122 surveys. In 118 surveys, they were asked their ideological identification. Our file contains 167,460 respondents from 48 states plus the District of Columbia. Of these, 157,393 revealed their party identifications by telling CBS/NYT interviewers they were a Democrat, Republican, or Independent. And 141,798 gave usable ideological identifications as "liberals," "conservatives," or "moderates."

The number of respondents per state is built up through aggregation by state and over time. The state sample sizes vary directly as a function of state population – the correlation between our state sample size and state 1980 population is .99. Since state populations vary substantially, so do the sizes of our state samples. While the state samples contain about 3,500 respondents *on the average* (certainly an adequate number), the variability is such that some states have more respondents than necessary and others not enough. At one extreme, over 14,000 Californians and over 11,000 New Yorkers were interviewed over the 1976–88 time period. At the other extreme, fewer than 600 respondents were interviewed in the least populous states of Wyoming, Delaware, South Dakota, North Dakota, and Nevada. Our smallest working "*N*" is the set of only 292 self-proclaimed liberals, moderates, or conservatives in the state of Wyoming.

An even greater concern than adequate *N*s for the state samples is the potential problem of unrepresentative samples at the state level. For periodic national *in-person* surveys conducted for the National Election Studies, for annual General Social Surveys, or for commercial polls like the Gallup poll, the pooling of respondents by states would produce misleadingly inefficient estimates. Typically, all of a state's respondents in a national survey will reside in only one or two counties (and a few neighborhoods within these counties). Moreover, for understandable reasons of convenience, survey organizations tend to maintain the same counties in their sampling frames for up to a decade or more. Thus, even with a large pooled *N*, a state's sample may be representative of only the small number of counties within the sampling frame.

Fortunately, the CBS/NYT surveys use a random-digit dialing design that largely overcomes this problem (Waksberg, 1978). The design has very small clusters compared to in-person surveys, and these are generally more widely dispersed geographically than interviews within the block clusters of personal interview samples. Rather than the 80 or so primary sampling units (or PSUs) typical of national in-person surveys, the CBS/NYT polls each have about 400 PSUs. This provides a wider dispersion of respondents and hence more efficient estimates of state opinion.

Technically, the CBS/NYT survey PSUs are defined by an area code and the first five digits of a valid residential exchange (e.g., [714] 527–09xx). Interviews are then taken from a sampling frame made up of hundreds of these sets of 100 possible numbers. Generally three interviews are taken from each exchange for a given survey. CBS/NYT surveys draw new sampling frames about once every two years. Aggregating over these different sampling frames increases the number of communities and areas from which respondents in these surveys, and hence from each state, have been selected. Thus, there is good reason to expect that these data, taken together, constitute valid samples of the individual states for the time period.

One final point deserves mention. For our construction of state measures of partisanship and ideology, we include CBS/NYT survey respondents in the relatively small number of "registered voter only" surveys. In a related decision, we count the "raw" numbers of respondents without employing the weights suggested by CBS/NYT surveys for improving the representativeness of the samples. The alternative would be to weight respondents, but also jettison the precious respondents from "registered only" samples. (For further discussion of the technical considerations, see Wright, Erikson, and McIver, 1985.) Strictly speaking, our state estimates are not strictly representative of state adult populations, but rather tilt slightly toward what might be called the "active electorate."

Presenting state partisanship and ideology

In the CBS/NYT surveys, respondents' partisanship is measured by their answers to the question, "Generally speaking, do you consider yourself a Republican, a Democrat, an Independent, or what?" Ideology is assessed by asking the questions: "How would you describe your views on most political matters? Generally, do you think of yourself as liberal, moderate, or conservative?" These questions are similar to the standard American National Election Study questions on partisan and ideological identification.

Tables 2.1 and 2.2 present the results of our state aggregations for the 48 contiguous states plus the District of Columbia. (No estimates are available for Alaska and Hawaii.) Shown are the percentages for each self-identified partisan and ideological category, as well as the number of usable respondents on which they are based. State positions on the two trichotomized measures are summarized as mean positions. These means

Table 2.1. *Partisan identification in the United States, 1976-88*

State	Republican	Independent	Democrat	Mean	N
Alabama	23.4%	32.2%	44.4%	21.1	2,419
Arizona	34.7	29.9	35.4	0.6	1,767
Arkansas	20.3	32.8	46.8	26.5	1,727
California	33.3	27.3	39.4	6.2	14,773
Colorado	32.6	38.8	28.6	-4.0	1,863
Connecticut	24.5	43.2	32.3	7.8	2,269
Delaware	28.7	40.6	30.7	2.0	443
District of Columbia	18.8	28.8	52.4	33.6	565
Florida	32.7	27.9	39.3	6.6	7,466
Georgia	21.0	31.0	48.0	27.0	3,814
Idaho	37.3	39.0	23.8	-13.5	724
Illinois	28.7	36.5	34.8	6.1	7,096
Indiana	32.9	36.0	31.2	-1.7	3,964
Iowa	32.4	38.1	29.6	-2.8	2,230
Kansas	38.3	32.7	29.0	-9.3	2,037
Kentucky	25.5	24.8	49.8	24.3	2,458
Louisiana	20.0	24.7	55.3	35.3	2,405
Maine	27.0	43.5	29.5	2.4	777
Maryland	24.2	29.4	46.4	22.2	2,996
Massachusetts	15.8	50.0	34.2	18.3	4,158
Michigan	29.8	38.3	31.9	2.1	6,806
Minnesota	27.3	35.8	36.8	9.5	3,181
Mississippi	27.0	29.2	43.8	16.7	1,416
Missouri	26.8	38.6	34.6	7.8	3,583
Montana	27.4	40.4	32.2	4.7	594
Nebraska	40.2	28.9	30.9	-9.3	1,252
Nevada	31.8	31.2	37.0	5.1	487
New Hampshire	31.8	46.3	21.8	-10.0	760
New Jersey	27.5	39.9	32.6	5.1	5,252
New Mexico	26.3	31.7	42.0	15.7	843
New York	29.7	32.6	37.7	8.0	11,599
North Carolina	27.6	25.8	46.6	19.0	3,885
North Dakota	36.2	36.6	27.3	-8.9	495
Ohio	31.0	33.6	35.4	4.4	7,778
Oklahoma	29.9	19.2	50.8	20.9	2,115
Oregon	31.2	30.2	38.6	7.4	2,063
Pennsylvania	34.8	26.8	38.4	3.7	8,710
Rhode Island	15.5	56.4	28.2	12.7	614
South Carolina	27.5	33.2	39.2	11.7	2,304
South Dakota	38.4	21.3	40.3	2.0	717
Tennessee	26.5	34.2	39.3	12.9	3,149
Texas	26.1	34.5	39.4	13.4	9,696
Utah	41.9	33.5	24.5	-17.4	966
Vermont	28.6	48.0	23.4	-5.1	448
Virginia	29.4	37.9	32.7	3.3	4,245
Washington	24.0	44.1	31.9	7.8	3,179
West Virginia	28.6	22.7	48.7	20.1	1,559
Wisconsin	27.1	38.7	34.2	7.1	3,413
Wyoming	34.5	35.1	30.3	-4.2	333

Table 2.2. *Ideological identification in the United States, 1976-88*

State	Conservative	Moderate	Liberal	Mean	N
Alabama	40.5%	42.0%	17.5%	-23.1	2,142
Arizona	37.4	43.4	19.2	-18.2	1,578
Arkansas	36.8	44.6	18.6	-18.3	1,528
California	31.6	43.1	25.4	-6.2	13,369
Colorado	31.3	46.1	22.6	-8.6	1,724
Connecticut	29.4	45.6	25.0	-4.4	2,095
Delaware	32.0	48.2	19.8	-12.2	409
District of Columbia	24.6	44.4	31.0	6.3	504
Florida	37.1	42.9	20.0	-17.1	6,735
Georgia	36.6	44.6	18.8	-17.7	3,443
Idaho	42.5	42.9	14.6	-27.9	666
Illinois	32.5	45.1	22.4	-10.1	6,456
Indiana	36.0	44.7	19.3	-16.7	3,510
Iowa	33.0	47.5	19.5	-13.5	1,980
Kansas	36.5	42.9	20.6	-15.9	1,810
Kentucky	33.7	45.8	20.5	-13.2	2,103
Louisiana	40.0	43.0	17.0	-23.0	2,119
Maine	36.1	42.6	21.3	-14.7	685
Maryland	30.4	44.8	24.8	-5.7	2,723
Massachusetts	28.2	44.5	27.3	-0.8	3,704
Michigan	31.6	45.6	22.8	-8.8	6,135
Minnesota	33.2	46.5	20.4	-12.8	2,942
Mississippi	41.2	43.0	15.8	-25.4	1,223
Missouri	34.4	46.7	18.9	-15.5	3,167
Montana	34.3	42.5	23.2	-11.1	551
Nebraska	37.5	43.7	18.8	-18.7	1,128
Nevada	29.6	41.0	29.4	-0.2	446
New Hampshire	34.2	44.5	21.3	-12.8	685
New Jersey	30.1	43.2	26.7	-3.4	4,833
New Mexico	36.2	43.6	20.2	-16.0	746
New York	30.4	42.4	27.3	-3.1	10,619
North Carolina	37.8	45.1	17.1	-20.7	3,326
North Dakota	40.5	45.6	13.9	-26.6	447
Ohio	32.4	45.2	22.3	-10.1	7,013
Oklahoma	42.0	43.4	14.7	-27.3	1,866
Oregon	32.8	42.3	24.9	-7.9	1,890
Pennsylvania	33.0	44.5	22.4	-10.6	7,783
Rhode Island	29.0	44.1	26.9	-2.1	562
South Carolina	39.8	41.8	18.4	-21.4	2,128
South Dakota	38.4	47.2	14.4	-24.1	627
Tennessee	36.6	43.3	20.1	-16.6	2,764
Texas	40.6	42.0	17.4	-23.2	8,745
Utah	44.1	39.7	16.1	-28.0	868
Vermont	34.8	41.7	23.5	-11.4	405
Virginia	37.0	43.9	19.1	-17.9	3,948
Washington	29.2	47.5	23.3	-5.9	2,915
West Virginia	32.2	44.8	23.0	-9.2	1,348
Wisconsin	32.6	45.4	22.1	-10.5	3,113
Wyoming	39.7	38.4	21.9	-17.8	292

are calculated by assigning a score of −100 to each Republican or conservative, a score of 0 to each Independent and moderate, and a score of +100 to each Democrat or liberal and then calculating the mean in the standard way. Measured in this metric, the mean has an easy interpretation as the relative percentage point difference between the Democrats and Republicans or between liberals and conservatives.

The reader may wonder why we score liberals and Democrats as positive and conservatives and Republicans as negative. We do so for one practical reason. Later in this volume, we relate state opinion to state policy. State policy variables are generally scored so that "high" scores are in the liberal direction (money spent, regulations enacted, etc.). It makes good sense to score the independent variable and the dependent variable with the same polarity.

Consider first the estimates of state partisanship. Based on our mean partisanship scores, the map in Figure 2.1 portrays the partisan landscape of the United States. At the national level, the Democratic Party has outnumbered the Republican Party in terms of party identifiers, even during the Reagan era. So, naturally, we must find a Democratic edge for the states as a whole. Indeed, Republican Party identifiers outnumber Democratic identifiers in only 11 of the 48 sampled states. These Republican states are generally found scattered throughout the rural West and Midwest. At the other end of the partisan spectrum, the most Democratic states cluster in the South and Border regions.

Consider next the estimates of state ideology. Based on our mean ideology scores, the map in Figure 2.2 portrays the ideological landscape of the United States. Just as Democrats have dominated the Republicans in terms of partisan identification, conservatives have numerically dominated liberals in terms of ideological identification. But whereas some states tilt in the Republican direction, every single state in the union (with the possible exception of Alaska and Hawaii for whom we have no data) contains more conservative identifiers than liberal identifiers. The only political entity for which we have data that is more liberal than conservative is not a state. The District of Columbia, also included in the CBS/NYT polling, displays a slight liberal tilt.

The ideological map presented in Figure 2.2 shows the geography of ideology to be quite different from partisan geography. The most conservative states are found in the Deep South and in the rural West. The most liberal states cluster along the Pacific rim and in the Northeast.

Figure 2.3 presents the data in still another way, as a scatterplot between state ideology and state partisanship. In general, there is no discernible statistical relationship between state ideology and state partisanship. Indeed, the correlation coefficient is a mere .08. Only if we separate out the southern states does even a mild ($r = .48$) statistical relationship

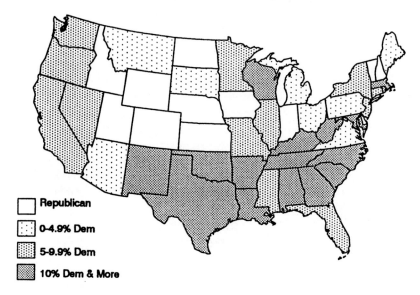

Figure 2.1 Map of State Partisanship (Percent Democratic minus Percent Republican).

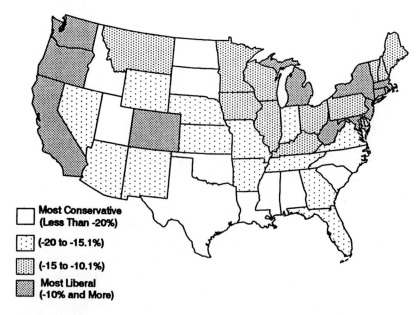

Figure 2.2 Map of State Ideology (Percent Liberal minus Percent Conservative).

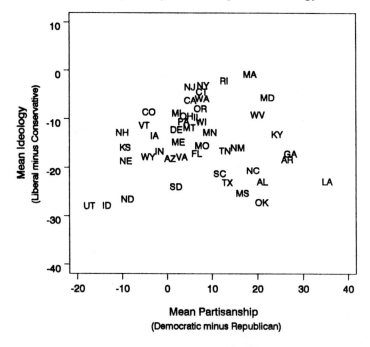

Figure 2.3 State Ideology and State Partisanship

emerge between the two indicators of mass political preference in the states. Figure 2.3 also shows clearly that the range of states on the mean partisanship index is considerably greater than the range of ideology. As statistical indicators, the standard deviations are 11.43 for the former and 7.30 for the latter.[1]

Nevada: A statistical outlier

In general, the estimates of state partisanship and ideology are quite reasonable. Even those estimates from states with relatively small samples generally possess a certain face validity. One exception, however, is the ideological score for Nevada. Based on the ideological preferences of 446 respondents, Nevada scores as the most liberal of all states, with almost a plurality preferring the liberal label. We believe that this score for Nevada

1. The District of Columbia and Nevada are omitted from the calculations for these statistical estimates of standard deviations and correlations. Except where otherwise noted, the statistics reported in this volume are based on calculations with the District of Columbia and Nevada removed. Regarding Nevada, see the discussion in the following section.

is so implausible that we substitute a more conservative coloring for the state in our map of state ideology.

Although Nevada certainly enjoys a reputation for what might be considered as social liberalism (legalized gambling and prostitution), there is little reason to believe it to be the hotbed of political liberalism that our pooled state survey would suggest. As judged by its presidential voting, the behavior of its congressional representatives, and the presence of a significant Mormon population, the signs suggest Nevada is quite politically conservative, like many of its western neighbors.

Important side evidence from CBS/NYT exit polls for Nevada clinches the validity of our concern about Nevada's ideology. Estimates of Nevada ideology based on over 2,000 CBS/NYT exit poll responses place Nevada clearly among the most conservative states. Among the 42 states with available CBS/NYT exit poll estimates of ideology, Nevada ranks 11th in conservatism! Our conclusion is that the observed ideology score for Nevada is a sampling fluke – a score that is substantively implausible but still within the range of remote statistical possibility, given the state's small sample size.[2]

This Nevada estimate presents a minor annoyance with no clearly ideal solution. We could ignore the problem and use the Nevada estimate in our analysis. Our results would be slightly less crisp than otherwise, due to our rigid inclusion of a clearly incorrect estimate. Alternatively, we could rig a simulated ideology estimate for Nevada, perhaps from exit polls. That solution, however, allows expectations to drive our measurement.

The solution we chose is simply to delete Nevada from our statistical analysis. This decision reduces our working N from 48 continental U.S. states down to 47. The forgone degree of freedom should not be missed any more than we would give serious regrets to the fact that Alaska and Hawaii have no estimates.

---

2. Readers with a statistical bent may wish to indulge in some details of the Nevada oddity. Given the Nevada sample size, the standard error of the Nevada ideology estimate is 3.2. This gives −0.2 ±6.4 as the approximate .95 confidence interval. The upper bound is −6.2, which would still be more liberal than most states. This might seem to be a compelling statistical argument for accepting the observed ideology mean for Nevada. Maybe the state is not as conservative as we thought. Consider, however, the exit poll evidence. Even though Nevada is a "small" state, it was administered statewide exit polls by CBS/NYT in 1982, 1986, and 1988, with a whopping total of 2,857 usable ideological responses. With our year-adjustment (set arbitrarily for the year 1982, see note 3), the exit poll sample estimate of Nevada's ideology is a quite conservative −20.4. Consider next the regression equation predicting our measure of state ideology from the CBS/NYT exit poll estimates, based on 41 states without Nevada. Forecast from this equation, an exit poll ideology of −20.4 translates to a predicted score of −18.3 on our scale. The standard error from the exit poll equation is 4.0 points. Thus, our observed estimate of −0.2 is 4.5 standard errors more liberal than the exit poll projection!

Measuring state partisanship and ideology
RELIABILITY AND VALIDITY

How reliable and valid are our estimates of state partisanship and ideology? Reliability refers to the replicability of an estimate, while validity refers to how well the measure taps the concept that it is intended to measure. The reliabilities of our estimates can be estimated easily by application of sampling and measurement theory. Validity would seem to present no difficulty here, in the sense that *accurate* survey estimates of party identification and ideological identification in the states would have strong face validity as evidence of state partisanship and ideology. We nevertheless examine the validity of our estimates by seeing whether our measures correlate with outside criterion variables in the expected manner. (See Carmines and Zeller's [1979] discussion of validity and reliability, as well as construct validity in particular.)

Reliability

Statistically, there exist two equivalent ways to define the reliability of a measure. One definition of reliability is as the theoretical correlation between the measure and its replication. The reliability of our ideology estimate, for example, would be the theoretical correlation between our observed measure and the parallel version we would obtain if CBS/NYT had somehow set up a "B" team to conduct a parallel set of surveys repeating the original methodology. A second, equivalent way to define the statistical reliability of a measure is as the ratio of the variance of the true score to the observed or total variance. For instance, if half of the total variance were true variance and the other half random error variance, then the reliability would be .50. If error variance can be estimated, the reliability of an indicator can be calculated.

Estimating reliability from sampling theory. Using sampling theory (e.g., Kish, 1965), we can estimate the error variance of the individual state estimates and average them to obtain estimates of the error variances for the state means on party identification and ideology. For each state, we computed the variance of partisanship and ideology around their respective means. Dividing the observed variance by the state N yields the state's estimated sampling variance. The estimated error variance for the full set of state scores is simply the mean of these estimated state sampling variances. Reliability is then estimated via the formula

$$\text{Reliability} = \frac{\text{total variance} - \text{error variance}}{\text{total variance}} = \frac{\text{true variance}}{\text{total variance}}$$

The resultant estimates for state mean party identification is a near perfect reliability of .967; for state ideological identification, the reliability is a commendable .923. One reason for the higher reliability for partisanship is the greater number of usable responses to the party identification question than the ideological identification question. A second reason is the greater amount of observed (total) variance in mean state partisanship.

These high reliability estimates are not surprising given the relatively large Ns for the state samples. They may represent an upper bound, however, because the estimated error variances are based on the assumption of simple random sampling. The clustering of CBS/NYT survey respondents by telephone exchange may slightly inflate the variance estimates – and therefore the reliability estimates as well.

Split-half estimates of reliability. Fortunately, we have one more way of estimating the reliabilities: the "split half" method from psychological and educational testing theory. Traditionally, the set of items used to form a scale are divided randomly into two subsets, and the observed correlation between them is used to estimate the reliability. Here, we first number our surveys by date; first, second, third, and so on. Next, we divide the set of surveys in half by assigning the odd-numbered surveys to one subset and the even-numbered surveys to a second subset. These subsets provide two parallel sets of estimates of partisanship and ideology for our 47 states for the period 1976 to 1988. The correlation between the odd and even half estimates are .955 for party identification and .865 for ideology, as shown in Figure 2.4.

These split-half correlations are not estimates of the reliability of our measures. Our measures of partisanship and ideology are based on roughly twice the number of surveys and twice the number of respondents as used for either split halves. To estimate the split-half reliabilities of our estimates, we "correct" the split half correlation by using the well-known Spearman-Brown prophesy formula.

$$\text{Reliability} = \frac{2r_{12}}{1 + r_{12}}$$

where r_{12} represents the split-half correlation. The resultant reliability coefficients are .977 for party identification and .927 for state ideology. *Concurring estimates.* The two methodologies lead to concurring estimates of the reliabilities. For state party identification, the reliability is a whopping .967 or .977. For state ideology, the reliability is a more than acceptable .923 or .927. To adjudicate the trivial disparity across methodologies, we split the differences and claim the reliabilities to be .972 for partisanship and .925 for ideology.

Technically, these estimates are upper bounds. To the extent state estimates represent sample clusters rather than state populations, the methodology based on sampling theory overestimates the true variance and,

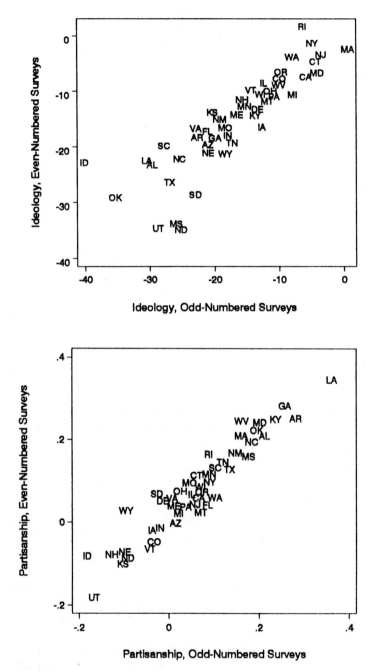

Figure 2.4 Split-Half Correlations for Ideology and Partisanship

therefore, the reliability. The split-half method also overestimates the reliabilities, for the reason that it reflects the stability of the split halves from the clusters employed and not the entire population.

The impact of sample size. Estimation error is concentrated among the smaller states with the smaller sample sizes. This pattern can be seen in Figure 2.5a. For the ideology measure, this figure shows the theoretical error variance as a function of sample size. Figure 2.5b presents the square root of this measure – the more familiar (estimated) standard errors, or the standard deviations of the states' sample means. Each state's .95 confidence interval, for instance, is approximately 1.96 standard errors around the mean. Note how sampling error clusters in the states with small sample sizes. From Figure 2.5, it is clear that we could obtain a further boost in reliability simply by jettisoning the smaller states.

Table 2.3 shows how reliabilities change when we restrict our states to those above the 25th, 50th, or 75th percentile in terms of sample size. The reliability of state party identification is always high, regardless of sample size. For ideology, we see a clear gradient as reliability increases with state sample size. Deleting the 12 smallest states raises the reliability from about .925 to about .96; deleting the 12 next smallest raise the reliability to about .97; and keeping only the 12 largest states pushes the reliability to about .98.

Validity

How valid are our measures? To be "valid," a set of scores must measure the concept that is intended to be measured. Most commonly, validity is established by "face validation." That is, do our measurements yield results that reasonable persons of diverse perspectives might agree look plausible? In essence, we have already asked the reader to join us in acknowledging the face validity of our measures when we offered the state scores for inspection in Tables 2.1 and 2.2 and accompanying maps. The scores are consistent with our stereotypes of where the different states belong relative to one another in terms of partisanship and ideology. Moreover, there is ample precedent for ascertaining Americans' partisanship by asking them whether they consider themselves Democrats, Independents, or Republicans or for ascertaining their ideology by asking whether they consider themselves liberals, moderates, or conservatives.

But we can make the validity test a bit more challenging. We can look for reassurance that our estimates of partisanship and ideology correlate with other variables with which they should correlate. For instance, partisanship and ideology as we have measured them should relate to other, more limited, attempts to measure these variables at the state level. In addition, our measures should relate to manifestations of partisan or ideo-

Measuring state partisanship and ideology

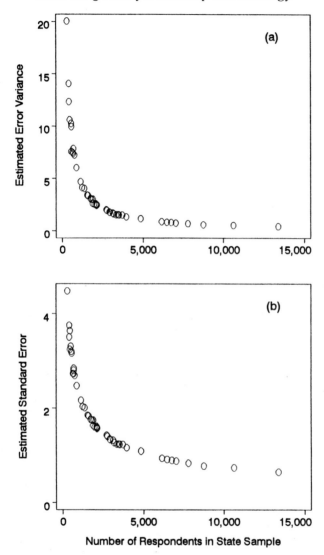

Figure 2.5 Sampling Error as a Function of Sample Size

logical behavior in the states. In this manner, we hope to demonstrate that our measures exhibit "criterion validity" (Cook and Campbell, 1979). *Exit polls.* In addition to their surveys of public opinion, CBS News and the *New York Times* have regularly conducted Election Day exit polls in selected states. Between 1982 and 1988, 42 states were the subject of at least one Election Day CBS/NYT exit poll in which voters were asked

Table 2.3. *Estimated reliability by sample size*

State Groups	Estimated from sampling theory	Estimated from split-half method
Partisanship		
47 states	.967	.977
Largest 35 states (state $N > 1,000$)	.979	.987
Largest 23 states (state $N > 2,400$)	.978	.989
Largest 11 states (state $N > 4,000$)	.978	.941
Ideology		
47 states	.923	.927
Largest 35 states (state $N > 900$)	.958	.959
Largest 23 states (state $N > 2,110$)	.971	.974
Largest 11 states (state $N > 3,600$)	.982	.976

their partisanship and ideology. For each of these 42 states, we pooled the exit poll estimates of party identification and ideological identification, adjusting for the year of the survey. Exit poll partisanship correlates at .92 with our measure of state partisanship; exit poll ideology correlates at .84 with our ideology measure.[3]

3. We used CBS/NYT exit polls of state elections, 1982–8. Exit poll estimates were year-adjusted by the following procedure. For states with more than one exit poll, exit poll estimates of partisanship and ideology were regressed on a set of election year dummies. The coefficients for these dummy variables were then used to estimate the partisanship for the base year (arbitrarily chosen) of 1982.

Measuring state partisanship and ideology

State polls. Our estimates of state partisanship and ideology are also generally consistent with the state aggregates from the polls taken by a myriad of state polling agencies across the last several decades. Correlations between our measures and previous estimates of state partisanship or ideology are shown in Table 2.4. These correlations fall within the satisfactory range of .79 to .86. Most impressive are the correlations between our partisanship and ideology measures and those from the much earlier 13-state Comparative State Elections Project (CSEP) of 1968. Given the 18-year time lapse between the CSEP interviews and the CBS/NYT surveys as well as differences in the methodology used to collect these data, we might expect estimates of state preferences to vary. Yet at the state level both party identification and ideology remained relatively stable.

Party registration. As part of our validity assessment, we can test whether our survey-based measurement of state party identification correlates with state party registration. Twenty-six states have registration by party (although the rules and procedures used by these states are quite diverse). For those states that do, party registration is closely aligned with public party preferences. Party registration data reported by Jewell and Olson (1988) permit us to demonstrate this connection. The correlation between party registration and mean state partisanship is .94.

Election returns. If mean state partisanship reflects the long-term partisan balance in the state electorate, we should see it related to the political behavior of state electorates. The Ranney index of interparty competition (IPC) summarizes partisan competition in state elections. It is constructed from three dimensions of party electoral success: (1) percentage of votes won in gubernatorial elections and seats won in state legislative elections, (2) the duration of party control of state legislature and governorship, and (3) the frequency of divided party control between governor and state legislature (Ranney and Kendall, 1954; Ranney 1976). Scores range from 0 (total Republican success) to 1 (total Democratic success). Following are the correlations between our two measures and IPC for recent years:

IPC	IPC/Partisanship	IPC/Ideology
1956–70	.78	.24
1962–73	.81	.20
1974–80	86	.10
1981–88	.82	.03

These results support the integrity of our measure of state partisanship. There is a continuing close relationship between state partisanship and competition between state Democratic and Republican parties.

Table 2.4. *Correlations between state partisanship, ideology, and measures of state partisanship and ideology from state polls*

State polls	State partisanship	State ideology
Network of state polls (Jewell, 1980)	.86 (*N*=7)	.79 (*N*=5)
14 state polls, 1974-78 (Jones and Miller, 1984)	.81 (*N*=14)	
12 southern states in 1980s (Swansbrough and Brodsky, 1988)	.86 (*N*=12)	
CSEP, 1968 (Black, Kovenock, and Reynolds, 1974)	.86 (*N*=13)	.79 (*N*=13)

State preferences should be reflected not only in state and local electoral campaigns but also in national political struggles. Table 2.5 reports how our measures of partisanship and ideology correlate with presidential elections returns, 1972–88. Here, we look for the vote to correlate with both partisanship and ideology. McGovern in 1972, Anderson in 1980, and Reagan in 1980 and 1984 are three candidates who sought to highlight ideological concerns. For each of these candidates, the state presidential vote correlated impressively with our ideology measure. In fact, ideology makes a generally impressive showing except for 1976. The 1976 Carter–Ford contest was almost certainly the least ideological of recent elections and perhaps the most partisan. State partisanship correlates more strongly with the 1976 vote than with the vote in any other recent election.

Summary. Our measures of state partisanship and state ideology correlate rather well with variables with which they are expected to correlate. Still, we have only considered a small number of the theoretically relevant correlations involving our two measures. Further evidence regarding the validity of these data will become apparent as we proceed through our analysis of the role of public opinion in state elections and state policy making.

Table 2.5. *Correlations between state partisanship, state ideology, and state presidential voting*

Presidential vote	Partisanship	Ideology
1972 McGovern	-.08	.72
1976 Carter	.81	.18
1980 Carter	.79	.26
1980 Reagan	-.61	-.61
1980 Anderson	-.43	.63
1984 Mondale	.46	.69
1988 Dukakis	.24	.69
1992 Clinton	.45	.47
1992 Bush	-.19	-.67
1992 Perot	-.13	.25

Note: $N = 47$ states. Vote is the percentage of the two-party vote, except for 1980 and 1992.

STABILITY AND CHANGE IN STATE OPINIONS

Our measures of state partisanship and ideology are actually estimates of mean scores over the 13 years 1976–88. We know that the national distributions of partisanship and ideology can change over the thirteen years of study. Our state means must therefore really measure average readings of changing scores. Change takes two different forms. "Across-the-board" change would be evidenced by movement over time in the mean score of the states. Across-the-board change affects the exact scoring of the states but does not affect their scores relative to each other. The second kind of change, which is a more important source of concern, is "relative" change around the (possibly moving) mean.

In the extreme, suppose states are constantly changing their relative positions, perhaps in response to short-term local shocks. States might move back and forth between the most liberal and conservative ends of the ideological spectrum or between the most Democratic and Republican ends of the partisan spectrum. If partisanship and ideology really are volatile, our 13-year average measure would represent too broad an averaging, and our scores would miss some politically important perturbations. On the other hand, if state partisanship and ideology are basically stable, then it makes considerable sense to average over as long a period as we have done. The more respondents one can gather into one's state samples, the better one can measure relative state differences.

Before we examine relative state change, it is helpful to get a fix on the degree of across-the-board change. Toward this end, we obtained separate measures of ideology and partisanship for each of the thirteen years, 1976–88. Figure 2.6 shows mean state partisanship and mean state ideology as a function of time. The figure tells different stories for the two measures.

Mean ideology was quite stable over the 13-year period. In other words, the popular notion that the electorate became more conservative during the Reagan presidency is not supported by CBS/NYT survey responses on ideological self-identification. While the electorate certainly preferred the conservative label under Reagan, it was no more conservative than before. For example, the lead of conservative identifiers over liberals was virtually the same during Reagan's second term (averaging 14.5 percentage points in the states) as during the Carter presidency (14.2)!

But in terms of party identification, the electorate did indeed change. As recently as the Carter presidency, the Democratic Party dominated the Republicans in terms of identification, with an average edge of 14.2 percentage points in the states. By Reagan's second term, this lead had shrunk to an average edge of only 2.8 points. Clearly, the Republican Party had made major gains, so that our average state partisanship scores represent the composite positions of moving targets.

In terms of across-the-board change, then, we find virtually none for ideology but a major movement for party identification. But what about *relative* change? Estimation of relative change is complicated because observed changes in the orderings of state means can result from measurement (sampling) error as well as from true change.

To investigate the degree of change in mean state positions, we separately measured state ideology and partisanship for the early ("time 1") and the late ("time 2") period of our analysis. Time 1 is defined as 1976–82, the late Ford administration through the early Reagan era. Time 2 is 1983–8, the postrecovery Reagan years. Each half contains approximately equal numbers of respondents.

Ideological stability

We consider state ideology first. The correlation between mean ideology scores at time 1 and time 2 is a hefty .857, indicating a considerable degree

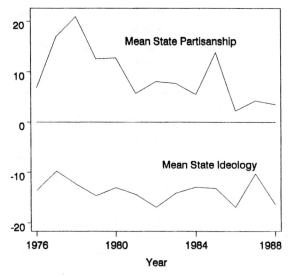

Figure 2.6 Partisanship and Ideology Over Time, 1976–88

of stability. The time 1 to time 2 ideology scatterplot is shown in Figure 2.7. The question is, Do the observed changes in mean ideology represent true change or do they represent the residue of sampling error? Our investigation shows the answer to be the latter. By any reasonable statistical interpretations, the observed differences in relative movement represent mainly random measurement error and only a little bit of real movement. Let us consider why this is so.

Just as we estimated the reliabilities for the 13-year average scores on partisanship and ideology, so too we can compute the reliabilities of the time 1 and time 2 scores. Then, we can adjust the observed correlations across administrations by the product of the square roots of the two reliabilities:

$$\text{Estimated true correlation } (x_1 x_2) = \frac{\text{observed correlation } (x_1 x_2)}{[\text{rel.}(x_1) \times \text{rel. } (x_2)]^{1/2}}$$

The estimated reliabilities and the resultant set of estimated true correlations are shown in Table 2.6. Using the reliabilities derived from sampling theory, we obtain

$$\frac{\text{Observed correlation } (x_1 x_2)}{[\text{rel.}(x_1) \times \text{rel. } (x_2)]^{1/2}} = \frac{.857}{(.865 \times .842)^{1/2}} = 1.004$$

31

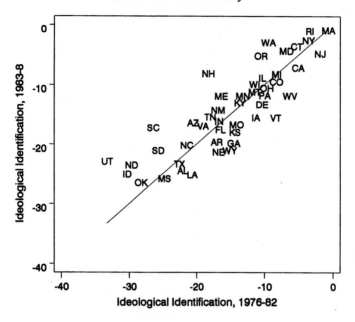

Figure 2.7 Change in State Ideology, 1976–88

for an estimate of perfect stability. The message is similar using the split-half derivation of the reliabilities:

$$\frac{\text{Observed correlation } (x_1 x_2)}{[\text{rel.}(x_1) \times \text{rel. } (x_2)]^{1/2}} = \frac{.857}{(.867 \times .889)^{1/2}} = .976$$

To split the difference, we call .99 the best estimate of the true correlation between state mean ideology in 1976–82 and 1983–8.

Consider why we obtain this estimate of near-perfect stability. First, note that the observed time 1–time 2 correlation of .857 is virtually as large as the .865 observed split-half correlation between odd- and even-numbered surveys for the 13-year period. If state ideology were at all unstable, the time 1–time 2 correlation would be visibly less than the split-half correlation involving two sets of observations that were intermixed across time. As additional evidence, the two time 1 and time 2 observed split-half correlations (time 1 odd with time 1 even; time 2 odd with time 2 even) are virtually identical to the temporally mixed correlations (time 1 odd–time 2 even; time 1 odd–time 2 odd; time 1 even – time 2 odd; time 1 even – time 2 even). Since the correlation does not noticeably fade with the time lapse between readings, the variation in observed readings must be almost all sampling error instead of true change. Finally, consider the split-

Table 2.6. *Reliability and stability of state ideology, 1976-82 and 1983-88*

Reliability	1976-82	1983-88
Derived from sampling theory	.865	.842
Derived from split-half method	.867	.889

Observed correlations	Split halves		Split halves	
	Odd	Even	Odd	Even
1976-82 split halves				
Odd	1.00			
Even	.77	1.00		
1983-88 split halves				
Odd	.80	.71	1.00	
Even	.71	.73	.80	1.00

Correlation	Full sample observed	Sampling theory correction	Split-half correction
1976-82 to 1983-88	0.857	1.004	0.976

half reliability of ideological change, or time 2 ideology minus time 1 ideology. The observed correlation between change for odd readings and change for even readings is a mere .127. Alternatively, the observed correlation between time 2 odd minus time 1 even readings and time 2 even minus time 1 odd readings is a mere .077. Neither correlation, of course, is significantly different from zero. Splitting the difference and computing the split-half reliability in the usual way yields a shaky "reliability" of about .17. Thus, almost all of the variance in observed ideological change is sampling error instead of true change.

As one clear revelation of the extreme stability of state opinion over the 1976–88 period, consider the observed time 1–time 2 correlation when the selected states are restricted to large states only, where the sample sizes are so large that there cannot be much sampling error. For these states, we should observe an extremely strong correlation, and we do. For the 11 states with over 3,600 ideological responses, we obtain a .97 time 1–time 2 correlation, which is shown in the scatterplot of Figure 2.8.[4]

Partisan stability

Next, we repeat our reliability exercise for time 1 and time 2 measures of partisanship. The time 1–time 2 partisanship correlation is a "mere" .809, suggesting less stability than found for ideology. This observed correlation is shown in Figure 2.9. The reliabilities of time 1 and time 2 partisanship are shown in Table 2.7, along with the corrected estimates of the time 1– time 2 correlation.

Suppose we estimate the true over-time correlation for state partisanship in the same manner as we did for state ideology. Using the sampling theory method of deriving reliabilities, we obtain

$$\frac{\text{Observed correlation } (x_1 x_2)}{[\text{rel.}(x_1) \times \text{rel. } (x_2)]^{1/2}} = \frac{.809}{(.943 \times .961)^{1/2}} = .863$$

Similarly, using the split-half reliabilities, we get

$$\frac{\text{Observed correlation } (x_1 x_2)}{[\text{rel.}(x_1) \times \text{rel. } (x_2)]^{1/2}} = \frac{.809}{(.867 \times .955)^{1/2}} = .842$$

Splitting the difference, we get .853 as the estimate of the true correlation between state partisanship for time 1 (1976–82) and for time 2 (1983– 88). Strong though this correlation is, it suggests a considerable amount of

---

4. One additional bit of evidence regarding the possibility of true change in state ideol- ogy is the correlogram of observed over-time correlations by smaller time segments, such as years. If true change is present, the over-time correlation should decay as the time lag between readings grows. We computed the 13-year correlogram for the 30 largest states in terms of sample size. Consistent with our finding of virtually no change, these correlations do not attenuate with time. Average correlation coeffi- cients by time lag, from 1 to 12 years are: .56, .63, .61, .54, .58, .59, .54, .60, .49, .46, .63, and .60.

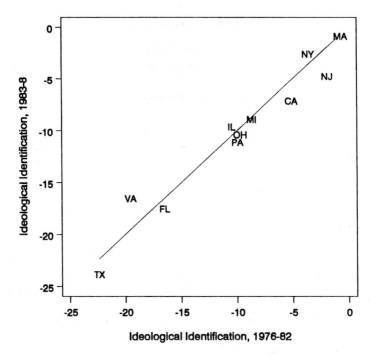

Figure 2.8 Change in Ideology for Large Sample States

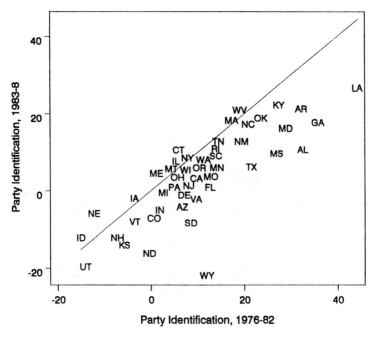

Figure 2.9 Change in State Partisanship, 1976–88

Table 2.7. *Reliability and stability of state partisanship, 1976-82 and 1983-88*

Reliability	1976-82	1983-88
Derived from sampling theory	.943	.967
Derived from split-half method	.931	.955

Observed correlations	Split halves		Split halves	
	Odd	Even	Odd	Even
1976-82 split halves				
Odd	1.00			
Even	.94	1.00		
1983-88 split halves				
Odd	.79	.79	1.00	
Even	.77	.77	.91	1.00

Correlation	Full sample observed	Sampling theory correction	Split half correction
1976-82 to 1983-88	0.809	0.863	0.842

real movement in the ordering of states on the partisan continuum. Indeed, the estimated split-half reliability of partisan *change* is a reasonable .811. This result suggests that the observed changes shown in Figure 2.9 are largely real instead of the result of sampling error. Given this measurement integrity, we present the map of partisan change in Figure 2.10. Regional differences are sketchy and inconsistent, but we can see a pattern of greatest Republican gains in the southern and western states.[5]

As one demonstration that much of the partisan change is real, consider the observed over-time partisanship correlation for large states only. The similar test for state ideology showed the underlying stability of that variable over time. For the 11 states with the largest number of partisan responses in the CBS/NYT samples, however, the time 1–time 2 partisanship correlation is a paltry .48. Figure 2.11 shows the scatterplot. Given the large samples (over 4,000 per state), the observed movement among these states represents meaningful change.[6]

Change, stability, and the measurement of state opinion

Our discussion of change and stability was motivated by concern that too much state movement would limit our ability to predict state means by averaging survey results collected over a 13-year period. For ideology, such concern should certainly be assuaged. For at least the 13-year period under question, the relative positions of the states in terms of ideological identification appear to be almost perfectly stable. Clearly the best way to measure state difference in ideological preference is to obtain the average state ideology for the full 13-year period.

For party identification, the message is more complicated. Averaging state scores over 13 years gives very reliable estimates for that longer time period. But the average scores smooth over some actual movement. Suppose we want to estimate state differences in partisanship for a shorter time frame than 13 years, say for the period 1976–82. We can measure state partisanship for the 7-year period only, with a quite acceptable reliability of about .953. In practice, it makes little difference which measure

---

5. The correlogram of annual readings of partisanship shows the decay pattern typical for true change. For the 30 states with the largest sample sizes, the average correlations are, in order of time lag from 1 to 12 years, .75, .70, .67, .70, .67, .64, .67, .67, .61, .54, .61, .48.
6. The small over-time partisanship correlation for the largest states reflects partisan movement plus the fact that large states are similar in their partisanship. The over-time correlations are, from smallest to largest quartile, .60, .86, .87, .48.

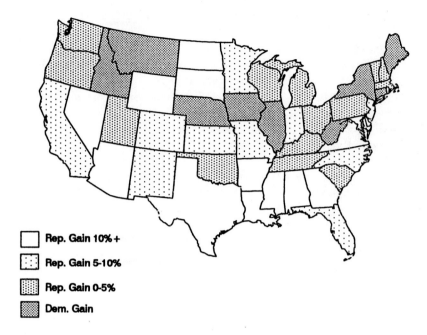

Rep. Gain 10% +

Rep. Gain 5-10%

Rep. Gain 0-5%

Dem. Gain

Figure 2.10 Map of Republican Gain 1976–82 to 1983–88

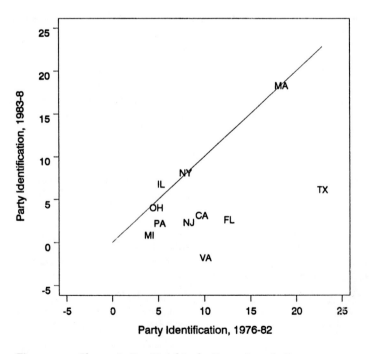

Figure 2.11 Change in Partisanship for Large Sample States

we use. We break the tie in favor of consistency. In subsequent chapters, we use the 13-year average as our estimate of state partisanship.[7]

IDEOLOGICAL POLARIZATION OF THE MASS PUBLIC

So far, we have presented data on the partisanship and the ideology of the states as strictly separate variables. An interesting further step is to present the state-to-state variation in the relationship between ideology and partisanship at the individual level. The most useful way of doing this is to present the mean ideological preferences of Republicans, Democrats, and Independents of each state separately and summarize these scores as the mean ideological distance between Republicans and Democrats within the state. These are presented in Table 2.8. The difference between Republican mean ideology and Democratic mean ideology provides a measure of the degree to which Democrats and Republicans differ ideologically. We refer to this difference as the "index of mass polarization."

In every state in the union, Republican identifiers are less liberal (more conservative) than Democratic identifiers, with Independents in between. Within all states, the Republican partisans naturally include more conservatives than liberals. On the other side of the ledger, while all state Democratic Party groups are more liberal than their Republican competitors, barely half of the state Democratic parties contain more liberals than conservatives. In 27 of 48 states, the liberals outnumber the conservatives, and in the remaining 21 conservatives hold the balance of power within the party. In large part, the difference is a matter of region. The southern wing of the Democratic Party displays a clear conservative bent while in the North the Democratic Party provides a haven for liberal identifiers.

The ideology scores of state Republican identifiers and state Democratic identifiers are shown together in Figure 2.12. The two partisan groups respond somewhat in tandem to the same ideological forces, with the ideological mean of state Democrats correlating at .40 with the ideological mean of state Republicans. (Independent ideology correlates at .75

---

7. How accurate is observed 1976–88 partisanship as a measure of partisanship for the narrower band of time 1 (1976–82) partisanship? We estimate this "reliability" to be .903. We compute this as the square root of the following quantity:

$$\frac{n_1 \times r_{11} + N \times r_{12}r_{22}}{n_1 + n_2}$$

where n_1 and n_2 are the time 1 and time 2 n's, r_{11} and r_{22} are the estimated time 1 and time 2 reliabilities, and r_{12} is the estimated true time 1–time 2 correlation.

Table 2.8. *Ideological polarization of state partisans, 1976-88*

State	Republicans' ideology	Independents' ideology	Democrats' ideology	Index of mass polarization
Alabama	-32.0	-30.7	-12.9	19.1
Arizona	-42.3	-10.4	0.2	42.5
Arkansas	-34.1	-11.8	-15.1	19.0
California	-37.4	1.6	15.2	52.6
Colorado	-33.9	-0.6	12.3	46.2
Connecticut	-33.5	-2.3	16.6	50.2
Delaware	-33.6	-2.1	1.7	35.3
Florida	-36.0	-11.8	-4.8	31.2
Georgia	-33.4	-21.0	-6.3	27.1
Idaho	-46.9	-18.2	-13.9	32.9
Illinois	-35.5	-2.9	4.9	40.3
Indiana	-33.8	-13.4	-1.6	32.2
Iowa	-30.5	-13.8	7.9	38.4
Kansas	-32.4	-11.2	2.0	34.4
Kentucky	-27.6	-14.6	-4.2	23.3
Louisiana	-38.1	-18.2	-19.4	18.6
Maine	-31.3	-8.2	-8.3	23.0
Maryland	-26.5	-3.7	4.8	31.4
Massachusetts	-27.4	0.1	10.8	38.2
Michigan	-31.8	-6.6	10.3	42.1
Minnesota	-39.9	-11.0	6.1	46.1
Mississippi	-38.1	-26.2	-16.5	21.6
Missouri	-38.4	-10.5	-3.1	35.3
Montana	-38.9	-3.6	5.4	44.3
Nebraska	-37.8	-11.7	-0.9	36.9
Nevada	-17.2	0.7	16.1	33.3
New Hampshire	-35.7	-8.0	10.4	46.1
New Jersey	-25.6	-1.7	13.2	38.8
New Mexico	-38.6	-10.2	-2.3	36.3
New York	-26.7	-0.9	14.5	41.2
North Carolina	-34.9	-19.2	-12.3	22.6
North Dakota	-43.7	-22.4	-16.1	27.6
Ohio	-31.5	-6.3	6.7	38.2
Oklahoma	-46.9	-25.4	-15.6	31.3
Oregon	-34.6	-0.2	8.1	42.7
Pennsylvania	-30.2	-5.5	4.2	34.4
Rhode Island	-31.0	-2.6	6.9	37.9
South Carolina	-38.5	-22.3	-9.3	29.2
South Dakota	-36.8	-22.8	-11.8	25.1
Tennessee	-31.8	-17.8	-5.2	26.6
Texas	-43.6	-21.8	-9.8	33.9
Utah	-50.0	-24.7	4.0	54.0
Vermont	-35.7	-1.1	1.1	36.8
Virginia	-39.3	-17.5	3.5	42.8
Washington	-32.8	-4.5	13.0	45.8
West Virginia	-25.7	-4.3	-0.6	25.1
Wisconsin	-36.1	-5.7	7.0	43.1
Wyoming	-37.8	-19.0	9.5	47.3

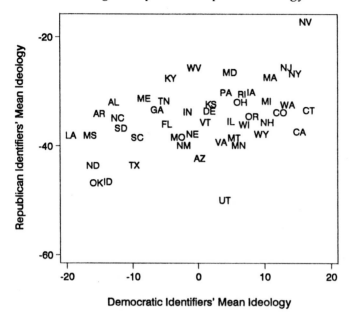

Figure 2.12 Republican Ideology by Democratic Ideology

with Democratic ideology and .52 with Republican ideology.) Note too that average Republican ideology in all states is to the right of average Democratic ideology in all states. The tails of the Democratic and Republican distributions of mean ideology do not quite meet. This is an impressive sign that the rank and file of the two parties are farther apart ideologically than one might believe.[8]

What about the ideological distance between each state's two parties? The most polarized states are widely dispersed geographically: California, Washington, Utah, Colorado, Minnesota, Connecticut, and New Hampshire. On the other hand, the least polarized states are concentrated in the South: Arkansas, Alabama, Louisiana, Mississippi, North Carolina, Kentucky, and (anomalously) Maine. In each of these least-polarized states, the local Democratic Party has more conservative than liberal identifiers.

Naturally, we can compute the reliabilities of the ideologies of each partisan group. Also, using the split-half method, we can even estimate the reliability of the measure of mass polarization. The split-half reliability estimates is .872 for Democratic ideology, which suggests relatively little

8. Here, however, the discarded case of Nevada is a slight exception. Our small and dubious sample of Nevada Republicans is the most liberal Republican group of all and slightly more liberal than Louisiana Democrats.

error except for the less populous states. For Republicans, the reliability is a smaller .651, due to the lesser number of Republicans and their greater ideological homogeneity. Finally, for the mass polarization index, the reliability is a respectable .700. We may place some real stock in this measure of the ideological distance between the two parties at the mass level.

CONCLUSION

In this chapter we have presented our measures of state partisanship and state ideology, based on CBS/NYT surveys from the latter half of the 1970s until the end of President Reagan's second term in office. These measures are based on state samples sufficiently large to be highly reliable statistically and appear to be reasonable estimates in terms of validity.

Easing the task of estimation, state differences in ideology are remarkably stable over the 13-year span. State partisanship is more volatile, but not to a degree that deters the measurement of state party identification by pooling estimates over time. Now that we are able to assess the stability and change found in these data, we are all the more comfortable that they paint a legitimate picture of the U.S. political landscape as it has existed for the span of the late 1970s through the 1980s.

Throughout the remainder of this book we will draw on these estimates of state opinion and state partisanship. With further reports on the relationships between our measures and other key political variables for the states, we will show the connection between state public opinion and policy making in the U.S. states.

Appendix: CBS/NYT polls, 1976–88

Year	ICPSR no./part	Survey month	Sample size	Sample population
1976	7760/1	February	1,458	Adults
	7660/2	March	1,524	Adults
	7660/3	April	1,464	Adults
	7660/4	May	1,501	Adults
	7660/5	June	1,454	Adults
	7660/6	September	1,703	Registered voters
	7660/8	October	1,761	Adults
	7660/9	October	2,025	Adults
	7660/11	November	2,042	Adults
		Total:	14,932	
1977	7817/1	January	1,234	Adults
	7818/1	April	1,707	Adults
	7818/2	July	1,447	Adults
	7818/3	July	1,463	Adults
	7818/4	October	1,603	Adults
		Total:	7,454	
1978	7818/5	January	1,599	Adults
	7818/7	April	1,417	Adults
	7814/1	September	1,451	Adults
	7817/3	September	973	Adults
	7817/4	December	1,011	Adults
		Total:	6,451	
1979	7819/1	January	1,500	Adults
	7819/2	February	1,113	Adults
	7819/3	March	1,221	Adults
	7819/4	April	1,158	Adults
	7819/5	June	1,422	Adults
	7819/6	July	1,192	Adults
	7819/7	July	895	Adults
	7817/5	October	1,514	Adults
	7819/8	November	1,385	Adults
		Total:	11,400	
1980	7812/1	January	1,468	Adults
	7812/2	February	1,536	Adults
	7812/3	March	1,468	Adults

Appendix: CBS/NYT polls, 1976–88 (continued)

Year	ICPSR no./part	Survey month	Sample size	Sample population
	7812/4	April	1,605	Adults
	7812/5	June	1,517	Adults
	7812/6	August	1,769	Adults
	7812/7	September	2,062	Adults
	7812/8	September	1,172	Registered voters
	7812/9	September	1,131	Registered voters
	7812/10	October	2,135	Registered voters
	7812/12	November	2,694	Registered voters
		Total:	18,557	
1981	7991/1	January	1,512	Adults
	7991/2	April	1,439	Adults
	7991/3	June	1,433	Adults
	7991/4	June	1,467	Adults
	7991/5	September	1,479	Adults
		Total:	7,330	
1982	9053/1	January	1,540	Adults
	9053/2	March	1,545	Adults
	9053/3	May	1,470	Adults
	9053/4	June	985	Adults
	9053/5	June	1,174	Adults
	9053/6	September	1,644	Adults
	9053/7	October	2,111	Registered voters
		Total:	10,489	
1983	8243/1	January	1,597	Adults
	8243/2	April	1,489	Adults
	8243/3	June	1,365	Adults
	8243/4	September	705	Adults
	8243/5	September	1,587	Adults
	8243/6	October	548	Adults
	8243/7	October	545	Adults
		Total:	7,836	
1984	8399/2	January	1,443	Adults
	8399/3	February	1,410	Adults
	8410/3	March	1,744	Registered voters
	8399/6	April	1,369	Adults

Appendix: CBS/NYT polls, 1976–88 (continued)

Year	ICPSR no./part	Survey month	Sample size	Sample population
	8399/7	June	1,267	Adults
	8399/8	July	943	Adults
	8399/9	August	1,616	Adults
	8399/10	September	1,546	Adults
	8399/15	September	1,748	Adults
	8399/16	October	1,809	Adults
	8399/17	October	1,463	Adults
	8399/18	November	1,994	Adults
	8399/20	November	2,875	Adults
	8399/22	November	866	Adults
	8399/23	December	1,340	Adults
		Total:	23,431	
1985	8550/1	January	1,525	Adults
	8550/2	January	1,534	Adults
	8550/3	February	1,533	Adults
	8550/5	May	692	Adults
	8550/6	June	1,509	Adults
	8547/1	June	508	Adults
	8547/2	June	542	Adults
	8549/2	July	1,569	Adults
	8550/7	September	762	Adults
	8550/8	September	1,277	Adults
	8550/9	November	1,659	Adults
	8550/10	November	927	Adults
	8547/4	November	800	Adults
	8547/5	December	1,072	Adults
		Total:	15,909	
1986	8695/1	January	1,581	Adults
	8695/3	February	1,171	Adults
	8695/5	April	1,090	Adults
	8695/6	April	704	Adults
	8801/1	April	1,601	Adults
	8695/7	June	1,618	Adults
	8695/8	August	1,210	Adults
	8695/9	September	1,525	Adults
	8695/11	October	2,016	Adults

Appendix: CBS/NYT polls, 1976–88 (continued)

Year	ICPSR no./part	Survey month	Sample size	Sample population
	8695/13	November	687	Adults
	8695/14	December	1,036	Adults
		Total:	14,251	
1987	8718/2	January	1,590	Adults
	8718/3	February	1,174	Adults
	8718/5	March	1,392	Adults
	8718/6	April	1,045	Adults
	8718/8	May	749	Adults
	8718/9	May	1,254	Adults
	8916/1	May	1,343	Adults
	8718/10	July	658	Adults
	8718/11	July	665	Adults
	8718/12	July	745	Adults
	8718/13	August	1,480	Adults
	8718/15	September	839	Adults
	8718/16	September	836	Adults
	8718/18	October	1,326	Adults
	8718/20	November	589	Adults
	8718/21	November	1,553	Adults
	8718/22	December	613	Adults
		Total:	17,851	
1988	9098/1	January	1,663	Adults
	9098/2	February	2,734	Adults
	9098/3	March	1,654	Adults
	9098/4	May	1,382	Adults
	9098/6	July	1,177	Adults
	9098/5	August	1,353	Adults
	9098/7	September	1,606	Adults
		Total:	11,569	
1976–88	Total		167,460	

ICPSR: Inter-university Consortium for Political and Social Research

3

Accounting for state differences in opinion

Chapter 2 described state-to-state differences in ideological and partisan identifications. With reasonable precision, that chapter identified which state electorates are most liberal and which are most conservative, as well as which state electorates are most Democratic and which are most Republican. Still to be answered, however, is why these state differences in mass preferences exist. The question is, Where do state-to-state differences in ideology or partisanship come from? Why, for instance, is Indiana more Republican than Missouri? Or for instance, why is Oklahoma more conservative than New York?

To some degree, state differences in political preferences follow simply from the states' group compositions. Each state electorate is a unique composite of political groupings, and these help to determine the state's political views. For instance, if a state electorate is composed primarily of the kinds of people who lean in the liberal direction, we would expect the state as a whole to tilt in the liberal direction. But collective sentiment can be more than the sum of views of the represented groups. A second potential source of state attitudes is state residence itself. It could be that from exposure to the predominant political culture of their state, citizens are influenced to hold political views they otherwise would not. For instance, if a state electorate is composed of groups that typically lean in the liberal direction, the state electorate could still tilt conservative due to a (perhaps intangible) conservative political culture in the state.

Political scientists often assume that political attitudes are shaped by the local political culture or the commonly shared and reinforced political values within the local community. The influence of geography is often conceptualized as the influence of region. "Region," defined in broad categories like the "Northeast," "South," "Midwest," and "West," seems to have a modest influence on how Americans think politically. Typically, political scientists use region as a surrogate for a common culture, often attributed to the unique historical, economic, or demographic composition of large areas of the nation. Region in this sense is used as an explanatory contextual variable in the analysis of individual-level attitudes and behaviors. Yet do regions as broad geographic categories adequately account for all geographic variation in political culture within the United States? Stated differently, do important variations within regions exist as unique subregional political cultures? If so, the usual regional definitions mask important differences in political culture within regions.

An intriguing possibility is that the unique political cultures of individual states exert an important influence on political attitudes. We are not alone in entertaining this possibility. A sizable literature documents apparent differences in state political cultures (Key, 1949; Fenton, 1957; Lockard, 1959; Fenton, 1966; and Patterson, 1968). By necessity, though, this literature is largely impressionistic. And the comparative component is implied more than it is demonstrated. The pioneering cultural mapping begun by Daniel Elazar (Elazar, 1966; Sharkansky, 1969) is forthrightly comparative, but it too is largely impressionistic in its assignment of contemporary cultural influences. Comparative analysis of the influence of political culture in the United States still awaits adequate measurement.

Under any circumstances, separating out the "contextual" effects of place of residence from the residue of group composition is a daunting task. One can never be sure, for example, that the effects of "context" are not the effects of some crucial group-level variable that has been omitted from the analysis. Sample size can be a particularly vexing problem. With a typical national sample of one or two thousand respondents, for example, one cannot hope to tease out the effects of states or other geographic units. State differences can be found, certainly, on any item in a national sample, even after the usual group-level variables are taken into account. But small sample sizes makes these differences too unreliable for any meaningful analysis.

The massive size of our cumulative CBS/NYT sample presents a golden opportunity to examine state context. For about 70 percent of our CBS/NYT respondents, information is available for several demographic classifications: education level, family income, race, religion, age, sex, and urbanism. The present chapter attempts to separate the two sources of differences in state ideological identification and state partisan identification. One source is demography – the ideological or partisan characteristics of the groups that make up the state sample. The second source is culture – the estimated effect of state residence itself apart from demography.

Here we analyze only the subset of the CBS/NYT surveys for which a full set of respondent demographic characteristics were ascertained. We examine the differing effects of 47 states, excluding Alaska and Hawaii (no interviews) and Nevada (an outlier sample, see Chapter 2). We have

116,450 respondents for our analysis of the effect of state on party identification and 113,244 respondents for our analysis of the effect of state on ideological identification.

The research that follows is a combination of individual-level and aggregate-level analysis. For the individual-level analysis, we examine geographic units as dummy variables among a larger set of independent variables predicting individual-level responses. For the aggregate-level analysis, we examine the extent to which the observed attitudinal differences across state samples conform to state boundaries, as represented by the state dummy variables from the individual-level analysis, rather than from state-to-state differences in demographic composition.

Our research strategy is first to run massive regressions of individual-level ideology and opinion on respondent demographics plus state "dummy" variables. The coefficients for the state dummy variables provide the estimates of state "effects" apart from demography. From the individual-level regressions, state samples can be decomposed into their demographic and cultural components. The demographic component is the mean prediction based on the coefficients for the group characteristics and the state sample means, or

$$\text{Demography} = \Sigma b_i \overline{D}_{ij}$$

where the D_{ij}s are dummy variables representing respondent demographic characteristics. The cultural component is the coefficient representing the state "effect,"

$$\text{Culture} = b_j S_j$$

where S_j is the state dummy variable. By definition, the two components equal the mean state estimate, so that for each state,

$$\text{Mean state estimate} = \text{demography} + \text{culture}$$

Note that state effects are estimated by separate dummy variables rather than residuals from a purely demographic analysis. One implication is that demographic and cultural components of state opinion are not constrained to be uncorrelated. If, for instance, opinion was influenced to generally go in the direction predicted by state demography, that would show up in the demography–culture correlation. Similarly, if state influence were to be unpredictable from state demography, that too would be observable from the lack of a strong demography–culture correlation.

DO STATES MATTER?

Are states influential on public opinion? Our first task is the estimation of state-level cultural effects from survey data. For each dependent variable, party identification and ideological identification, we run four regression equations. First, we include 25 dummy variables representing the available categories on the demographic variables for the CBS/NYT surveys as the independent variables. (The dummy variables represent categories on respondent's age, education, family income, religion, race, gender, and urbanism.) Next, we add three dummies representing the four major regions: the Northeast, Midwest, South, and West. Then, we switch to dummies representing a more detailed breakdown of eight separate regions: New England, Mid-Atlantic, Great Lakes, Plains, Deep South, Border South, Mountain, and Pacific. Finally, we replace the region dummies with separate dummy variables for each of 48 states. At each stage our primary interest is to see how the more complex breakdown of geography improves the explanation of the political attitudes in question.

Once we reach the point where each state becomes a dummy variable, we have 73 independent variables, which with multiple thousands of cases can be handled easily. In fact the large data set allows the luxury of including missing data ("don't know," "no answer") for each demographic variable as its own dummy variable.

Table 3.1 shows the demographic side of two regression equations predicting party identification and ideological identification from selected demographic variables plus state of residence. The regression coefficients conform to expectations. (Almost all are highly significant, as we would expect given the large sample sizes.) Having a high income, being a Protestant, being white, being male, and living in the suburbs or rural areas all appear to result in being Republican and conservative. Age is also related to conservatism, but its effect on partisanship is not clear. Education is the one variable that clearly pushes partisanship and ideology in opposite directions. High education levels appear to promote Republican partisanship but also liberal ideological identification.

Our major interest here is in the consequences of adding dummy variables representing geographic location to the set of independent variables. Table 3.2 displays the statistical evidence. As can be seen, each further refinement of geographic location does add to the prediction of partisanship and ideology: Four regions add significantly to what demographics alone explain; eight regions add significantly beyond what four regions explain; and states add beyond what eight regions explain. Knowing a person's state, therefore, does add to our ability to forecast a person's partisanship or ideology beyond what we know from the person's

Table 3.1. *Regression of party identification and ideological identification on selected demographic variables*

Demographic variable	Party identification		Ideological identification	
	Regression coefficient	Standard error	Regression coefficient	Standard error
Education				
Not high school graduate				
High school graduate	-5.1***	0.7	3.2***	0.7
Some college education	-13.3***	0.7	5.1***	0.7
College graduate	-17.9***	0.8	7.5***	0.7
Don't know or refused	-0.7	3.7	-2.0	4.0
Income				
Low				
Low middle	-5.8***	0.7	-0.8	0.7
High middle	-8.4***	0.8	-1.7	0.7
High	-19.2***	0.8	-4.6***	0.8
Don't know or refused	-14.4***	1.2	-11.4***	1.2
Age				
18-29				
30-44	9.4***	0.6	-6.6***	0.6
45-64	10.0***	0.6	-15.1***	0.6
65 and older	0.1	0.8	-20.1***	0.7
Don't know or refused	-3.9	4.3	-18.0***	0.4
Race				
White				
Black	59.4***	0.9	15.3***	0.8
Other minority	19.1***	1.3	4.4**	1.3
Don't know or refused	21.2***	3.7	7.1	3.6
Religion				
Protestant				
Catholic	24.4***	0.6	8.1***	0.5
Jewish	55.9***	1.4	39.0***	1.3
Other religion	4.5*	1.4	7.3***	1.4
No religion	11.8***	1.3	19.0**	1.2
Don't know or refused	10.2***	2.6	4.4	2.5
Gender				
Male				
Female	4.2***	0.5	4.4***	0.4
Size of Place				
Rural				
Large city	2.0*	0.7	5.4***	0.6
Suburb	-4.6***	0.6	1.8*	0.6
Small city	1.5	0.8	2.5**	0.7
Don't know or refused	1.6	13.7	-4.0	13.0

Note: Coefficients are estimated while controlling for state dummies.
*Significant at .01; **significant at .001; ***significant at .0001.

Table 3.2. *Significance of regions and states as predictors of party identification and ideological identification*

Variables	Adjusted R^2	Change in Adjusted R^2	F for Change	Degrees of freedom	Significant at .001
Predicting party identification $(N = 116,450)$					
Demographics only	.08174				
Demographics plus four regions	.08467	.00353	149.46	3 and 116,421	Yes
Demographics plus eight regions	.08708	.00241	76.83	4 and 116,417	Yes
Demographics plus 47 states	.09134	.00426	13.99	39 and 116,378	Yes
Predicting ideological identification $(N = 113,244)$					
Demographics only	.03186				
Demographics plus four regions	.03492	.00306	119.66	3 and 113,215	Yes
Demographics plus eight regions	.03525	.00033	9.68	4 and 113,211	Yes
Demographics plus 47 states	.03673	.00148	4.46	39 and 116,378	Yes

demographic characteristics alone or even beyond what we know from the person's demographics and region together.

Of course, the increments in the adjusted R^2 values for each new refinement in the measurement of geography are minuscule. Seemingly it took tens of thousands of cases to make states collectively a statistically significant set of predictors for political attitudes. This statistical "proof" that the state of residence helps explain political attitudes by itself does not demonstrate the substantive significance of the coefficients for the state dummy variables. Are these estimates of state-to-state differences in political culture large enough and statistically reliable enough to merit detailed attention? To these questions we turn next.

Table 3.3 shows the regression coefficients and standard errors for the state dummy variables as predictors of partisanship and ideology, with demographics controlled. Coefficients and standard errors are shown for each of the 48 states. (The estimates for Nevada, however, are not included in our statistical analyses.)[1] In place of omitting one state to serve as the base category (the usual procedure in dummy variable analysis), the intercept is omitted. (The two procedures give equivalent equations.) Suppressing the intercept serves two functions. It gives coefficients representing state effects that are relative to the mean respondent (more precisely, the mean respondent in the base category on each set of demographics) rather than relative to the effect of one arbitrarily chosen base state. Second, it results in standard errors that represent the error in the estimate of the state effect by itself rather than the error in the relative difference between the state effect and the effect of the arbitrarily chosen base state. We will see this to be an important advantage.

The best way to evaluate the magnitudes of the estimated state effects of Table 3.3 is to compare them with the magnitudes of the effect of the demographic categories, shown in Table 3.1. This comparison shows that the effect of living in one state instead of another is often of about the same magnitude as the difference between one demographic category and another. Consider, for example, the apparent effects of living in the relatively liberal and Democratic state of Minnesota rather than the relatively conservative and Republican state of Indiana. Comparing these states' relevant regression coefficients suggests that living in Minnesota instead of Indiana produces a difference of 12.8 percentage points on the three-point party identification scale and a difference of 3.4 points on the three-point ideological identification scale. These differences are about two-thirds the size of the difference between being in the highest rather than the lowest income category (see Table 3.1): a difference of 19.2 points on party identification and 4.6 points on ideological identification. In other words, the effect of living in the Indiana rather than the Minnesota politi-

---

1. Except for Nevada, all reported coefficients in Table 3.3 are from an analysis based on 47 states. The Nevada coefficients are from a separate analysis including Nevada as the 48th state. Note the extreme outlier estimate of the state effect for Nevada on ideology, 5 percentage points more liberal than any other state. This offers the diagnostic clue that the erroneous Nevada estimate (see Chapter 2) is due to an overly liberal estimate of the state effect rather than due to an oversampling of liberal demographic groups in Nevada.

Table 3.3. *Effects of state culture on party identification and ideological identification*

State	Party identification		Ideological identification	
	Regression coefficent	Standard error	Regression coefficient	Standard error
Alabama	19.3	2.0	-24.3	1.9
Arizona	0.3	2.3	-19.9	2.2
Arkansas	26.1	2.3	-16.2	2.2
California	4.4	1.3	-12.0	1.2
Colorado	1.4	2.3	-13.5	2.2
Connecticut	2.4	2.2	-10.5	2.1
Delaware	1.9	4.3	-14.3	4.0
Florida	3.8	1.4	-20.7	1.4
Georgia	20.7	1.7	-19.6	1.6
Idaho	-11.6	3.4	-29.0	3.2
Illinois	1.7	1.5	-14.0	1.4
Indiana	-1.1	1.7	-17.2	1.6
Iowa	1.7	2.1	-13.9	2.0
Kansas	-4.6	2.2	-14.0	2.1
Kentucky	24.4	2.0	-13.5	2.0
Louisiana	23.7	2.1	-26.8	2.0
Maine	-4.9	3.4	-14.9	3.2
Maryland	17.4	1.9	-10.9	1.8
Massachusetts	13.1	1.7	-6.7	1.8
Michigan	-1.1	1.5	-11.5	1.4
Minnesota	11.9	1.8	-13.8	1.7
Mississippi	12.9	2.5	-23.9	2.4
Missouri	8.5	1.7	-16.5	1.7
Montana	7.7	3.8	-13.2	3.5
Nebraska	-7.6	2.7	-18.6	2.6
Nevada	4.8	4.2	-1.4	3.9
New Hampshire	-14.7	3.5	-16.7	3.3
New Jersey	-2.5	1.6	-9.9	1.5
New Mexico	7.5	3.2	-16.7	3.1
New York	-4.8	1.3	-12.6	1.3
North Carolina	14.3	1.7	-22.1	1.7
North Dakota	-12.3	4.1	-30.6	3.9
Ohio	3.1	1.4	-12.2	1.3
Oklahoma	23.4	2.2	-27.7	2.1
Oregon	9.9	2.2	-9.6	2.1
Pennsylvania	-1.2	1.4	-13.6	1.3
Rhode Island	4.4	3.8	-7.5	3.5
South Carolina	2.8	2.1	-23.5	2.0
South Dakota	2.1	3.5	-21.3	3.3
Tennessee	10.2	1.8	-17.3	1.8
Texas	13.4	1.3	-26.3	1.3
Utah	-9.3	3.1	-28.6	2.9
Vermont	-7.8	4.4	-12.4	4.3
Virginia	1.3	1.7	-20.5	1.6
Washington	10.5	1.9	-8.9	1.8
West Virginia	20.4	2.4	-6.7	2.3
Wisconsin	0.5	1.8	-14.4	1.7
Wyoming	-0.9	4.9	-16.4	4.7

Note: $N = 47$ states.   Coefficients are state effects controlling for state demographics.

cal culture approaches the political magnitude of the effect of having a very high instead of a very low income.

Our examples of Minnesota and Indiana effects are not the most extreme cases. The most Democratic state effect is estimated to be the effect of living in Arkansas (+26.1); the most Republican state effect is estimated to be the effect of living in New Hampshire (−14.7). The coefficients of Table 3.1 suggest that the difference in party identification produced by the difference between the political cultures of Arkansas and New Hampshire (40.8 points) approaches the partisan consequence of being Jewish instead of Protestant (55.9) or of being black instead of white (59.4)! And remember that the state coefficients are derived from an analysis in which all major demographic variables are controlled. These differences in state effects on partisanship are *not* a function of the measured state demographics.

Considering ideology, Table 3.3 identifies West Virginia and Massachusetts (−6.7) as the most liberal states relative to their demographic composition. The most conservative state political culture is that of Idaho (−29.0). The magnitude of the difference between these two extremes (22.3 points) exceeds the maximum difference across categories on all demographic variables with the exception of religion. The evident ideological impact of living in West Virginia or Massachusetts rather than in Idaho exceeds by a considerable amount the effect of being Catholic rather than Protestant. But our West Virginia/Massachusetts versus Idaho differential does not quite compare in size to the ideological impact of being Jewish rather than Protestant.

Clearly, as estimated by the coefficients for state dummy variables with controls for demographics, the effects of state political culture seem to be reasonably large. But how reliable are these estimates? To have confidence in the size of these state effects, we need to be convinced that they represent true state differences (with demography controlled) and not the result of sampling fluctuations. To ascertain the reliability of the state estimates, we exploit the standard errors of the state effects, shown in Table 3.3.[2] For both partisanship and ideology, we wish to estimate the reliability of the 47 estimates of state effects represented by the state dummy variables. By the standard statistical definition, the reliability of each variable is the ratio of true variance to observed variance. True variance cannot be esti-

---

2. Recall that these standard errors are determined from the form of the equation in which the base state replaces the intercept. This is important. These standard errors are equivalent to sampling errors for state means, but with demographics held constant. If a base state were omitted (as with the normal routine of dummy variable analysis), then the standard errors would be equivalent to the standard error for a difference of means test comparing the effect of the particular state with the effect of the base state.

mated directly. But since the observed or total variance is the sum of the true variance plus the error variance, we can estimate the true variance by subtracting the error variance from the observed variance.

At the practical level, our steps are as follows: First, we square the standard errors for the state coefficients and obtain their mean, which serves as the estimated error variance for the state coefficients. Second, we compute the observed variance as the variance of the state coefficients. Third, we subtract the error variance from the observed variance to estimate the true variance across states in cultural differences. Fourth, we divide the estimated true variance by the observed total variance to estimate the reliability.

For party identification, the estimated reliability of the dummy variable coefficients is .94. For ideology, the estimated reliability of the state effects is an only slightly less impressive .86. Thus, our estimates of state effects on both partisanship and ideology with demographic effects controlled can be accepted with considerable confidence.[3]

Let us review our findings so far. First, states make a statistically significant contribution to the prediction of partisanship and ideology beyond what demographics plus a detailed breakdown of region can do. Second, the estimates of specific state effects range sufficiently to compare in magnitude with the measurable effects of standard respondent demographic variables such as race, religion, income, education, and age. Finally, these coefficients for estimated state effects are quite reliable. This means that the state estimates accurately measure state-to-state differences in individual responses to survey items about partisan and ideological identification, adjusted for the effects of the included demographic variables.

CULTURE VERSUS DEMOGRAPHY AS SOURCES OF STATE OPINION

So far we have examined the effects of state residence on individual attitudes and how these effects compare with the effects of standard demographic variables on individual attitudes. In this section, the state rather than the individual respondent is the unit of analysis. Here we try to ascertain the extent to which state-level differences in partisanship and ideology are a function of unique state cultures rather than the different group characteristics of the states' residents.

For this analysis, we decompose the observed mean party identification and the observed mean ideological identification of each state into its

3. The same procedure can be used to estimate the reliabilities of the "raw" state opinion estimates without the demographic controls. That is, we can estimate state opinion from state dummy variables alone, and proceed as described. These are our sampling-theory-based reliability estimates from Chapter 2. Those reliabilities are slightly higher than those presented here for state effects.

cultural component and its demographic component. The cultural components are our estimates of the effect of state political culture on individual attitudes: The dummy variable coefficients of the state impact on partisanship and ideological identification independent of demography (see Table 3.3). The demographic components are the average of the respondents' predicted responses based on demography, controlling for state effects. More precisely, the demographic components are the average of the responses predicted by the regression coefficients but with the effects of the state dummy variables subtracted out. Tautologically, the cultural and demographic components of partisanship (and of ideological identification) add up to exactly the states' mean responses.

We display these state differences with both maps and scatterplots. Figures 3.1 and 3.2 map the distributions of cultural and demographic partisanship for the U.S. states. In similar fashion, Figures 3.3 and 3.4 map the distributions of cultural and demographic ideology. (Nevada's uncertain ideology coefficient is depicted as in the second most conservative quartile.) Figures 3.5 and 3.6 show the scatterplots of the states' cultural and demographic components, for partisanship and ideology, respectively. The horizontal axes represent the estimated effects of demography: The farther right the state's position on the horizontal axis, the more Democratic or the more liberal the demographic components of state attitudes. The vertical axes represent the estimated effect of state residence: The higher the state's position on the vertical axis, the more Democratic or the more liberal is the state effect.

For convenience, both the cultural and the demographic components are rescaled for the scatterplots in Figures 3.5 and 3.6, so that zero represents the mean state position. The diagonal line represents the mean state position in terms of summed demographic and cultural influences. States to the right and above the diagonal lines in the two figures are relatively Democratic (Figures 3.5) or relatively liberal (Figure 3.6). States to the left and below the diagonal line are relatively Republican (Figure 3.5) or relatively conservative (Figure 3.6).

Observe first that for both partisanship and ideology, the demographic and cultural components are remarkably uncorrelated only .16 in the case of partisanship and −.03 in the case of ideology. Demographically, the most Democratic states are mostly nonwhite and non-Protestant, wherever they are located geographically. Culturally, however, the Republican–Democratic continuum shows a strong North–South gradient.

For ideology, the demographic picture parallels that for partisanship, with the most nonwhite and non-Protestant states cast as the most liberal. The cultural picture, however, is not the North–South gradient of cultural partisanship. Instead, we see a pattern of bicoastal cultural liberalism versus interior cultural conservatism.

57

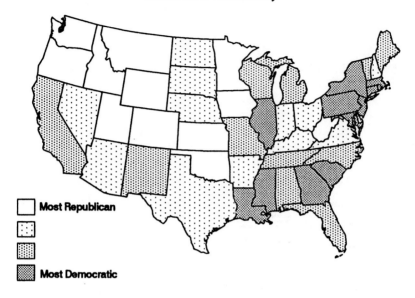

Figure 3.1 Demographic Component of State Partisanship

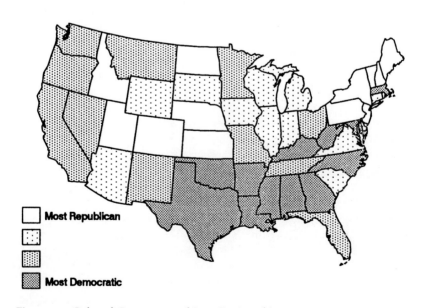

Figure 3.2 Cultural Component of State Partisanship

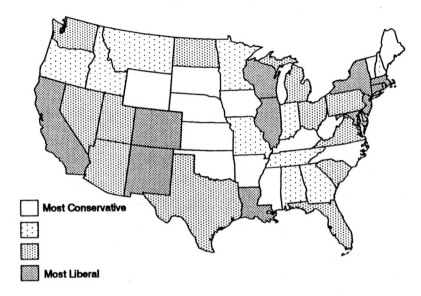

Figure 3.3 Demographic Component of State Ideology

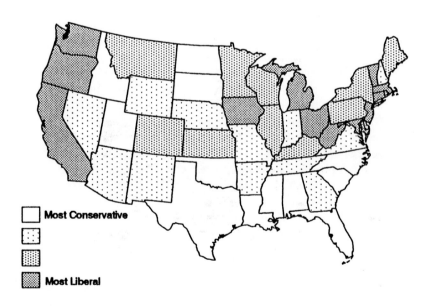

Figure 3.4 Cultural Component of State Ideology

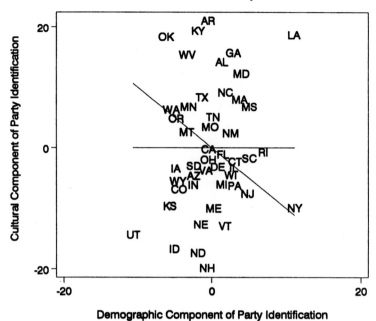

Figure 3.5 Demographic and Cultural Components of Party Identification

The two sets of demographic scores – ideology and partisanship – correlate fairly strongly at .61. This is expected, because each demographic category that predicts liberalism generally predicts Democratic identification, and each that predicts conservatism generally predicts Republicanism. An exception is education level, with high education predicting liberalism and Republicanism. For this reason, mismatches on demographic ideology and demographic partisanship generally are those states with unusually high or low education levels.

The demographic component of ideology receives a strong reflection in the kinds of aggregate demographic variables normally used to measure socioeconomic development. The demographic component of ideology correlates at .60 with median family income and .78 with urbanism (measured as percent of the population in standard metropolitan statistical areas or SMSAs). These strong positive state-level correlations are remarkable because, at the individual level, wealth is associated with conservatism, and urbanism is only weakly associated with liberalism. The reason why both state wealth and state urbanism correlate strongly and positively with state liberalism at the aggregate level is that the types of individuals who call themselves liberal – blacks, Catholics, Jews, and the educated – concentrate in wealthy, urban states.

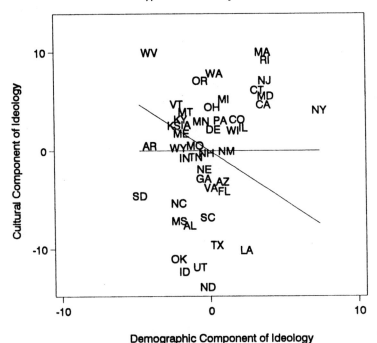

Figure 3.6 Demographic and Cultural Components of Ideological Identification

For both partisanship and ideology, the cultural component varies far more than does the demographic component. For partisanship, the ratio of variances is 5.8 to 1; for ideology, the ratio of variances is 6.7 to 1.[4] Adjustment for measurement error modifies these estimates only slightly. We can adjust the two cultural variances to purge our estimates of the error variances identified from the reliability exercise. Generously, let us assume that the demographic component is measured perfectly, thus allowing a slight inflation of the variance estimate for demography. The resultant ratios still resoundingly favor culture as the predominant source of state variance, by 5.5 to 1 (partisanship) and by 5.7 to 1 (ideology).

The interpretation of these findings is straightforward and intriguing. Since the cultural components have the higher ratio, most of the variance in state partisanship and state ideology is due to state-to-state differences that cannot be accounted for by the demographic variables measured here. Only a relatively small proportion of the variance in state partisan-

4. Although the cultural and the demographic components add up to define the state means, the variances do not add up in similar fashion. The slight covariance of the two components gets in the way.

ship and ideology is due to state-to-state variation in the demographic characteristics – race, religion, income, education, and so on – that we might think account for state-to-state differences in state attitudes. Put another way, such differences in partisanship and ideology are far more than the sum of their demographic parts.

One implication of this result is to question the validity of the procedure of "simulating" state public opinion from the attitudes of the state's known demographic groups. Simulation of state opinion from state demographics has often been employed as a substitute for unavailable state survey estimates (Pool, Abelson, and Popkin, 1965; Weber et al., 1972). But the simulation of opinion can be misleading if state attitudes are more than the reflection of state demographics. Here we provide ample evidence that the partisanship and ideology of state electorates are not determined exclusively from state demographic compositions, but rather are largely the product of the unique political context within each state.

THE CONSEQUENCES OF OMITTED VARIABLES

The analysis of this chapter is an exercise in "contextual" analysis. As usually defined, "contextual" analysis means that individual-level variables are explained in terms of both individual-level and aggregate-level (contextual) variables. One problem with contextual analysis is that the estimated effects of the aggregate-level independent variable might actually represent in part the effects of unmeasured individual-level variables (Stipak and Hensler, 1982). Thus, if one does not adequately control for relevant individual-level independent variables one risks exaggerating the effects of the contextual variables.

Here, this worry applies to the possible consequences of the incompleteness of the demographic controls. We have dummy variables for categories of education, income, race, religion, age, gender, and urbanism. Are omitted individual-level variables contributing to the apparent cultural effects? Probably they are but in most instances only at the margins. An extreme illustration is the absence, in the measurement of religion, of a separate dummy variable for Mormonism. The Utah dummy variable has regression coefficients indicating a conservative and a Republican influence of culture in this state. But part of this cultural effect for Utah probably would disappear if we could control for Mormon affiliation. Mormons are both homogeneous in their political attitudes and geographically concentrated, particularly in Utah. Consequently, Mormon religious affiliation may have a significant impact on the attitudes of Utah residents. Most (omitted) demographic variables, however, are less salient, less homogeneous and less concentrated and, consequently, would have a lesser impact.

We have seen that observed standard demographic variables account for only a small portion of the observed state-to-state differences in opinion. If these demographics contribute so little to state differences in aggregate opinion, incorporating additional group characteristics seemingly would make little further difference. But the validity of this conclusion is not guaranteed. Whether omission of a particular demographic variable causes us to exaggerate state "cultural" effects can depend on several statistical considerations. Is the missing variable highly correlated with the included variables? If so, its influence would be picked up by its included correlates and would therefore offer little distortion in the estimate of state effects. Second, does the concentration of the missing variable vary much across states? If homogeneously distributed, the missing variable cannot masquerade as state effects and therefore presents little problem. The gender breakdown of states into men and women, for instance, is quite uniform across states. Failure to consider gender would present little distortion of the state estimates.

We consider the consequences of two omitted variables: union membership and fundamentalist Protestantism. Union members are more liberal and Democratic. Fundamentalists may not be more Republican in party identification but certainly are more conservative than other Protestants in terms of ideological identification.

Union membership

In our survey data, union membership is measured for about two-thirds of the respondents. We chose not to use this variable in our primary analysis, partly because of the loss of cases. A second reason was that union membership (or its absence) is not necessarily causally prior to opinion. For instance, Democrats and liberals may be more likely to join unions. Or Democratic or liberal state electorates could promote pro-union legislation that expands union membership. Either way, union members would be more Democratic and liberal, apart from membership affecting partisanship or ideology. But such concerns need not bother us here, since for current purposes we need only that union membership be a predictor of partisanship and ideology and that frequencies of union membership vary across state lines.[5]

5. To see why causal ambiguity is of no concern for this test, consider the extreme case, where union membership does not cause attitudes but where being a liberal or a Democrat cause unionism and/or where liberal or Democratic state cultures pro-

Union membership makes a useful test variable for determining the robustness of the analysis against omitted variables. Union membership is a good marker of both partisanship and ideology. When added to the regression equations, union membership shows regression coefficients at about the same magnitudes as the standard demographic variables. (Compare union membership's 20.4 coefficient for party and 8.2 coefficient for ideology with the coefficients of Table 3.1.) Since union membership is unevenly spread across states, with heavier clustering where the Democratic Party and political liberalism thrive, possibly some of our cultural effects for party and ideology can be attributed to union membership instead.

Happily for our enterprise of estimating the effects of state culture, our cultural estimates survive this threat. For both party and ideology, the 47 state dummy variable coefficients computed without a union membership control correlate almost perfectly (.99+) with a new set of state coefficients computed with union membership as an additional control. Moreover, the variances of the state coefficients are not greatly affected – declining 11 percent on ideology and actually gaining 1 percent on partisanship.[6] These results suggest that our state effects are not seriously contaminated or underestimated by the omission of union membership.

Religious fundamentalism

Religious fundamentalism presents a different story. Unfortunately, the CBS/NYT polls do not include a breakdown of Protestants by denomination or inclination toward religious fundamentalism versus liberalism. Thus, the consequences of the omitted fundamentalism category cannot be tested directly. However, a rough indirect estimate is possible.

Using the National Election Studies (NES) surveys for 1976–88, we generated regression equations predicting trichotomous ideology and party identification from demographics plus states. These equations are similar to those in Tables 3.1 and 3.3, except for the addition of a dummy variable for membership in a fundamentalist Protestant denomination. This variable is measurable from the NES's coding of specific Protestant denominations. We coded as Protestant fundamentalist all denominations

mote union membership. Union membership at the individual level would still predict ideology and partisanship, so that states (or state samples) with the most union membership would show up as more *demographically* liberal and Democratic, and by default, less *culturally* liberal and Democratic.

6. When comparing state coefficients with and without union membership in the equation, our comparison is limited to equations for respondents with an actual union membership code.

coded as "neo-fundamentalist" in NES codebooks, plus all Baptists and the Latter Day Saints (Mormons).[7]

From this NES analysis, our fundamentalist coefficients are a somewhat trivial 6.3 for predicting party identification but a rather substantial −20.7 for predicting ideological identification.[8] The question is, How much does this conservatizing effect of religious fundamentalism at the individual level distort our estimates of the division between cultural and demographic ideology at the state level?

To attempt an answer to this question, we estimated from a religious census (Johnson, Picard, and Quinn, 1974) the proportion of each state's population belonging to a fundamentalist denomination. We then regressed the state's cultural components on the percentage of a state's population who belong to fundamentalist denominations. This test suggests that fundamentalism is a missing ingredient for the prediction of state ideology, although not state partisanship. Thus, although our omission of fundamentalism does not distort our estimate of the cultural component of state partisanship, it may cause us to exaggerate the cultural component of state ideology.

Table 3.4 shows a series of regressions predicting the state cultural components of ideology. All contain religious fundamentalism as an independent variable. Fundamentalism is always a considerable predictor of the cultural component of ideology. Fundamentalism shows a regression coefficient of −0.29 in the bivariate equation and declines only slightly with controls. Assuming that state Protestant fundamentalism is reasonably uncorrelated with the demographic component of the state ideology,

---

7. Denominations coded as fundamentalist are – in addition to generic Baptists and Latter Day Saints – United Missionary, Church of God, Nazarene, Church of God in Christ, Plymouth Brethren, Pentecostal, Church of Christ, Salvation Army, Primitive Baptist, Seventh Day Adventist, and Missouri Synod Lutheran. This coding combines the politically conservative and "nontraditional" Latter Day Saints with "Evangelical Protestant" denominations often associated with the political right. Our classification appears to be consistent with the division used by Wald (1992).
8. NES codes ideology as a seven-point rather than CBS/NYT's three-point scale. For our NES analysis, we trichotomized ideology so that the midpoint (4) equals moderate, while all points to the left (1, 2, 3) are liberal and all to the right (5, 6, 7) are conservative. Another difference in surveys is that NES filters out more nonresponses. The lesser amount of noise in the dependent variable is the major reason why the NES equation can explain a greater amount of variance (7 percent) in the ideology dependent variable. Our estimate of a −20.7 fundamentalist effect on ideology is from counting as fundamentalist only those who belong to fundamentalist denominations and belong to the top three categories of church attendance (through "once or twice a month" but excluding "a few times a year" or "never"). This coding counts 16.8 percent of the cumulative NES sample as "fundamentalist" while the mean state percent fundamentalist from the religious census is 15.5 percent. The more frequent the reported church attended, especially among fundamentalists, the greater the conservatizing effect.

Table 3.4. *Predicting cultural component of state ideology from religious*
fundamentalism and other variables

Variable	(1)	(2)	(3)	(4)	(5)
% Fundamentalist	-0.29***	-0.24***	-0.22***	-0.24◊**	-0.20**
	(-5.77)	(-4.47)	(-3.89)	(-4.42)	(-3.40)
The South		-3.19	-2.39	-4.88*	-3.86
		(-1.78)	(-1.23)	(-2.37)	(-2.99)
Median family income[a]			0.41		0.85
			(1.07)		(1.71)
% High school graduates				-0.14	0.29
				(-1.08)	(1.71)
% Black					-0.07
					(-0.47)
Adjusted R^2	.413	.440	.442	.442	.457

Note: Coefficients are *b*'s, with *t*-values in parentheses.
*Significant at .05; **significant at .01; ***significant at .001.
[a] In thousands of dollars.

this coefficient suggests that membership in a fundamentalist denomination is worth as much as 29 points in the conservative direction on the ideological scale.[9]

The importance of the fundamentalism variable derives not only from its ability to account for individual-level votes, but also from its high concentration in certain states. Table 3.5 depicts this concentration, largely in the South but also (counting Latter Day Saints in our fundamentalist category) in the Mountain region. The regression equations of Table

9. Precise alignment of the fundamentalist effect at the individual level and the state level is made complex because all Protestants, not just nonfundamentalists, are included in the base religious category. For instance, extrapolating state-level consequences of a −20.7 effect at the individual level depends on how many Protestants are in the state population. Note also that taking into account the fundamentalist effect alters our understanding of Catholic–Protestant ideological differences. In our main analysis, the Catholic dummy variable coefficient is 8.1, as an estimate of the Catholic–Protestant differential. In the NES analysis, the Catholic dummy coefficient is a lesser 4.4, reflecting the presence of only a minor ideological difference between Catholics and mainline (base category) Protestants.

Table 3.5. *Membership in fundamentalist Protestant denominations by state*

Alabama	33.9	Nebraska	11.3
Arizona	14.2	New Hampshire	3.4
Arkansas	29.6	New Jersey	2.1
California	6.8	New Mexico	16.5
Colorado	9.8	New York	2.0
Connecticut	2.2	North Carolina	28.6
Delaware	2.8	North Dakota	7.9
Florida	15.3	Ohio	6.8
Georgia	31.2	Oklahoma	33.1
Idaho	34.8	Oregon	10.5
Illinois	8.6	Pennsylvania	2.5
Indiana	12.9	Rhode Island	3.5
Iowa	8.6	South Carolina	32.1
Kansas	12.5	South Dakota	9.2
Kentucky	31.4	Tennessee	31.9
Louisiana	18.4	Texas	24.4
Maine	6.0	Utah	76.3
Maryland	5.6	Vermont	3.4
Massachusetts	2.2	Virginia	17.8
Michigan	6.5	Washington	6.7
Minnesota	7.0	West Virginia	15.5
Mississippi	33.0	Wisconsin	7.4
Missouri	21.0	Wyoming	17.5
Montana	8.5		

Note: Measures are the percentages of the state populations belonging to fundamentalist Protestant groups.
Source: Computed from Johnson, Picard, and Quinn, 1974.

3.4 show that whereas no other contextual variables contribute statistically to the explanation of cultural liberalism, fundamentalism by itself accounts for 41 percent of the measured variation in cultural liberalism among the states. Most of this net effect of fundamentalism probably should be attributed to an individual-level effect (that was otherwise missed) and perhaps a small amount to the contextual effect of fundamentalism on state culture apart from demographics.

To see the importance of fundamentalism in terms of understanding state ideological differences, consider the extreme case in which the statistical contribution of fundamentalism to ideology is entirely attributed to individual-level effects. Moving the fundamentalism component from culture to the demographic component results in a revised partition, with almost 60 percent of the variance in state ideology due to demography (from the individual-level equation plus aggregate fundamentalism).

ACCOUNTING FOR STATE DIFFERENCES IN POLITICAL CULTURE

By whatever accounting, a sizable share of the variance in state partisanship and ideology is attributed to state effects rather than the influence of demography. But what accounts for these state effects, apart from a possible contextual effect of religious fundamentalism? Several hypotheses can be advanced to account for differing state influences on partisanship and ideology.

Region

Most obviously, we can look for a geographic pattern of common state effects within regions or among geographically similar states. Earlier we saw that state effects contribute significantly to the prediction of individual partisanship and ideology beyond what effects from our eight regions can do. But this does not preclude the possibility of regional patterning of state effects. Referring to Table 3.3, one can see some regional patterns. For instance, southern and border states show party effects that are considerably more Democratic than the norm. Southern and interior western states show ideology effects that are more conservative than the average.

The eight-way regional breakdown can account for 39 percent of the variance in the state coefficients for party identification and 35 percent of the variance in the state coefficients for ideological identification. Most of this regional predictability is due to the Democratic and conservative South. Excluding southern and border states, region dummies account for none of the variance in state coefficients for party identification (adjusted $R^2 = -.013$). With southern and border states excluded, region does account for 29 percent of the ideology coefficients. However, this is without a control for religious fundamentalism. With all the fundamentalism-induced variance partialed out, and with southern and border states removed, region accounts for a nonsignificant 9 percent of the variance in the cultural component of ideology.

Therefore, setting aside the cultural distinctiveness of the South, the effect of state cultures on partisanship and ideology does not follow a consistent geographic pattern. Classifying a state as Mid-Atlantic, Mountain, and so forth, does not tell us much about the effect of residence in the state on partisan or ideological identification.

Elazar's political culture

Daniel Elazar has presented the most well-known classification of U.S. states according to political culture. Elazar classifies the predominant culture of states as "moralist," "individualist," and "traditionalist." We devote Chapter 7 to Elazar's classification scheme. Here, we note, however, that state scores on Elazar's classification are unrelated to our cultural components of partisanship and ideology. Elazar's traditionalist states are almost coterminous with the combined southern and border states, preventing the effects of Elazar's traditionalism from being effectively disentangled from southern regionalism. Therefore, the one relevant question about Elazar's categorization is whether his distinction between moralistic and individualistic states predicts the cultural components of partisanship and ideology. They do not. With traditionalistic states set aside, the moralist–individualist distinction accounts for a trivial 2 percent of the cultural component of partisanship and 6 percent of the cultural component of ideology. Thus, while Elazar's classification has considerable appeal as a taxonomy of elite subculture (see Chapter 7), his scheme is by no means a surrogate for state effects on partisanship and ideology.

"Social context" effects

Studies of the contextual effects of small geographic units such as neighborhoods have given special attention to the hypothesis that peoples' attitudes are influenced by the aggregated attitudes of those around them. Rationales include the possibilities that people respond to social norms or are influenced by social interactions. Local attitudes are typically operationalized as the attitudes of the locally predominant social groups. The effect of social context might be examined, for example, by seeing whether neighborhood effects on the vote correlate with the vote predicted from residents' individual characteristics (Huckfeldt, 1979, 1984). At the state level, the social context hypothesis offers an obvious prediction. If state effects reinforce state attitudes that result from individual citizen characteristics, then the demographic component of state opinion (due to individual characteristics) should be related to the cultural component (due to residence in the state apart from individual effects).

Interestingly, the data offer no support for a social context effect at the state level. For state partisanship, the demographic and cultural components are correlated at .16 for 47 states, and an even lesser –.03 with southern and border states are removed. For ideology, the two components are correlated at .32 for 47 states and .37 when southern and border states are removed. Thus, the partisan and ideological leanings that a state obtains from its demographic composition do not seem to affect the directions of the cultural components of state partisanship and ideology. Perhaps surprisingly, although the state of residence appears to have a major impact on political attitudes, these state effects are not influenced by the attitudinal predispositions of the states' demographic groups.

Statehouse democracy

Specific demography: Income, education, race

Even though a social context explanation fails, we might expect that specific components of state demography influence the partisan or ideological direction of state culture. Consider state income: Wealthy states are often suspected of being more liberal even though individual wealth breeds Republicanism and conservatism. Consider education. It might be that a more educated populace affects the political climate – perhaps encouraging liberalism, but possibly Republicanism as well. Consider race. The size of the local black population sometimes makes whites more racially reactive (Wright, 1977).[10]

None of these speculations holds up well from an inspection of the data. Table 3.4 presents several regressions with state median family income, education levels (percent high school graduates), and percent black predicting cultural *ideology*. None of these variables presents a statistically significant contribution. In the case of cultural *partisanship* (not shown), the predictions from these variables are even worse, once regional controls for southern (11 former Confederate states) and border states are imposed.[11]

Commonality to partisan and ideological effects?

Although we cannot identify the specific causes of state effects on partisanship or ideology, perhaps the unidentified causes of the two sets of cultural effects are related. If so, the state effects on partisanship and on ideology would correlate with each other. But even this expectation is not borne out by the data. The two are correlated at a surprisingly low .04. But here is an instance where excluding southern and border states boosts the correlation – due to the conservative but Democratic effects of southern states. With southern and border states excluded, the correlation between state effects for partisanship and ideology is .38, suggesting some mild commonality.

10. We do not include urbanism among the set of potential contextual variables influencing cultural ideology for the reason that the individual-level urbanism dummies already control for urban context. In any event, urbanism (percent SMSA) does not statistically contribute to the explanation of cultural ideology. Neither do the variables of percent Catholic or percent Jewish.

11. Under some specifications, union membership appears to have a modest contextual effect on cultural ideology, although not cultural partisanship. The proper way to investigate this contextual effect is to use the measure of cultural ideology that controls for individual-level union membership. When union membership is entered into the equations predicting the regular measures of cultural ideology or partisanship, it is statistically significant, picking up both the individual-level and contextual effects of union membership.

Discussion

This quest for causes of the measured state effects ends on a puzzling note. As we saw, indigenous "state" effects, which we attribute to state-to-state differences in political culture, account for far more of the interstate variance of partisanship and ideology than does interstate variation in the demographic compositions of state populations. A state's partisan or ideological bent seems more a function of its political history and development than of the characteristics of its population. But these important differences in political culture are not easily accounted for. Apart from the uniqueness of the South, with its Democratic but conservative culture, states seem to develop relatively conservative versus liberal cultures, or relatively Republican versus Democratic cultures, without any pattern that we can yet discern. The natural follow-up question is how to account for the clear and important differences in state-level effects. Apart from identifying part of the cultural component as the likely reflection of religious fundamentalism, the exact sources of these state effects remain a mystery.

In subsequent chapters, we examine the linkages between state-level ideological identification and state policy. For that analysis, state ideology is treated as "exogenous," which (in statistical parlance) means that it is treated as given, a variable used to explain other variables. As we will see, variation in the electorate's ideological preferences is the driving force behind many of the political differences among U.S. states. This crucial variable originates in part from the states' specific group interests. But as we have seen in this chapter, state ideology is also shaped by locally generated idiosyncratic differences in ideological taste.

State partisanship is an intermediate variable in our subsequent analysis. State partisanship, we will see, affects state policy. But state partisanship is also "endogenous" (in statistical parlance), meaning that it is affected by other identifiable variables. We will see that the cultural component of state partisanship – that portion due to state effects – is not quite as mysterious as presented here. We will see that state partisanship is partially a response to the two parties' relative abilities to represent state opinion. The mysterious state differences in partisanship that cannot be explained by state demographics are partially a result of the representation process in the states.

CONCLUSIONS

This chapter presents a detailed examination of the effects of different state political cultures on political attitudes in the United States. For each state, we report reliable estimates of the influence of the state political culture on the partisanship and ideology of its individual citizens.

At the individual level of analysis, the state of residence produces at least as much variation in partisanship and ideology as does the typical demographic variable. With the state as the unit of analysis, we find that much of the variance in state-level partisanship and ideology is due to state-level differences in political culture rather than the demographic characteristics of residents of different states.

Our identification of idiosyncratic state culture as a source of state-to-state differences in ideology and partisanship is only partially complete. It is complete in the sense of demonstrating that state of residence is important both as a source of state attitudinal differences and in actually measuring state effects. These we regard as important accomplishments.

Our analysis is incomplete because it leaves open several intriguing questions. Most obviously, while we can identify state effects, the underlying causes of interstate differences in state effects remain a mystery. Speculatively, are state-to-state differences in cultural effects the result of idiosyncratic historical development of state political culture? What role do state political elites and, especially, major state media play in determining the variation? We also are ignorant regarding how the effects of state culture are transmitted. For instance, at what point in a person's life does the state political culture exert its influence? Are the state effects we have measured the result of childhood socialization (assuming most people grow up near where they live as adults) or the subtle influence of the state environment on the attitudes of adults? Finally, the geographic variation in the effects of state political culture requires further inquiry. Do the geographically concentrated effects of political culture spill over state lines? Indeed the geographic sources of the variation in political opinions measured here may extend beyond discrete cultures separated by state boundaries. "State" effects captured by state boundaries may represent in part the sum of the effects of regional variation within states, or even of variation that transcends state lines. In any case, it is clear that the political attitudes of Americans vary in important ways on the basis of where in the United States they live.

4

Public opinion and policy in the American states

In theory, one major advantage of the U.S. federal system is that rather than always having one national policy to fit all circumstances, individual states can tailor their policies to local needs and preferences. Of course, federal guidelines and regulations sometimes structure a certain uniformity of state policy. The states' common participation in programs like Medicaid or AFDC are cases in point. Even where states are quite free (within constitutional constraints) to experiment boldly, innovation is often the exception. Observers generally depict the state policy process as a pattern of occasional innovation by some states followed by widespread copying by others (e.g., Walker, 1969; Gray, 1973). Still, even though states may seem more similar than different in terms of the policies they enact, the differences that do exist are often important. Moreover, these differences reflect more than random policy mutations. Behind many differences in state policy one can detect differences in the policy preferences of state citizens.

To illustrate, we select the states of Oklahoma and Oregon for comparison. These two states are similar in many respects besides adjacency in alphabetical order. They are both in the West and similar in size, urbanism, and average income levels. Yet when we compare their policies in force in or about the year 1980, we find many differences.

We can begin with spending for public schools, an important matter that normally accounts for about a quarter of a state's spending. Oregon chose to spend about 40 percent more per pupil than did Oklahoma ($3,130 vs. $2,230), suggesting a considerable difference in the two states' interest in investing in education. Next, consider welfare. Oregon not only spent more per AFDC or Medicaid recipient but also had more generous eligibility guidelines, expanding the base roughly 10 percent more than if it had used Oklahoma's criteria. We also find a difference in taxation policy. Oklahoma relied more on the "regressive" sales tax than the "progressive" income tax. Oregon obtained most of its revenue from an income tax and did not even have a sales tax.

Other policy arenas also reveal differences between our comparison states. In terms of criminal justice policy, circa 1980 Oklahoma had a death penalty (with over 30 inmates on death row); Oregon had no capital punishment. To take another indicator, Oregon had decriminalized marijuana; Oklahoma had not. Additional differences are found for consumer legislation. By one count of 28 possible "litmus test" pieces of consumer legislation, Oregon had enacted 21 and Oklahoma only 7. The two states also varied in their policies regarding various forms of legalized gambling. Oregon permitted both horse and dog racing, plus poker card rooms. Oklahoma's one bow to legalized gambling was bingo. Finally, consider womens' rights. Oregon appeared to be the more responsive to womens' concerns, having passed the Equal Rights Amendment while Oklahoma did not.

In their accumulation, most political observers would describe the net policy difference between Oregon and Oklahoma as a matter of some considerable substantive significance. Moreover, there exists an obvious common denominator to these differences. Across the board, the policies we have described for Oregon are liberal in comparison with those in Oklahoma, which are more conservative.

When we ask why Oklahoma has such conservative and Oregon such liberal policies, speculation can turn to several sources. Although the two states are similar demographically, Oregon's population is better educated. We can note too that Oklahoma is a border state with a southern exposure; while Oregon is decidedly northern, with a historical pattern of settlement by New England emigrants. Politically, Oklahoma is dominated by the Democratic Party (in terms of party identification and state legislative elections), while Oregon is competitive with only a slight Democratic tilt. But none of these differences is the decisive factor that accounts for Oklahoma's policy conservatism and Oregon's policy liberalism. The decisive factor is public opinion on the ideological continuum. Oklahoma's electorate is more conservative than Oregon's in its political preference. This basic difference in public attitudes is the reason why Oklahoma has the more conservative policies of the two states.

To assert an opinion–policy causal explanation for Oklahoma's and Oregon's policy differences, we obviously need some evidence. Toward that end, the present chapter explores the statistical connection between state ideology and state policy. As described in Chapter 2, state ideology is measured as mean ideological identification, which represents state "public opinion" in the broad sense – a summary measure of the state electorate's ideological taste rather than state preferences on specific policies. For short, we here refer to mean ideology as "state opinion." To relate to state

74

opinion, we identify state policies that themselves have an ideological flavor.

MEASURING STATE POLICY

Because state public opinion is measured as ideological identification, we selected policy variables that reflect the usual ideological divisions between liberals and conservatives. Also, we chose to go beyond simply examining how state ideological preferences relate to each of a set of separate policy indicators. Our ultimate measure of state policy is a grand index of state policy, which we label "composite policy liberalism." This index is a combination of state policies on eight issues, each chosen to represent a separate aspect of state liberalism, circa 1980.[1]

These eight policy measures are as follows:

Education. Public educational spending per pupil. (Source: January 1984 report by the U.S. Department of Education.)

Medicaid. Hanson's (1983) measure of the "scope" of Medicaid, or the state's extension of eligibility for Medicaid beyond the minimal levels required by federal regulations.

AFDC. Hanson's (1985) "scope" of AFDC eligibility, analogous to the Medicaid measure.[2]

Consumer protection. Sigelman and Smith's (1980) index of state responsiveness to the consumer movement, based on enactments through 1974 of legislation in 28 areas such as unit pricing, open dating, drug advertising, cooling-off periods, small claims courts, construction standards, and the like.

Criminal justice. Our index of state support for "liberal" approaches to criminal justice. The scale is based on the presence of state laws concerning victim compensation, domestic violence (injunction relief and shelter services), the decriminalization of marijuana possession, and the absence of the death penalty. (Data source: *The Book of the States* 1982–3.)

Legalized gambling. Our index of state legalization of 10 different kinds of legalized gambling: lotteries, numbers, sports betting, off-track betting, horse racing, dog racing, jai alai, casinos, card rooms, and bingo. Nevada

---

1. State policy studies rarely create general indices of policy by combining policies with different subject matter. One early exception was Sharkansky and Hofferbert's (1969) measurement of two broad policy factors for the 1960s. More recently, Klingman and Lammers (1984) built a measure of "state policy liberalism" by combining six distinct policy indicators. Unfortunately, not all their indicators clearly represent contemporary liberalism–conservatism (e.g., Walker's index of policy innovation). Still, we owe a debt to Klingman and Lammers's effort. Two of our eight policy issues also were used by them.

2. Another way of measuring state AFDC policy and Medicaid policy is in terms of per recipient benefits, which we examined as alternatives to our "scope of eligibility" measures. They give very similar results when substituted in the analysis.

Table 4.1. *Pearson correlations among indicators of state policies*

Indicator	ED	MC	AFDC	CON	GAM	CJ	ERA	TAX
ED	1.00							
MC	.56	1.00						
AFDC	.61	.69	1.00					
CON	.56	.52	.53	1.00				
GAM	.70	.42	.51	.48	1.00			
CJ	.44	.48	.40	.62	.23	1.00		
ERA	.51	.52	.30	.43	.43	.39	1.00	
TAX	.57	.61	.57	.48	.29	.56	.41	1.00

Note: Each of the indicators is described in detail in the text. The nmemonic names are ED, state educational expenditures per pupil; MC, scope of eligibility for Medicaid assistance; AFDC, scope of eligibility for Aid to Families with Dependent Children; CON, scale of state consumer legislation; GAM, scale of state gambling legislation; CJ, scale of state criminal justice restrictions; ERA, state support of the Equal Rights Amendment; TAX, scale of state tax progressivity.

(excluded from this study) allows for 9 of these forms of gambling. The remaining states range from 6 legalized and operating activities to none permitted. (Data source: *The Book of the States*, 1982–3.)

Equal Rights Amendment. Number of years from ERA ratification (if any) until 1978 (Boles, 1979).

Tax progressivity. Phares's (1980) scale, which is the only systematic evaluation of state tax systems that considers the allocation of tax burdens across income categories within each state. Lowery (1985) argues convincingly that Phares's calculations provide the best measure of tax progressivity.

The intercorrelations among these eight items are shown in Table 4.1. A perusal of this table shows that the correlations tend to be uniformly high. Twenty-five of the 29 correlations are between .40 and .70. When the correlations are factor-analyzed, they conform to a single factor model. The primary factor accounts for over 60 percent of the common variance, and no other factor is represented by an eigenvalue greater than 1.0. The

Table 4.2. *State scores on standardized index of composite policy liberalism*

Alabama	-1.45	Nebraska	0.44
Arizona	-1.05	Nevada	-0.35
Arkansas	-1.54	New Hampshire	-0.14
California	1.49	New Jersey	1.34
Colorado	0.48	New Mexico	-0.99
Connecticut	1.19	New York	2.12
Delaware	1.11	North Carolina	-0.96
Florida	-0.37	North Dakota	-0.52
Georgia	-1.04	Ohio	0.64
Idaho	-0.87	Oklahoma	-0.98
Illinois	0.41	Oregon	1.39
Indiana	-1.20	Pennsylvania	1.01
Iowa	0.44	Rhode Island	0.68
Kansas	0.24	South Carolina	-1.53
Kentucky	-0.32	South Dakota	-0.95
Louisiana	-1.04	Tennessee	-0.85
Maine	-0.02	Texas	-0.65
Maryland	0.85	Utah	-0.44
Massachusetts	1.64	Vermont	0.79
Michigan	1.18	Virginia	-0.84
Minnesota	0.79	Washington	0.35
Mississippi	-1.51	West Virginia	0.12
Missouri	-0.55	Wisconsin	1.23
Montana	0.60	Wyoming	-0.70

Note: State policy values are based on standardized scores of 47 states, Nevada excluded. The score for Nevada (not used in our analysis) is based on the set of 48 states.

single factor nicely supports the notion that the eight policy variables represent one single dimension of policy liberalism.

Since each of the eight items loads similarly on the common factor, we constructed the composite policy liberalism index in the simplest manner: by summing the standardized scores on the eight component items. This composite policy liberalism index is reliable, as reflected by a Cronbach's alpha of .89. The index should be an accurate reflection of the liberal–conservative tendency of states' policies. Table 4.2 presents these scores on the composite index of policy liberalism. For convenience, these scores are standardized, with mean zero and standard deviation one, so that each unit represents a standard deviation of policy liberalism.

The distribution of policy liberalism across the states is shown in Figure 4.1. This presents our composite index of state policy liberalism as a map

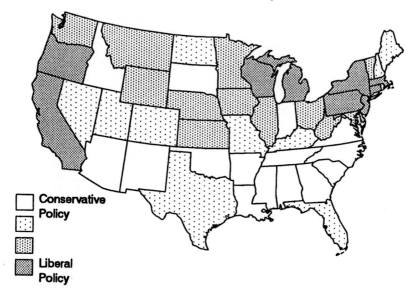

Conservative
Policy

Liberal
Policy

Figure 4.1 Map of State Policy Liberalism

of the states running from the most conservative to the most liberal. Notice that policy liberalism in the states has clear regional associations with
the South and Mountain regions generally conservative and the Mid-
Atlantic, upper Midwest, and Pacific regions being more liberal. In general outline, this pattern is similar to that which we reported for state ideology in Chapter 2 (see Figure 2.2). Let us now turn to a more quantitative
assessment of the opinion–policy connection in the states.

THE OPINION–POLICY CORRELATION

The relationship between public opinion and state policy can be summarized by the the simple correlation between states' mean ideological
identification (1976–88) and the composite policy index. This correlation
is a strong .82. The accompanying *b* coefficient is .113, meaning that for
every percentage point movement on the –100 to +100 ideology scale,
policy moves one-tenth of a standard deviation. Figure 4.2 presents the
striking scatterplot of this relationship. Clearly the most liberal states –
mainly in the Northeast – tend to enact the most liberal policies while the
most conservative states – mainly in the South and Mountain regions –
tend to enact the most conservative policies. Remarkably, only a few states
fall (ever so slightly) in the off-diagonals with opinion more liberal than
the average but policies more conservative than the average or vice versa.

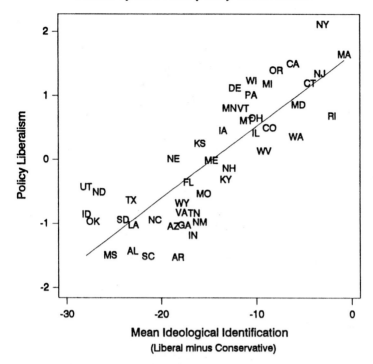

Figure 4.2 State Policy and Public Opinion

No states show composite policy positions that are far different from predicted by the bivariate regression line shown in Figure 4.1. As we will see, the strongest departures tend to be the least populous states, where the opinion measure is most likely to err due to small state samples. When one considers that the opinion measure is imperfect, albeit with an estimated reliability of about .93 (Chapter 2), the observed relationship shown in Figure 4.1 becomes even more impressive. With some basic statistical manipulation, one can readily conclude that underlying the "observed" correlation of Figure 4.1 is a "true" correlation in the high .80s or even .90 or above.

Consider that the observed correlation between two variables represents the "true" correlation times the product of the square roots of the two variables' reliabilities, so

$$\text{True } r_{xy} = \frac{\text{observed } r_{xy}}{(r_{xx} \, r_{yy})^{1/2}}$$

where r_{xx} and r_{yy} are the estimated reliabilities of x and y. As mentioned, the estimated reliability of state opinion is .93. As estimated from Cron-

79

bach's alpha, the estimated reliability of state policy liberalism is .89. Applying the formula,

$$\text{Estimated true opinion–policy } r = \frac{.82}{(.93 \times .89)^{1/2}} = .91$$

Based on statistical considerations, then, we obtain the remarkable estimate of about .91 as the true correlation between state opinion and state policy on the ideological continuum!

This argument can easily be supported by statistical demonstration. In principle, we should obtain a truer (and therefore stronger) statistical relationship when we restrict our analysis to states with large state samples for the measurement of state opinion. We can directly observe how measurement error attenuates the opinion–policy relationship by noting how the observed correlation varies with the number of respondents sampled for the measure of state ideology. Figure 4.3 makes the presentation by showing the opinion–policy scatterplot separately for two groups of states divided by whether their sample exceeded the median sample size. Twenty-three states have state samples greater than 2,110; 24 states (recall that Alaska, Hawaii, and Nevada are omitted) have smaller state samples. Among the latter, the observed correlation is "only" .75. Clearly, restricting cases to those with greater measurement error on the independent variable attenuates the observed correlation. Among the largest 23 states (i.e., with sample sizes greater than 2,110), the observed correlation is a hefty .91! This observed correlation is virtually identical to the theoretical true correlation, adjusted for reliability. (The accompanying *b* coefficient increases too, from 0.086 to 0.149.) For large states, sample sizes are sufficiently large that errors in the measurement of state opinion are of little statistical consequence.

The same result can be seen from a four-way division of states from smallest to largest, based on sample size. To approximate a division into quartiles, we set the sample size cut points at 900, 2,110, and 3,600. Figure 4.4 shows the results. In the 12 states with the smallest state samples (Group 1), the opinion–policy correlation is "only" .73, with a *b* of 0.068. This rises to .78 (b = 0.114) for the 12 states in Group 2 and .88 (b = 0.139) for the 12 states in Group 3. Finally, for Group 4, 11 states with state sample sizes over 3,600 – or about twice the average *N* of a national survey – the correlation is an excessive .94, with a *b* equal to 0.134. For these 11 states, measurement error is minimal, and the observed opinion–policy correlation is near-perfect.

The awesome strength of the opinion–policy correlation is reason to give pause. Our evidence is not just that state opinion is strongly or signifi-

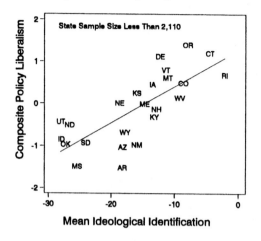

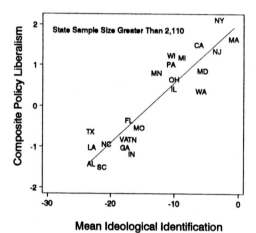

Figure 4.3 Opinion–Policy Relationship by
State Sample Size

cantly related to the ideological tendency of a state's policies. With an
imputed correlation of about .91, state opinion statistically explains over
80 percent of the variance in state policy liberalism. This leaves little variance to be accounted for by other variables. Thus, state opinion is virtually the *only* cause of the net ideological tendency of policy in the state.
Moreover, even seemingly small difference in state ideological preferences
appear to have major policy consequences. A mere 1 percentage point
difference in a state electorate's relative preference for the conserva-

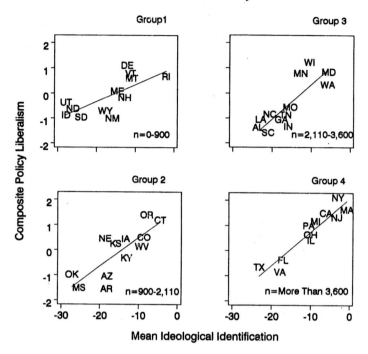

Figure 4.4 Opinion–Policy Relationship by Quartile of State Sample Size

tive or liberal label translates into a tenth of a standard deviation difference in policy liberalism.[3]

CONTROLLING FOR SOCIOECONOMIC VARIABLES

So far, we have ignored the fate of socioeconomic variables that the literature on state policy has shown to be powerful predictors of state policy variables (e.g., Dye, 1966; Hofferbert, 1966, 1974). Let us, therefore, reinvestigate the opinion–policy relationship, but with appropriate controls for socioeconomic variables. To keep the analysis manageable, we

3. As a further exploration of the opinion–policy correlation, we examined the correlation based on state opinion observed for the years 1976–82 only. As reported in Wright, Erikson, and McIver (1987), this correlation is .80. When both measures of state ideology (for 1976–82 and 1976–88) are used to predict policy in a multiple-regression analysis, the partial measure shows a trivial, nonsignificant effect. We also tried the opinion estimate using the CBS/NYT exit poll measure (see Chapter 2). For 41 available states, this variable correlates at only .66 with policy liberalism.

have chosen a set of three socioeconomic variables that are typical of those employed in the state policy literature. These are median family income, percent population residing in SMSAs, and percent population 25 years or older who are high school graduates. We will refer to these variables as income, urbanism, and education, respectively.

Table 4.3 shows the correlations among three socioeconomic variables themselves and with state ideological preference. The table also shows the results of a regression equation predicting state ideological preferences from the three socioeconomic variables. State ideology is clearly related to the socioeconomic variables, with income being the best predictor. Ironically, income is positively related to state opinion liberalism, even though the wealthiest individuals tend to be the most conservative. These patterns illustrate the familiar lesson that relationships can differ at the individual and aggregate levels of analysis.

An interesting question is *why* income is so strongly correlated with state ideology. One plausible hypothesis is that wealth exerts a liberalizing contextual effect on state opinion apart from the conservatizing effect of individual wealth on individual opinion. But we know this hypothesis to be untrue from our analysis of Chapter 3: There we saw that the cultural component of state opinion is largely unrelated to income and other state-level socioeconomic variables. The answer instead is that ideologically liberal groups tend to populate wealthy and developed states. The demographic component of ideology strongly correlates with socioeconomic development – .60 with income and .78 with urbanism.

Table 4.4 shows the results of a series of multiple-regression equations that race our measure of state opinion against the socioeconomic variables as predictors of policy liberalism. The table presents equations for each of the eight components of the policy index in addition to the overall index of policy liberalism. For each dependent variable, the table summarizes the results of three separate equations that predict policy from socioeconomic variables alone, from state opinion alone, and from environment and opinion together. Equations are standardized, meaning that the regression coefficients represent the estimated effect on the dependent variable (in terms of standard deviation units) of one standard deviation movement in the independent variable. Standardization facilitates the comparison of effects across variables.

If we look first at the equations explaining policy from socioeconomic variables alone, we see that these variables do seem to contribute to the explanation of state policy, as the literature suggests. But note what happens when we allow state opinion to enter the equation. With or without the socioeconomic variables in the equation, state opinion is significantly related to each policy variable. On the other hand, with state opinion in

Table 4.3. *Relationships between state ideology and selected socioeconomic variables*

| Variable | Correlations | | | | Standardized regression coefficients (dependent: ideology) |
	Wealth	Urbanism	Education	Ideology	
Wealth: median family income	1.00	.58*	.60*	.61*	0.55*
Urbanism: % state population in metropolitan areas	.58*	1.00	.07	.52*	0.21
Education: % state residents (age 25 and over) with a high school degree	.60*	.07	1.00	.24	-0.10
Adjusted R^2					.37

Note: *Significant at .05.

the equation, only a scattering of the socioeconomic coefficients are significant. The seemingly dominant socioeconomic variables are overwhelmed when the contribution of state opinion is taken into account.

The analysis focusing on composite policy liberalism produces the most intriguing results. Since this index is based on the sum of state responses to the eight separate policy indicators, it should reflect a common component of policy liberalism and little else. Therefore, this index should show the clearest effect of opinion on policy. This expectation is born out handsomely. The coefficient describing the impact of public opinion on the composite measure is a sizable 0.70, down only slightly from the original coefficient of 0.82 without the socioeconomic controls.

Without state opinion in the equation, the socioeconomic variables, and income in particular, seem to do a fair job of predicting composite policy liberalism. But note the fate of income when state ideology is entered. The standardized coefficient for income drops from 0.46 to 0.09, a statistically insignificant effect.

Table 4.4. *Regressions of state policies on state socioeconomic variables and opinion*

Dependent variable	Independent variables				
	Income	Urbanism	Education	Opinion liberalism	Adjusted R^2
Per pupil	.67*	.05	.06		.508
educational				.75*	.558
expenditures	.38*	-.06	.11	.52*	.674
Medicaid: scope	.33	.21	.07		.209
				.67*	.433
	.00	.09	.12	.59*	.413
AFDC: scope	.42*	.26	.13		.427
				.66*	.423
	.20	.18	.17	.40*	.517
Consumer policy	.15	.30	.34		.316
				.56*	.313
	-.06	.22	.38*	.39*	.396
Criminal justice policy	.26	.16	.10		.122
				.46*	.194
	.06	.09	.13	.34*	.177
Legalized gambling policy	.21	.25	.17		.197
				.76*	.575
	-.22	.09	.25	.79*	.580
Equal rights policy	.46	-.26	.14		.178
				.55*	.291
	.11	-.39	.21	.64*	.402
Tax progressivity	.28	.03	.17		.119
				.49*	.218
	.04	-.06	.21	.44*	.222
Composite policy	.46*	.17	.20		.453
liberalism				.82*	.680
	.09	.03	.26*	.70*	.755

Note: Coefficients are standardized regression coefficients.
*Significant at .05.

The absence of a direct link between income and policy has important implications. The statistical importance of income in previous studies has been one of the primary pillars of the economic determinism interpretation. Our results show that high income predicts liberal state policies largely because income is correlated with the degree of liberal sentiment of state public opinion. Rather than concluding that state policy is inevitably determined by state wealth, we report with some confidence that the liberalism or conservatism of state policy results largely from the source that democratic theory would direct us to: the relative liberalism or conservatism of the state's electorate.

We may even question whether the socioeconomic variables (or at least the three we have chosen) present a collectively significant set of effects on the index of policy liberalism when state opinion is controlled. The appropriate F-test, however, shows that collectively, these variables are highly significant at .003. Education appears to lead the way, with a coefficient that is significant at the .05 level in its own right.

There is statistical evidence, however, that even this residual socioeconomic influence on policy is an artifact of the imperfect measurement of state opinion. Suppose we divide our 47 states at the median again, in terms of sample size for the estimation of state opinion. Suppose also for each group that we replicate our equation predicting policy liberalism from opinion, education, median family income, and urbanism. The results are shown in Table 4.5, Columns 1 and 2. For the larger states, the collective significance of the three socioeconomic variables is .64, or even less than the expected .5 value if the null hypothesis were true. For the smaller states we also find a lack of significance – due to the halving of the sample size – but with a p-value of .07. Some clarification results when education stands by itself as the only socioeconomic variable in competition with state opinion (Columns 3 and 4). Education is significant in the small states but not the large states. Similar results (not shown) obtain when we substitute the eight separate policy dependent variables and examine the effects of socioeconomic variables for the 23 states with the largest sample sizes. We obtain but one significant "effect" when state opinion is held constant – an evident pro-gambling effect of urbanism.

We conclude from this statistical exercise that socioeconomic variables add very little to the prediction of state policy beyond that predicted by state opinion. Even when socioeconomic variables (notably education) appear as significant in a regression equation, the result appears to be an artifact of sampling error in the measurement of state opinion. Restrict the analysis to states with large opinion samples and all evidence of independent socioeconomic effects disappear. Socioeconomic variables do predict policy liberalism, of course, when state opinion is omitted from the equa-

Table 4.5. *Policy regressions by size of state sample*

Independent variables	Opinion and Demographics		Opinion and Education	
	(1)	(2)	(3)	(4)
	Large sample states	Small sample states	Large sample states	Small sample states
	(*N*=23)	(*N*=24)	(*N*=23)	(*N*=24)
State opinion	0.73*	0.69*	0.81*	0.75*
Wealth	0.04	0.15		
Urbanism	0.07	-0.01		
Education	0.13	0.26	0.13	0.36*
Adjusted R^2	.809	.627	.819	.654
Collective significance of socioeconomic variables	.64	.07	.38	.01

Note: Coefficients are standardized regression coefficients. *Significant at .05.

tion. This is because state socioeconomic variables reflect the ideological division of state opinion.[4]

REVERSE CAUSATION?

The previous section showed that the strong relationship between state opinion and state policy survives some obvious controls. But spuriousness

4. It is conceivable that some additional unmeasured variable may be a common cause of the eight policy indicators. Evidence would be a pattern of strong partial correlations among the policy indicators when state opinion is held constant. We examined these partial correlations for the 23 states with the largest samples for the state opinion measure. Of the 28 partial correlations, only 2 are statistically significant. A reasonable interpretation is that other than state ideological preference, the causes of these variables are essentially idiosyncratic to the particular indicator.

is not the only potential threat to the inference that state opinion drives state policy. Another possibility is that we have the causal flow reversed. Conceivably, it is the policy tendency of the state that drives public preferences rather than the other way around. How could this reverse process come about? We can imagine that state elites determine the ideological tone of state policy and then successfully sell it to a passive state public. Or state publics may obligingly support whatever they learn the policy tendency of the state to be: For example, conservative policies may cue voters to call themselves conservative.

To separate the effect of opinion on policy from contamination by any reverse causal flow, it is necessary to employ a simultaneous equation estimation procedure, such as two-stage least squares (2SLS). Two-stage least squares estimation requires one or more instrumental variables that predict the independent variable in question (here, state opinion) but are causally unrelated to the dependent variable (here, state policy). Fortunately, we have a good set of instrumental variables for this purpose: the numerical strengths of various religious groups in the state.

Our instrumental variables are percent Jewish, percent Catholic, and percent fundamentalist Protestant in the states.[5] As instrumental variables, we argue, these variables influence state opinion but do not influence the ideological direction of state policy except indirectly, as determinants of state opinion. In the first stage, these measures of religious affiliation are employed along with our initial set of socioeconomic variables (income, urbanism, education) as predictors of state opinion. In standardized form, this equation is

$$\overset{\wedge}{\text{Opinion Liberalism}} = 0.18(\text{income}) + 0.22(\text{urbanism})$$
$$- 0.04(\text{education}) + 0.03(\%$$
$$\text{Catholic}) - 0.51(\% \text{ fundamentalist}) + 0.16(\% \text{ Jewish})$$

Adjusted R^2 = .628

For the second stage, the relationship between state opinion and state policy controlling for socioeconomic variables is reestimated with one important difference. The predicted values for state opinion liberalism (from the first-stage equation) are substituted for its actual values in the

---

5. Church membership by state was obtained from the National Council of Churchs' *Church and Church Membership in the United States,* Johnson, Picard, and Quinn, eds., 1974. Protestant denominations coded here as "fundamentalist" include all Baptists, Latter Day Saints, and those denominations coded as "neofundamentalist" in the National Election Studies codebooks. Percent Jewish by state was obtained from *American Jewish Yearbook 1972,* vol. 73 (New York: American Jewish Committee and the Jewish Publication Society of America, 1972), pp. 386–7, as reported in Leo Rosten (1975), 564–5.

policy equation. With state opinion standardized by actual rather than predicted values, this equation is

$$\overset{\wedge}{\text{Policy Liberalism}} = 0.86(\overset{\wedge}{\text{opinion liberalism}}) + 0.00(\text{income})$$
$$- 0.03(\text{urbanism}) + 0.27(\text{education})$$

Adjusted R^2 = .656

The result is clear. Using 2SLS estimation, the coefficient for state opinion is substantially larger than the original OLS (ordinary least squares) regression estimate, with a t-value of 5.1 statistically significant at the .001 level. Except for conceivable slippage due to religious variables influencing policy by bypassing state opinion, or state policies determining religious affiliations, the conclusion seems inescapable. The influence of state opinion on state policy is not seriously contaminated by the reverse process.[6]

WHY IS THE OPINION–POLICY CONNECTION SO STRONG? A DISCUSSION

State public opinion, as measured by the ideological disposition of state electorates, is strongly related to the ideological content of state policies. It may not surprise many readers to find that a reliable measure of state-level ideological preferences is related to liberal–conservative state policies in a way that is causally convincing. What may surprise the reader, however, and what deserves discussion, is the strength of the estimated effect of state opinion on state policy. Why does state opinion affect state policy so strongly?

Several plausible political mechanisms exist to translate the ideological preferences of a presumably inattentive public into an ideologically compatible pattern of sometimes obscure and invisible state policies. We may

---

6. The one-way nature of the causal process can be illustrated in an additional way. In Chapter 3, we separated state opinion into a "demographic" component due to measurable causes of state opinion and a second "cultural" component due to residual cultural factors. Conceivably, the cultural component of state ideology could be influenced by state policy; but certainly, the demographic component – race, religion, income, and the like – is not caused by state policy. Therefore, we should check the relative effects of the demographic and cultural components on state policy liberalism. If there is reason to worry about reverse causation, the cultural component would show an inflated "effect" that the demographic component would not. To compare the two effects properly, we employ unstandardized measures of the two state opinion components. In every variation on this equation, both components are highly significant, with the demographic component showing a significantly higher unstandardized coefficient. This is the opposite of what we would expect if the cultural component of state ideology were responsive to state policies.

start with elections: As elections allow voters to choose from among competing elites, state electorates will tend to place in the state legislature candidates who share their political values and reject those who do not. This electoral connection may be as simple as the electorate's relative preference for the state's Republican and Democratic parties. The state's two major parties display different shadings of ideology for the state electorate to choose from. The state electorate chooses a balance of Democrats and Republicans for state office. The resultant mix of elected officials then enacts an ideologically predictable set of policies.

We explore this electoral connection in Chapters 5 and 6. Enhancing the process, the recruitment of candidates from the same constituencies as the voters they hope to represent means that the values of the legislators should reflect state ideology to some extent, even apart from any issue voting or ideological voting by the state electorate. From this "sharing" of political values between voters and candidates (Erikson, Luttbeg, and Tedin, 1991), enhanced by the electorate's sorting of candidates into winners and losers on the basis of issues and ideology, state electorates tend to elect legislators who want the same things they do.

Legislators can also go against their own values to follow public opinion. This may happen circuitously, for instance, when interest groups exert their influence: The proposals that interest groups urge for the legislative agenda presumably reflect the ideological tone of the state. Of course, legislators also react to public opinion directly from fear of electoral sanctions. The policies in question are often salient to segments of the state electorate. Further, state legislators and other relevant actors perceive that the public is watching on these issues.

The policies represented by our various policy indices include such matters of heightened public concern as the death penalty, ERA ratification, state income tax, and state lotteries. Legislative votes on these matters are known to concentrate the attention of state electorates. Whether these matters become the stuff of electoral mandates, state legislators prefer to avoid becoming victims of public outrage by voting incorrectly.

Not all the state legislative actions that created state scores on our policy indicators were visible to much of the state electorate. But consider some more of the issues involved. Probably a tier below capital punishment, the ERA, state lotteries, and a state income tax in public visibility are state issues like horse racing, victim compensation, consumer protection packages, and changes in education spending. State decisions regarding welfare issues such as AFDC and Medicaid sometimes are also made under a strong public spotlight. On the issues we have mentioned, legislators would be mindful of the potential reactions from various segments of the public. These reactions may be difficult to gauge. But when legislators assess possible public readiness for policy changes on these issues, they may refer to their sense of their constituencies' overall degree of liberalism or conservatism.

To account for the strong opinion–policy correlation, it is important to consider that state policy liberalism is the product of numerous policy decisions and nondecisions summed across not only multiple policy areas but also across time. The weighted sum of a state's policies at any one time reflects the accumulation of state policies over many years and even decades. We need not conceptualize the opinion–policy linkage as an immediate responsiveness of state policy in any year to the voice of public opinion in that year. Such a conceptualization is certainly unrealistic. The cross-sectional patterns we have examined represent the accumulation of governmental responses to public opinion over a reasonably long time period. Except for extreme in- or out-migration, we have no reason to suspect much volatility in the relative positions of state electorates over time. Indeed, as described in Chapter 2, we have strong evidence that state differences in ideological preference were virtually stationary for the period 1976–88. We might further surmise that our measure of state ideology in the late 1970s and early 1980s is a reasonable reflection of state ideology throughout, say, most of the post–World War II era. In fact, the limited historical evidence does suggest considerable continuity to state ideology over the long haul, although not as extreme as the near stasis of recent times (see Chapter 9). We can state our central finding this way: State opinion over the recent era is strongly related to the accumulation of liberal versus conservative policies during the same era.[7]

This line of speculation is not overly bold. To account for the strong relationship between opinion liberalism and policy liberalism, we need not posit some implausibly deterministic effect of general liberalism–conservatism as the dominant cause of specific policies. Policy liberalism is manifested only from multiple legislative decisions aggregated across policies and across time. This long-term inclination of the state to enact a certain mix of liberal and conservative policies is largely determined, in a variety of ways, by state public opinion.[8]

---

7. Although state opinion may be largely static, policies can change and new policy questions arrive on state agendas. For one study of policy change as a function of an early version of our state opinion measure, see Lowery, Gray, and Hager (1989).
8. As a technical matter, we can speculate how to model the time-series process underlying our discussion. An interesting possibility is an "error corrections" model where most of the action is in the error term. By an application of the error corrections model, the public opinion that matters for state election outcomes is the public's attitudes toward policy change – too much/too little – rather than which absolute level is just right. By this second model, one ends up with two integrated time series (opinion and policy), which have an equilibrium relationship through time and in which deviations from equilibrium at time t produce compensation at $t + 1$.

CAUSATION IS NOT CONGRUENCE: A DISCLAIMER

We have shown that the most liberal states enact the most liberal policies and the most conservative states enact the most conservative policies. However, we must avoid any claim about the exact fit between state preferences and state policy. The reason, of course, is that opinion liberalism and policy liberalism do not share a common metric. This limitation in no way weakens our ability to make causal inferences about how opinion liberalism affects policy liberalism. But it does mean that we cannot discern whether any particular state has more liberal or more conservative policies than its electorate wants. This is an obvious point, but perhaps one worth considering in detail. Figure 4.5 presents some different projections of our opinion–policy scatterplot on a hypothetical grid where opinion and policy are scored on a common hypothetical scale. As the base for this scale, state opinion is represented in standardized units, with mean state opinion equaling zero and a standard deviation of 1.0.

Consider first the "ideal," shown in Figure 4.5a, where the expected policy equals state opinion. As depicted in Figure 4.5a, the regression of policy on opinion yields a slope of 1.0. Given $b = 1.0$, any opinion change would bring about a corresponding one-to-one change in policy. And given an intercept of zero as well as $b = 1.0$, average policy equals average opinion. If this is the correct calibration, then policy matches opinion whenever state policy falls directly on the regression line that forecasts policy from opinion.

However, even if opinion influences policy in the manner reflected by the opinion–policy correlation, sources of bias can push policies systematically in one ideological direction away from what the state electorates want. For instance, on issues in which business groups have an interest, we might find legislatures consistently enacting policies somewhat more conservative than what the state electorate wants. This possible conservative bias is depicted in Figure 4.5b. Or perhaps on some social issues, the values of the legislators themselves could generate policies somewhat more liberal than what the public wants. This possibility is depicted in Figure 4.5c. In short, variables other than the preferences of the general public may systematically push state policies off center from the mean (or median) voter position, even as state opinion is determining the positions of the states relative to one another on the liberal–conservative policy continuum.

Statistically, if there were a common metric for opinion and policy, these biases would be reflected in the intercept of the regression equation predicting opinion from policy. In addition to not knowing the bias because the intercept is unknown, we are also ignorant of the true "slope" of the opinion–policy relationship. The slope has consequences for represen-

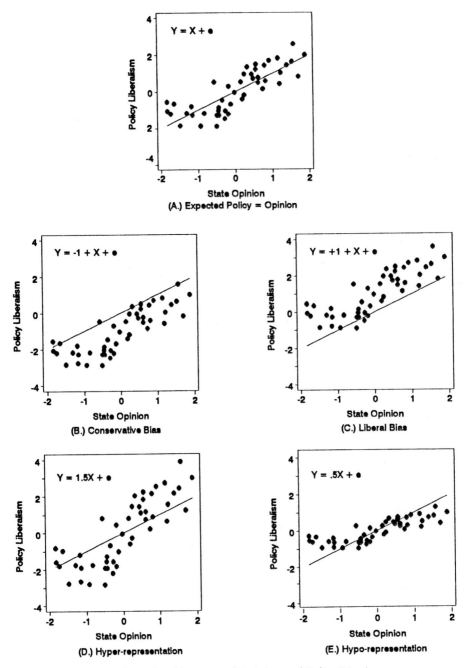

Figure 4.5 Hypothetical Calibrations of Opinion and Policy Metrics

tational accuracy too. From a representational standpoint, the ideal true slope is the value 1.0, reflecting a one-to-one policy response to opinion.

We can imagine a slope greater than 1.0. Assuming a zero intercept, this would mean that policies tend to be too liberal in liberal states and too conservative in conservative states. This possibility is shown in Figure 4.5d. This outcome of "hyper-representation" is not far-fetched. It could occur, for example, if liberal states misjudge and elect too many liberal Democrats and conservative states elect too many conservative Republicans.

The opposite possibility would be sluggish hyporepresentation with a slope less than the ideal of 1.0. The result would be policy that is too conservative in liberal states and too liberal in conservative states. This possibility of is shown in Figure 4.5e.

We could show even more possibilities by both moving the intercept off zero and the slope off 1.0 in the same graph. To imagine one example, there could be hyporepresentation with a conservative bias. We might also ask, as we consider the myriad of possibilities, what shreds of certainty are left in our causal interpretation? Opinion certainly appears to cause policy, but there is a lot about the nature of this process that we do not know and, given the lack of a common metric, seemingly cannot know.

What we surely know is that the strong correlation between opinion and policy represents a causal process in equilibrium. Measured in terms of mean ideological preference, opinion is stable in the long run, at least for the 13-year span we have examined. Opinion for 1976–88 is strongly related to policy as coarsely measured for a swath of time around the year 1980. Presumably, our opinion measure would be equally correlated with policy liberalism as measured for a later time as well. Whether this is so is an empirical matter of some interest.

As a dynamic causal process, we could imagine a state undergoing the shock of a sudden or gradual ideological movement. Suppose, for example, that the mass public of Oklahoma suddenly turns liberal. What would happen? Our strong inference is that, over time, policy would become more liberal to match the ideological movement of the electorate. Our evidence strongly suggests that states rarely make major ideological lurches of this kind. But states must sometimes undergo at least gradual ideological movement, and when they do, policy should adjust in the same direction. And when a state's policies are more liberal or more conservative than in other states with similar ideological preferences, the state's policies presumably would gradually return to equilibrium. In these ways our analysis sustains the democratic faith that opinion determines policy. But whether this equilibrium is more conservative or more liberal than state opinion, or undershoots or overshoots the exact mean of mass preferences, we cannot be sure.

CONCLUSION

This chapter only begins our exploration of the terrain that needs to be mapped to understand the relationships between state publics, political institutions, and policy making. Our central conclusion reverses that of much of the state policy literature of the past twenty years. State politics – elections, legislatures, and executives in all their variations – do matter. State political structures appear to do a good job of delivering more liberal policies to more liberal states and more conservative policies to more conservative states. Across an impressive range of policies, public opinion counts, and not just a little.

5

State parties and state opinion

Political parties hold a special place in modern theories of democracy. They were not popular when anticipated by the founders of the U.S. Constitution (see Madison's Federalist Paper no. 10), and they are not generally thought well of by the general U.S. public today (Dennis, 1978; Wattenberg, 1986). Nevertheless, it is difficult to envision representative democracy in complex societies without competitive political parties.

Two different models of party competition are commonly presented, usually as if the two models are in direct competition with one another. One is the "responsible parties model," which as a prescriptive doctrine promotes ideologically distinct political parties. The other, sometimes called the "public opinion" model (Page, 1978), is more commonly called the "Downs" model after the theorist Anthony Downs (1957). While it is common to juxtapose these two models as competing with one another, they are in fact complementary, each drawing on different aspects of party motivation. The responsible parties model emphasizes the policy or ideological motivations of party elites, which push party positions away from center. The Downs model emphasizes the electoral incentives pushing politicians toward the center in order to get elected. As we will see, the positions of state political parties represent both sets of forces.

The responsible parties doctrine was a product of political science thinking in the 1940s and 1950s. Inspired by British electoral experience, its advocates (Schattschneider, 1942; Committee on Political Parties, 1950) favored strongly disciplined and cohesive political parties that would offer distinct policy programs. According to the design, responsible parties were to be internally democratic, so that party activists would control the content of party programs. In U.S. politics the responsible parties doctrine would translate as a competition between a cohesively liberal Democratic Party and a cohesively conservative Republican Party. U.S. institutional arrangements – particularly federalism and the separation of powers – prevent a responsible parties system from catching hold in this country in anything like the fashion envisioned by its promoters. Still, the responsible parties model emphasizes one aspect of party and electoral behavior that makes politics interesting: Democratic and Republican politicians participate in politics to achieve policy or ideological goals that matter to them.

The second – and often decisive – motivation of politicians is to get elected and stay elected. This motivation is the center of Anthony Downs's (1957) model, as described in his classic book *An Economic Theory of Democracy*. Downs presented members of the electorate as generally voting for the candidates or political parties that are closest to their particular ideological viewpoint. To the extent that ideology is electorally decisive, candidates and parties must compete for the favor of the pivotal voters in the ideological center. (Strictly speaking, the median voter determines purely ideological elections.) To win, parties and candidates must appeal to the center even as they may prefer more ideologically "extreme" positions themselves. To the extent the Downs model works, elections are close contests between two similar centrist parties or candidates rather than an ideological battle of polar opposites. Downsian outcomes may be less interesting than ideological warfare, but they enhance the abstraction we call representative democracy by handing control of policy to the voters in the center of the ideological spectrum.

To address variations on the themes of responsible parties versus the electoral incentive of the Downs model, it is helpful to focus on differences in the factors that motivate party officials in the two models. In the responsible parties model, the parties are motivated by concerns with policy. They are constituted by teams of like-minded people with the goals of winning office in order to achieve their policy objectives. In the Downsian model, the party motivation is simply to win office. Downsian parties treat policy stances as a means of winning, not as ends to be achieved. In reality, American state parties experience both of these motivations: The political ideologues' calls for ideological purity persistently conflict with the electoral incentive for ideological moderation.

To some extent, these conflicting motivations separate the parties' activist elites from their electoral elites. Ideology can motivate a party's activists to work for its success, free of the responsibility that comes with trying to get elected themselves. When party elites become candidates themselves, the chance of getting elected can compel more moderate postures. Thus, we hypothesize a possible ideological distinction between a party's activist elites and its electoral elites. We expect to find activists more ideologically extreme and electoral candidates more responsive to public opinion.

In this chapter, we explore the ideological preferences of state party elites and the degree to which they represent the ideological preferences of

state electorates. For this analysis, we introduce measures of the ideologies of Democratic and Republican state party elites. These new measures are compiled from data gathered in several previous studies. We
define the party "elites" broadly to include those who are the activists
(campaign volunteers, contributors, convention delegates, and party officials) and those who seek office and sometimes get elected under the ban-
ners of the parties. Following the responsible parties model, we examine
the ideological similarities of party elites and their mass counterparts –
parties' rank-and-file voters or, more precisely, their party identifiers within the electorate. Following the Downs model, we also examine the party
elites' ideological similarities to the electorate as a whole. We find evidence that parties are pulled in two opposite directions – toward their
ideological poles by their own activists and toward the political center of
their states, where the votes are.

MEASURING STATE PARTY ELITE IDEOLOGIES

In Chapter 2, we assigned ideological scores to state electorates and to
their constituent sets of Democratic and Republican (plus Independent)
party identifiers. In this chapter, we measure the ideologies of the state
Democratic and Republican party elites. For this task, we are fortunate to
draw on several data sources developed by other scholars. Borrowing
from the efforts of other researchers, we have assembled four separate
indicators of the ideological preferences of Democratic and Republican
state elites.

1. *Congressional candidates' conservatism–liberalism.* Using the 1974,
    1978, and 1982 CBS/NYT surveys of congressional candidates, we are
    able to estimate the ideological positions of all congressional candi-
    dates who ran in these three elections. First, the issue responses to the
    CBS/NYT candidate surveys were summed to create ideological
    scores (Wright, 1986; Wright and Berkman, 1986). Second, to make
    the scores equivalent across surveys, scores were standardized on the
    basis of the scores for incumbents who served throughout the period.
    Third, state means were calculated as the mean ideology scores for all
    Democratic and all Republican candidates cumulated for the state in
    the CBS/NYT surveys. The result is the measurement of the mean
    ideological position of each party's congressional candidates for each
    state.
2. *State legislators' conservatism–liberalism.* For a study of legislative
    decision making, Uslaner and Weber (1977) surveyed more than a
    thousand state legislators in 1974. Among the issues addressed were
    the legislators' opinions on the death penalty, abortion, pollution reg-
    ulation, gun control, teachers' unions, and the legalization of mari-

juana. From the legislative responses, we constructed factor scores to represent the legislators' composite ideological positions. Mean factor scores were calculated for the legislators of each state party.[1]

3. *Local party chairpersons' conservatism–liberalism.* For a study of state and local party organizations, Cotter et al. (1984) ascertained the ideological identifications of county party chairpersons in 1979–80. Ideological identification was measured as position on the National Election Studies' seven-point scale from "extremely conservative" to "extremely liberal." Mean ideological identifications of Republican and of Democratic county chairpersons in each state serve as our third measure of party elite ideology.

4. *National convention delegates' conservatism–liberalism.* Miller and Jennings collected the ideological self-identifications of delegates to the 1980 Democratic and Republican national conventions (Miller and Jennings, 1987). The self-identifications are self-ratings on the National Election Studies seven-point scale.

We have, then, eight different measures, four for each of the two major parties, for 46 states. These measures tap ideological tendencies or sentiment for different elite party groups during a short interval of time. In the process, we drop one more state from analysis – Nebraska. We exclude Nebraska because of its strictly nonpartisan legislative politics and the absence of any measure of state legislative liberalism.

Our next task is to establish the structure of the relationships among these indicators. Table 5.1 shows the correlations among the indices, first within each of the political parties, then between Democrats and Republicans, and then pooling Democratic and Republican parties together. Within each party, the four indices intercorrelate in the .5 to .7 range. The measures clearly share a common source of variance, presumably ideology, plus considerable unique variance of their own. Across parties (e.g., Democratic legislators with Republican party chairs), the correlations are considerably lower. When we pool the Democratic and Republican measures, the correlations are substantially stronger, averaging .81. This increase is expected, because the pooling of Democratic and Republican parties expands the variance.

We use a simple factor analysis to uncover the structure of the relationships among the eight measures. Not unexpectedly, this exercise reveals that the party elite ideology is structured primarily by party affiliation. Table 5.2 displays the rotated principle factor components solution. All the Democratic measures load on one factor, while the measures of Re-

---

1. The Weber-Uslaner data contained no South Carolina Republicans. We estimated the ideological score for South Carolina Republican legislators from the South Carolina Republican scores on the other three elite ideology variables.

Table 5.1. *Correlations among components of state party elite ideology*

State Democratic elites (N=46)

	County chairs	Convention delegates	State legislators	Congressional candidates
County chairs	1.00			
Convention delegates	.56	1.00		
State legislators	.53	.63	1.00	
Congressional candidates	.68	.63	.73	1.00

State Republican elites (N=46)

	County chairs	Convention delegates	State legislators	Congressional candidates
County chairs	1.00			
Convention delegates	.56	1.00		
State legislators	.52	.69	1.00	
Congressional candidates	.59	.58	.69	1.00

Cross-party comparisons (N=46)

	Republican			
Democratic	County chairs	Convention delegates	State legislators	Congressional candidates
County chairs	.25			
Convention delegates	.46	.29		
State legislators	.50	.42	.49	
Congressional candidates	.54	.66	.57	.63

Total combined (N=92)

	Democratic & Republican			
Democratic & Republican	County chairs	Convention delegates	State legislators	Congressional candidates
County chairs	1.00			
Convention delegates	.91	1.00		
State legislators	.71	.72	1.00	
Congressional candidates	.89	.88	.80	1.00

Note: N=46; Alaska, Hawaii, Nebraska, and Nevada are omitted.

Table 5.2. *Rotated principal components factor solution for eight indicators of party elite liberalism*

Party Elites	Republican	Democratic
Republican		
State legislators	.86	.23
Convention delegates	.79	.31
Congressional candidates	.83	.23
County party chairs	.67	.36
Democratic		
State legislators	.32	.79
Convention delegates	.04	.90
Congressional candidates	.52	.75
County party chairs	.27	.75

publican elites load on the other. This result, reflecting the correlations of Table 5.1, supports our decision to construct a composite measure of party elite ideology. The four sets of Democratic scores go together in one factor (intercorrelate), presumably because they all reflect a common source: the unique ideological tendency of the state's Democratic Party leadership. The four sets of Republican scores go together for the similar reason: the common source of a unique ideological tendency of the state Republican Party leadership. Suppose that counter to our findings we discovered the presence of but one single factor resulting from the factor analysis. Then we would naturally choose a single-factor solution also. But we would also have to argue awkwardly that the two groups of party elites in the state shared the common variance of one common ideological tendency, relative to the parties' norms.

We combine the different elite indicators into composite measures of Democratic and Republican party elite liberalism–conservatism. Multi-indicator measurement of party elite ideology mitigates the effects of idiosyncratic measurement errors of the individual indices. For our composite measures, we first created standardized measures across all 92 party elites for each of the four components. We then sum the four Democratic measures for a measure of Democratic ideology and sum the four Republican measures for a measure of Republican ideology. This procedure implicitly assumes that all four types of party elites have the same mean ideology and, within each type, the same standard deviation. We do not assume the parties are equally far apart on each of the indicators, nor that the distributions within the parties are equal.

On balance, we have ample reason to believe in the integrity of our measures of state party elite ideology. There is a simple face validity that is persuasive; we have measures of four different groups of elites that together make about as good a sample of party elites as we could construct if we were gathering the data from scratch. The numbers of cases on which particular state estimates for individual measures is smaller in a few cases than we would like; but this is mitigated by our access to four measures, which helps to overcome the vagaries of the individual estimates. Ideologies of the different party elite groups are correlated in a manner to suggest that the different index components measure similar things.[2] We are ready to discuss the actual estimates of party elite ideology.

PARTY ELITE IDEOLOGY

Our analysis begins with a look at the scores of party elite ideology, presented in Table 5.3, which shows the state scores for the activist (county chairs plus convention delegates) and electoral (congressional candidates plus state legislators) components as well as for the overall samples of party elites. The most conservative elites are Texas Republicans (-6.03), and the most liberal are the California Democrats (7.54). The most conservative elites of both parties tend to be in the South, with this pattern truer for Democrats than for Republicans. The correlation of region (a 1,0 dummy variable for South–non-South) is $-.64$ for Democratic elites and $-.50$ for Republican elites.

Republican scores are overwhelmingly negative, indicating conservative positions, while Democratic state party elites are overwhelmingly positive, meaning liberal. Almost all Republican state parties, in other words, are more conservative than almost all Democratic state parties. Ideological differences between the leaderships of the two parties are certainly no surprise and may be regarded as a matter of common knowledge. In the political science literature, studies spanning several decades

2. We also have evidence that party elite liberalism is temporally stable. For the congressional candidate data, we have estimates for 1974, 1978, and 1982. For the liberalism of the states' Democratic candidates, the three intercorrelations are .73 for 1974–8, .67 for 1974–82, and .60 for 1978–82. For Republicans, the correlations are .58 for 1974–8, .63 for 1974–82, and .69 for 1978–82. Note that the correlations do not seriously attenuate for the longer (1974–82) time interval. We are also able to compare the state mean 1980 convention delegates' ideologies to state means from Miller and Jennings's later study of 1984 delegates. The correlations are .70 for Democrats and .83 for Republicans.

Table 5.3. *Party elite ideology scores*

State	Democratic elites			Republican elites		
	Activist	Electoral	Overall	Activist	Electoral	Overall
Alabama	0.69	-1.24	-0.55	-2.18	-0.64	-2.83
Arizona	2.28	2.34	4.62	-1.47	-1.85	-3.32
Arkansas	0.73	0.19	0.92	-1.96	-2.71	-4.68
California	3.44	4.03	7.47	-2.12	-1.28	-3.44
Colorado	2.27	3.02	5.29	-2.65	-0.93	-3.58
Connecticut	1.86	3.30	5.17	-0.96	0.15	-0.80
Delaware	0.67	0.48	1.16	-1.46	0.10	-1.35
Florida	1.11	0.49	1.61	-2.73	-2.00	-4.74
Georgia	0.57	-0.49	0.07	-2.46	-2.26	-4.72
Idaho	2.28	0.03	2.31	-2.43	-3.16	-5.60
Illinois	1.74	2.09	3.83	-1.55	-.85	-2.41
Indiana	1.18	2.27	3.46	-1.46	-1.87	-3.34
Iowa	2.74	2.88	5.63	-0.74	-0.87	-1.61
Kansas	1.92	2.41	4.34	-1.68	-0.63	-2.32
Kentucky	1.16	0.16	1.32	-1.81	-1.44	-3.26
Louisiana	0.64	-1.27	-0.62	-2.64	-2.25	-4.89
Maine	3.12	1.52	4.64	-1.50	-0.32	-1.83
Maryland	2.07	2.38	4.46	-1.06	-0.83	-1.89
Massachusetts	2.26	3.13	5.39	-1.08	0.60	-0.47
Michigan	2.53	2.75	5.28	-0.96	0.12	-0.84
Minnesota	3.10	2.78	5.89	-1.07	-0.46	-1.54
Mississippi	0.71	-1.42	-0.71	-2.23	-3.35	-5.58
Missouri	1.00	0.39	1.40	-2.01	-2.06	-4.08
Montana	2.43	1.32	3.76	-2.56	-1.94	-4.51
New Hampshire	2.56	1.61	4.17	-1.57	-0.74	-2.31
New Jersey	2.02	2.74	4.77	-0.49	0.07	-0.41
New Mexico	0.90	0.58	1.49	2.70	-2.27	-4.97
New York	2.05	2.82	4.88	-0.63	-0.03	-0.67
North Carolina	1.10	-0.08	1.01	-2.64	-3.20	-5.84
North Dakota	2.64	1.72	4.36	-1.65	-1.73	-3.38
Ohio	1.97	2.43	4.40	-1.81	-1.52	-3.33
Oklahoma	0.70	-0.77	-0.07	-2.83	-2.96	-5.79
Oregon	2.63	2.47	5.11	-0.89	0.28	-0.60
Pennsylvania	2.09	1.73	3.83	-1.00	-0.09	-1.09
Rhode Island	1.34	1.46	2.80	-1.12	0.55	-0.56
South Carolina	1.21	0.34	1.56	-2.44	-2.85	-5.30
South Dakota	1.90	2.30	4.21	-1.91	-2.67	-4.58
Tennessee	1.16	0.73	1.90	-1.65	-2.50	-4.16
Texas	0.83	1.06	1.90	-2.89	-3.15	-6.05
Utah	2.16	-0.36	1.79	-1.81	-2.82	-4.63
Vermont	2.55	1.64	4.20	-1.63	1.23	-0.40
Virginia	1.92	-0.11	1.81	-2.36	-2.63	-4.99
Washington	2.11	2.37	4.49	-1.95	-0.34	-2.30
West Virginia	1.09	0.88	1.98	-2.33	-1.66	-3.99
Wisconsin	3.23	3.39	6.62	-1.36	-1.20	-2.57
Wyoming	2.15	0.64	2.79	-2.39	-2.15	-4.55

have shown Democratic and Republican elites to be ideologically divergent.[3]

An overview of the political geography of the two parties is shown in Figure 5.1. Here we have shaded the states according to degree of liberalism–conservatism using our overall measure of party elite ideology. (Note, however, that this shading represents within-party tendencies; the Republican state parties are, individually and as a group, much more conservative than the Democratic state parties, as can be readily seen from the figures of Table 5.3.) The patterns overlap some, with the most conservative elites of both parties well represented in the southern states. Republican conservatism, however, extends more thoroughly through the western states than is the case for the Democratic Party. The more liberal wings of both parties are found among the states of the Mid-Atlantic and upper Midwest regions. It is not the case, however, that the two parties always move together. Notice the contiguous states of Oregon and California for example. The Democratic Parties of both states are quite liberal, as are Republican party elites in Oregon. The Republican leadership in California, in contrast, is relatively conservative. These intrastate variations can be observed more systematically in Figure 5.2.

Figure 5.2 plots the relative liberalism–conservatism of the states' two parties. For each state, the Democratic position is located on the horizontal axis and the Republican position is located on the vertical axis. Figure 5.2 clarifies the ideological polarization of the state parties. In every state, the Democratic party elite is more liberal than the state's Republican elite – and with ideological room to spare. Thus, as estimated by the ideological preferences of party elites, state parties offer a true ideological choice.

But just as states' party elites are pulled ideologically apart, they are also pulled together by some common force. We see this from the modestly impressive correlation (.63) between the Democratic and Republican elite ideological positions shown in Figure 5.2. The more liberal a state's Democratic elite, the more liberal too (relatively speaking) is the state's Republican elite. Our suspicion is that state opinion is the source of this correlation. Our next task is to examine this possibility.

3. A large literature has documented the very real ideological division between Democratic and Republican party activists. In addition to the sources of our elite ideology variables, consult the following. Regarding convention delegates, see McCloskey, Hoffman, and O'Hara (1960), Soule and McGrath (1975), Kirkpatrick (1976), Kweit (1986), Browning and Shaffer (1987), and Baer and Bositis (1988). Regarding candidate views, see Sullivan and O'Conner (1972), Backstrom (1977), and Erikson and Wright (1980). Regarding roll calls, see Bullock and Brady (1983), Poole and Rosenthal (1984), and Browning and Shaffer (1987). For theoretical discussions of party activists in the context of Downs-type modeling, see Aldrich (1983), Wittman (1983), and Calvert (1985).

State parties and state opinion

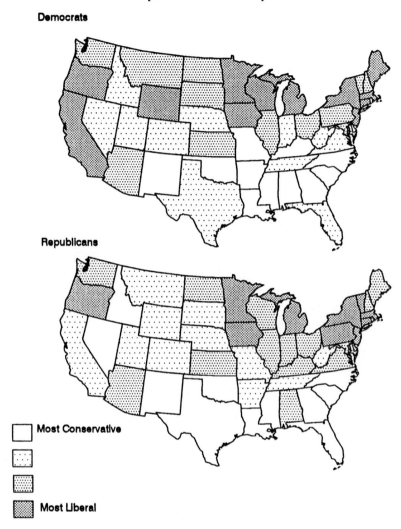

Figure 5.1 Map of State Party Elite Ideology

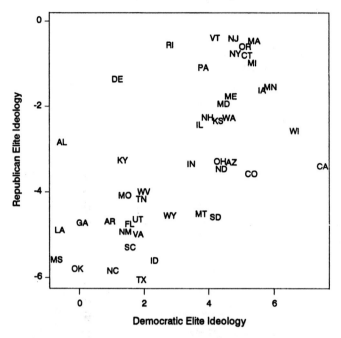

Figure 5.2 Democratic and Republican Elite Ideology

STATE OPINION AND PARTY ELITE IDEOLOGY

In Chapter 2, we presented the mean ideological identifications of state electorates. These mean ideology scores serve as a composite of state public opinion. It is time now to see how strongly state public opinion correlates with the ideological positions of state party elites. Figure 5.3 presents the scatterplots for both Democratic and Republican party elites. The correlations are a modest .62 for Democrats and a somewhat higher .77 for Republicans. Although our measures of state opinion and party ideology are on different scales, Figure 5.3 gives the strong impression that Democratic parties are generally to the left and Republican parties are generally to the right of state electorates.

Impressive as the correlations between the party elite ideology measures and state opinion may seem, they are not strong enough to offer a full statistical explanation for the .63 correlation between Republican and Democratic elite ideologies. For state opinion to be the sole cause of the elite-level correlation, the product of the two elite measures' correlations with state opinion would need to approximate the .67 correlation of the two elite measures. At .47 (i.e., .77 × .62), the observed product falls considerably short of the mark.

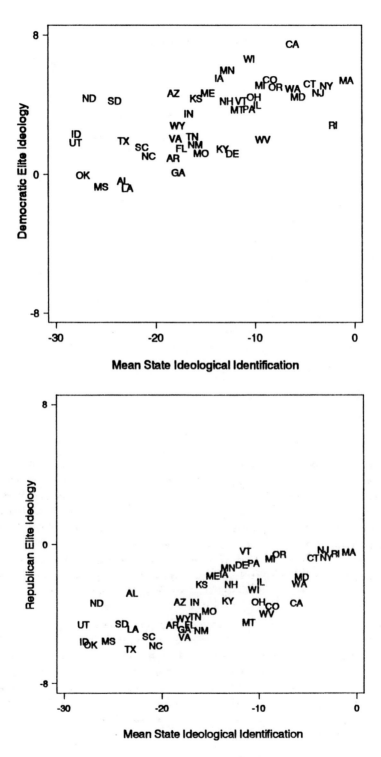

Figure 5.3 Party Elite Ideology by State Ideological Identification

However, there is a quite satisfactory resolution of this shortfall. If we adjust for the measurement error in state opinion, the expected result appears. We can see this quite simply by dividing the states into two equal portions based on the sample size for the state opinion measure. (The half of the states with more respondents in the 13-year sample all have over 2,110 respondents.) In the states with larger, more reliable samples, the correlation between the two party elite measures is .67, about the same as we found for the total sample. For these states, state opinion correlates at a very strong .82 and .83 with Democratic and Republican elite ideologies, respectively. The product of these two numbers, .68, is actually a point larger than the target value of .67. We can readily conclude that for states with minimal measurement error, the influence of state opinion fully accounts for the correlation between state Democratic elite ideology and state Republican elite ideology. Meanwhile, for that half of the states with lesser sample sizes, the two party elite measures correlate at .59, offering satisfaction that these two measures are not attenuated for relatively unpopulous states. But due to the sampling error in the opinion measure, the Democratic and Republican elite measures correlate at only .42 and .73, respectively, with state opinion. The product equals a mere .31, but we partially attribute this low number to sampling error in the selection of states with small sample sizes for the opinion measure.

ACTIVIST ELITES, ELECTORAL ELITES, AND STATE OPINION

We can also separate out the state opinion–party elite correlations for activist elites (convention delegates and county chairpersons) and for electoral elites (state legislators and congressional candidates). Electoral leaders face the incentive to shade toward moderation, away from their party's ideological extreme. The amount of this pressure should be a function of state liberalism–conservatism. A Democratic candidate, for example, would be more pressured to moderate in a state with conservative voters than one with liberal voters. Of course, the same applies to a Republican in the other direction; the strength of the pull away from conservative extremism should be proportional to the liberalism of the state. Activists should feel this pressure much less, if at all.

The correlations shown in Table 5.4 and pictured in Figure 5.4 support these conjectures. State opinion more strongly correlates with the ideologies of electoral elites than that of activists. We can also examine the measures of elite opinion as a function of both state opinion and party affiliation. This entails pooling Democratic and Republican party elites in the same data set (N = states $\times$ 2 = 92). Table 5.5 shows a set of regressions that tells an interesting story. We regress both activist and electoral elite

Table 5.4. *Correlations between elite ideology and state opinion*

Elite type	Democratic elites	Republican elites
Activist	.37	.60
Electoral	.70	.78
Overall	.62	.77

Note: Table entries are Pearson product moment correlations between the ideology score for each elite group and state opinion liberalism.

ideologies on state opinion and party. Compare Equation 1 for activist ideology and Equation 2 for electoral elite ideology. That comparison shows that activist ideologies are the more responsive to party (3.61 vs. 2.75) while electoral elite ideologies are the more responsive to state opinion (.05 vs. .13). Equation 3, with electoral elite ideology as the dependent variable, has activist opinion as an explanatory variable, along with state opinion and party affiliation. Here, the coefficient for party actually vanishes–it changes sign and is not statistically significant. This means that the addition of activist opinion to the analysis completely explains the partisan differences between Democratic and Republican electoral elites. Here, then, we obtain firm empirical evidence for what "party" means when we say, for example, that party affiliation is an important variable in legislative policy making. "Party" in this sense stands for the issue stances and ideological values of the self-recruiting issue-motivated party elites in the states and districts in which legislators develop their political careers, get nominated, and eventually get elected. (See Wright, 1989 for parallel evidence in the case of roll call voting in the U.S. Senate.)

This points to an important – indeed fundamental – finding about state parties. The values and ideologies of party activists are what give shape and definition to what the parties stand for in state politics. There is considerable variation across the states in the relative liberalism–conservatism of party activists, and these differences are only weakly correlated with public opinion in the states. While we do find that electoral elites take moderate positions more congruent with those of voters near the ideological center of their states, we also find a remarkably powerful effect for activists in influencing the ideological positions of state electoral elites.

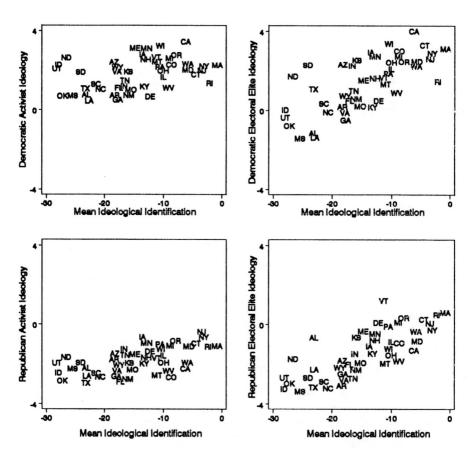

Figure 5.4 Party Activist and Electoral Elite Ideology by State Ideology

Table 5.5. *Regressions of state elite ideology on state opinion and party*

Independent variable	Activist ideology (1)		Electoral elite ideology (2)		(3)		(4)	
	b	Beta	*b*	Beta	*b*	Beta	*b*	Beta
Party (Democrat=1; Republican=0)	3.61*	0.93	2.75*	0.73	-1.41	-0.11		
State Opinion	0.05*	0.18	0.13*	0.51	0.09*	0.35	0.10*	0.37
Activist Ideology					0.87*	0.90	0.77*	0.80
Adjusted R^2	.891		.782		.870		.870	

Note: N=92.
*significant at .001. *b*'s without asterisks are not significant, even at the .05 level.

A further question is whether, when electoral elites respond to state opinion, they weigh the opinions of different kinds of partisans differently. Since activists are drawn from the state pools of party identifiers, we would expect that activists would represent mainly their own partisan grouping. Electoral elites may have a Downsian incentive to weigh the views of Independents higher because electoral marginality makes them a crucial swing group (Wright, 1989; Erikson and Romero, 1990). Testing these conjectures carries us toward the limits of what our data might be expected to reveal. Yet the data are generally supportive of our speculation.

Table 5.6 shows the two sets of elites (activists and elected officials) as a function of state opinion once more, but this time opinion is divided into the ideological means for three groups – their own party, the opposite party, and Independents. Opinion is weighted in proportion to each group's share of the electorate, so that any inequity in the coefficients represents only the differential weighting for the three partisan groups, and not their proportions of the electorate. In Table 5.6, for electoral elites we also include party activists' mean ideology.

Table 5.6. *Regressions of elite ideology on party and state opinion, by partisan groupings*

Variable	Activist Ideology	Electoral Elite Ideology		
	(1)	(2)	(3)	(4)
Party (Democrat= 1; Republican = 0)	2.83**	1.61**	-0.81	
Same party opinion x Same party proportion of state electorate	0.08**	0.16**	0.09**	0.09*
Opposition party opinion x Opposition party proportion of state electorate	0.00	0.05	0.04	0.06*
Independent opinion x Independent proportion of state electorate	0.04	0.17**	0.13**	0.14**
Activist opinion			0.85**	0.72**
Adjusted R^2	.894[a]	.790[a]	.870	.867

Note: Coefficients are unstandardized *b*'s.
*Significant at .01; **significant at .001.
[a]Significant (.05) improvement over the base equation where Democratic, Republican, and Independent opinions are weighted equally.

The activist equation (Equation 1) is remarkably consistent with our expectations. Activist opinion within a state party is a function of party affiliation and the opinions of the activists' rank-and-file partisans. But according to the equation, opinions of the opposition party's partisans and of Independents do not matter.

Equations 2, 3, and 4 present a different story for electoral elites. Mirroring Table 5.5, they show that electoral elites respond to both activist opinion within their party and state opinion at large. With state opinion divided into three partisan categories, we see that opinions of Independents appears marginally more important than partisan opinions. Although not statistically significant, this tendency is in the direction predicted. But Independent opinion is not all that matters. When activist opinion is omitted (Equation 2), "same party" opinion matters considerably – reflecting an indirect effect via activists. On net balance, opposition party opinion matters least in determining the opinions of electoral elites.

In summary, the ideological postures of electoral elites represent a compromise between the ideological preferences of party activists and the moderating forces needed to get elected. State electoral elites present a composite of activist opinion plus mass opinion. The data present an intriguing but modest hint that electoral elites weigh the opinions of Independent swing voters most heavily. But electoral elites' own partisan voters are influential indirectly, because they comprise the pool from which activists are drawn. The electorate's task is to distribute the two contesting sets of elites into office, in proportion to their representation of mass ideological preferences. That performance is the subject of subsequent chapters.

PARTY MIDPOINT AND PARTY POLARIZATION

In addition to separately scoring the individual Democratic and Republican elites of the states, we can classify states according to their combination of Democratic and Republican elite ideologies. There are two ways to combine the elite measures to score the party "system." One obvious way is to simply average the ideologies of the two party elites. We refer to this average as the "party midpoint." A second measure is the ideological distance between the two party elites. We refer to this as the "polarization" score for state parties. For any given party midpoint, any value of party polarization is theoretically possible. Consider, for instance, a centrist party midpoint. In the case of Downsian parties offering centrist policies, the moderate party midpoint would be accompanied by a low level of polarization. However, with parties behaving in the responsible parties fashion, parties could on average present a centrist midpoint but with a polarized ideological choice.[4]

The midpoint and the polarization scores are shown graphically in the scatterplot of Figure 5.5. We can divide the states into four types as represented by particular states. Vermont for example has a relatively liberal and relatively unpolarized party system. At the opposite extreme,

---

4. The party midpoint is the mean of the Democratic and Republican "overall" scores reported in Table 5.3. The party elite polarization index is the difference between these two overall scores. The polarization measure can be divided into its four components – the party difference on each of the four elite measures. These four polarization components are modestly correlated, with an average intercorrelation of .23.

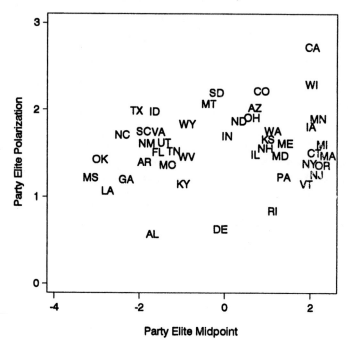

Figure 5.5 Party Elite Polarization and Party Elite Midpoints.

Texas is an example of a relatively conservative and relatively polarized party system. California and Wisconsin exemplify states that are liberal and polarized. Opposite from them is Louisiana, conservative and un-polarized. Each type, one might anticipate, enjoys a somewhat distinct brand of politics – in terms of contentiousness and predictability of the policy process.

Since the party midpoint is simply the average of the Republican and Democratic elite positions for the state, like its two components it should correlate strongly with state opinion. Indeed, this correlation is a healthy .76. We have strong reason to suspect that this correlation would be much higher if measurement error in state opinion were removed. Dividing the states in two groups based on state opinion sample size, we find that the midpoint correlates at a very high .90 for the 23 states with sample sizes above 2,110 and a lesser .64 for the remainder.

We would not expect party polarization to correlate with the direction of opinion, and it does not. The correlation is a meaningless –.05. Party elite polarization should correlate, however, with the polarization of state opinion. Recall from Chapter 2 our measure of mass polarization as the difference between the mean ideology of a state's Democratic identifiers and the mean ideology of the state's Republican identifiers. This variable does correlate with party polarization at a modest .42. We expect this observed correlation to be attenuated due to measurement error, so that its moderate magnitude may indicate an interesting effect. To explore this further, we estimate the correlation between the estimated mass polarization and party polarization for the 23 states with the largest CBS/NYT survey samples. Now we find the correlation rises to a much higher .65. (For the 23 states with lesser sample sizes, the correlation falls to .20.) Thus we have identified a major source of party polarization. When the state electorate is polarized ideologically, so too are the party elites.

PARTY SYSTEMS AND PARTY CONFLICT

Several studies have classified political systems in the U.S. states according to the nature of state political conflict. Here, we assess the relationships between our classification of party systems based on our measurement of party elite ideology on the one hand, and the relevant classification schemes found in the literature, on the other. Whereas our ideological measurement of state parties is based on composite surveys of party elites, other researchers have inferred party differences from patterns of policy making or from relatively unsystematic observations of the states and their parties. We will contrast our measures with the party classifications offered by John Fenton (1966), Edward Jennings (1979), Thomas Dye (1984), and James Garand (1985). Each of these scholars has provided a classification of states based on a dimension of substantive differences between the parties.[5]

The first two classifications we consider include only a few states each. John Fenton's classic study, *Midwest Politics* (1966), examines six states, classifying three as primarily "issue-oriented" (Michigan, Wisconsin, and Minnesota) and three as primarily "job-oriented" (Illinois, Indiana, and Ohio). This division nicely parallels the distinction between the "new style" and "old style" politics described by Sorauf and Beck (1988, chap. 16) and dovetails nicely with the theoretical distinction between responsible parties (more issue-oriented elites) and Downsian parties (more pragmatic elites). Thus, we anticipate greater levels of party polarization in the issue-oriented states than in the job-oriented states.

A similar distinction is pursued by Edward Jennings (1979), who classifies eight states as "class-based" or "non-class-based" over the period 1932–70. Jennings reports some of the strongest evidence available that policies change when the voters change the governing party – but

5. Some readers might expect us to include Daniel Elazar's (1966, 1972) typology of states according to political culture in our analysis here. We present a detailed analysis of Elazar's model in Chapter 7.

only when the parties are clearly different on policies. Two of the states in Jennings' analysis changed the nature of their politics, and hence their classification, during the period. We use his classification as of the end of that period. From Jennings's discussion it is clear that his nonclass-based parties are nonideological more generally. They battle for the patronage spoils of office rather then for high principles of governance. We would expect to find, therefore, higher polarization scores among Jennings's class-based party states.

Thomas Dye's (1966) research on comparative state politics has helped to set the agenda for much of the subsequent work in the field. Dye found that measures of economic development of the states were better predictors of state expenditure policies than were available measures of political variables, such as relative strengths of the two parties. Our explanation for why political parties do not matter is that the parties may stand for different things in different places. Dye (1984) expands on this observation to make the argument – similar in spirit to that offered by Jennings – that party control will matter only when the policy programs and electoral constituencies of the parties are significantly different from each another. Accordingly, Dye offers a classification of the states based on whether their parties were "policy relevant." He bases this classification on a time-series analysis of when welfare expenditures change with party control. When the changes are in the expected direction – expenditures go up when Democrats come into office or down when Republicans come into office – the parties are deemed to be policy relevant. When the expected policy change does not occur, Dye concludes that the parties are not policy relevant. Our hypothesis is the obvious: Party polarization should be larger among the states Dye classifies as policy relevant.

James Garand (1985) takes a similar theoretical approach as Dye but uses a different basis for classifying the states. From his survey of the literature, Garand combines the various descriptions of the states into a scale of "policy differentiation" between the parties. He finds some of the states have high levels of policy differentiation between the parties, others medium, and still others low differentiation. Garand's measure presents a strong parallel, conceptually, to our measure of party polarization: States given scores of high levels of policy differentiation should be our states with the greatest ideological polarization of party elites.

The analysis of these four classifications in terms of our party system variables is shown in Table 5.7. For each we have a clear hypothesis that polarization scores should be higher in systems that posit greater party distances. For the most part, however, we have no hypothesis about the midpoint of party elite ideology; there is no *a priori* reason to expect a relationship between the relevance of issues to the parties and the direction, liberal or conservative, of the party system.

Table 5.7. *Party elite liberalism and party polarization by selected party classifications*

Classifications of State Party Systems	Party Elite Liberalism	Party Polarization
Fenton (1966)		
Issue-oriented (N=3)	2.17	7.52
Job-oriented (N=3)	.43	6.95
Significance	$F_{1,4}$=69.5***	$F_{1,4}$=0.28
Jennings (1979)		
Class-based (N=6)	1.61	6.94
Nonclass-based (N=2)	-1.33	5.60
Significance	$F_{1,6}$=5.0	$F_{1,6}$=1.3
Dye (1984)		
Policy-relevant (N=18)	.94	6.93
Not policy-relevant (N=29)	-.57	6.00
Significance	$F_{1,45}$=10.2**	$F_{1,45}$=3.4
Garand (1985)		
Policy Differentiation:		
High (N=15)	1.60	6.18
Moderate (N=16)	-.13	6.72
Low (N=16)	-1.35	6.16
Significance	$F_{2,44}$=21.3***	$F_{2,44}$=0.51

Note: Table entries are category means.
*Significant at .05; **significant at .01; ***significant at .001.

The pattern that we find in Table 5.7 is quite intriguing. Our primary hypothesis, that there should be a relationship between our polarization measure and the classification systems, received no support in any of the four tests. Some of the relationships are in the predicted direction, but they are small and not statistically significant. Overall, party ideological distances do not coincide with the classification schemes of the literature.

The other surprise is that the party elite ideological midpoints *do* coincide with the various classification schemes. In all four tests, where the parties are believed to be more ideological or issue/class-oriented we find that the party systems are significantly more liberal. The theoretical reversal here is remarkable. We had strong theoretical reasons to expect polarization to be related to party classification, and instead we find that party elite liberalism is – and this occurs with striking consistency across frameworks developed over quite a time period and with quite different methods.

How is it that a set of keen observers of state politics could think they were seeing class-based or issue-based differences in the party systems, whereas what they really distinguish is the overall liberalism–conservatism of the party systems? It could be that these observers were just wrong, that they did not know what they were seeing when they looked at state politics. Such a conclusion would be hasty, perhaps impertinent, and worse, it would leave us with no explanation for the pattern that we do find. Instead, let us review our findings again. We expected to find that the policy distances between the parties would be larger in policy-oriented or class-based party systems. This does not turn out to be the case. Rather, our panel of highly informed observers have identified states with liberal party elites as the states possessing strong class or policy division between the parties.

What is actually varying, then, in these classification schemes is not the ideological distance between party elites, but rather the location on the ideological spectrum where the most salient party conflict occurs. Here, we believe, is the resolution to the puzzle. For a party system to be called "class-based" or "policy-relevant," political scientists are conditioned to look for partisan division over classic issues of redistribution. For such a partisan division, the more liberal (Democratic) party must visibly appeal to the have-nots, welfare recipients or other groups whose interests constitute class-based or policy-relevant politics. Where the parties are more conservative, not even the Democratic Party facilitates the expression of the interests of the have-nots. Conservative party systems may contain substantial ideological gaps between the parties, but the division is simply to the right of the ideological zone generally identified with meaningful issue or class conflict. Arguably, these less visible divisions have been too long ignored. Perhaps state policy analysts should give greater consideration to variability in the policy concerns of the constituencies of the two parties across the states, not just where obvious class conflict is manifest.

CONCLUSIONS

This chapter has shown that the ideologies represented by the state party elites are a reflection of state opinion. Democratic elites are to the public's left, and Republican elites are to the public's right. But within each party, the degree of liberalism among the leadership is correlated with the degree of liberalism of the state public. The process is complex. Party activists are drawn from the state public at large, with liberals moving into the Democratic elite and conservatives into the Republican elite. Each party's electoral elite must respond not only to activist sentiment but also to the views of the electorate. The electorate's complicated task is to sort this all out. From the conflicting programs of Democratic and Republican parties, both perhaps too extreme for average tastes, the electorate must do the proper sorting to determine who gets elected and who does not. In subsequent chapters, we will see how the electorate's performance of this task is an important part of the electoral process.

6

Legislative elections and state policy

One central question about modern democracies is, How much do partisan elections contribute to the effective representation of public opinion? In theory, programmatic parties provide the electorate with a clear choice of policy options, with election results followed by predictable policy consequences. But empirically, does it matter which party (or coalition) governs? Most recent cross-national comparisons of Western democracies answer affirmatively. Socialist or leftist party participation in national governments is associated with a high inflation to unemployment tradeoff (Hibbs, 1977), growth of the governmental sector (Cameron, 1978; Lange and Garrett, 1985), high public expenditure (Tufte, 1978; Castles, 1982), welfare spending (Castles, 1982; Hicks and Swank, 1984), quality-of-life (Moon and Dixon 1985), and income equality/ redistribution (Tufte, 1978; van Arnhem, Corina, and Schotsman, 1982; but see also, Jackman, 1975, 1980). In sum, nations where leftist parties are most influential also tend to have the kinds of policies and policy consequences with the greatest appeal to leftist constituencies. Time-series analyses for individual nations also show policy consequences resulting from party control (Hibbs, 1977, 1987; Alt, 1985). Party control does matter.

It may be the case, however, that party control matters only in terms of the sharp divisions between European socialist parties of the left and parties of the right. In the U.S. context, it is by no means clear that major policy differences flow from variation in Democratic versus Republican control. At the national level, while some time series find policy consequences from party control of the presidency and/or Congress (Hibbs, 1977, 1987; Kiewiet and McCubbins, 1985), the role of parties remains in some dispute (Beck, 1982; Browning, 1985; Lowery, 1985).

At the state level, the policy relevance of party control has been viewed with particular skepticism. Indeed, in state policy research, the apparent irrelevance of political parties has been a persistent puzzle. Presumably,

Legislative elections and state policy

Republican states would have the most conservative policies and Democratic states the most liberal policies. But this is not the case. The relative strengths of the Republican and Democratic parties in state politics appear to be statistically unrelated to policy directions in the states, even after the imposition of rigorous controls (Dye, 1966; Winters, 1976; Plotnick and Winters, 1985). Only time-series analyses show any evidence of the expected party effects, with welfare spending responsive to party control in some states but perhaps not in others (Jennings, 1979; Dye, 1984; Garand, 1985).

The nonrelationship between party control and state policy appears to deny common, seemingly informed, stereotypes of how politics in the United States works. Most observers would agree that Democratic and Republican elites differ ideologically in terms of their political values and as manifested in certain behaviors such as roll call votes. Could this be an illusion? Could it be that the two parties have become indistinguishable on policy substance, just what spatial models of party competition predict should happen with electorally driven parties (Downs, 1957)? Clearly the answer is no. As Chapter 5 showed, Democratic and Republican party elites are quite ideologically distinct in individual states. If party control makes no difference, the reason is not that the leaderships of the two parties are not ideologically different.

Then, perhaps the seeming irrelevance of parties is confirmation of the general theory that policy outcomes are determined by environmental rather than political variables (Dye, 1966, 1979). Indeed, the failure of party control to predict policy may be the strongest evidence available in support of the environmental theory. Although Republican and Democratic candidates diverge in their campaign rhetoric and even in their personal values, perhaps Republican and Democratic politicians ultimately enact the same policies when given the responsibility of governing. By this scenario, politicians in office respond to the social needs and economic constraints of the state at the expense of campaign pledges or other ephemeral political considerations.

A BROKEN ELECTORAL LINKAGE?

Does electoral politics in the states really not matter? Consider our .82 correlation between the net ideological identification of state opinion and our composite measure of state policy liberalism. Clearly, the ideological preferences of state electorates play an important role in determining the ideological tone of state policies. Partisan elections would seem a likely conduit for this flow of causality, with liberal states electing Democrats who enact liberal legislation and conservative states electing Republicans who enact conservative legislation. This simple model is diagrammed in Figure 6.1.

But our data do not fit this simple model. Echoing earlier findings, we find Democratic Party control of state legislatures unrelated ($r = -.22$) to our eight-item measure of state policy liberalism (described in Chapter 4). Moreover, even if party control could account for policy, the linkage between opinion and policy via parties would be broken at the front end. The correlation between the liberalism of state publics and Democratic control is only .01. Thus, liberal and conservative states do not differ in their tendencies to elect Republicans or Democrats to state office. The strong effect of state opinion on state policy would seem to bypass the electoral process.

State-to-state differences in mean party identification add to the puzzle. Not only are the ideological preferences of state electorates uncorrelated with the partisan composition of state elected officials, but they are also unrelated to the electorate's partisan preferences. The mean liberalism of state public opinion correlates at only .06 with mean Democratic Party identification. State party identification, however, does correlate with party control ($r = .87$) just as one would think that it must.

Democratic states do elect the most Democrats to state office. But the most Democratic state electorates are not unusually liberal. And the Democratic legislatures they elect do not enact unusually liberal legislation. All this would seem to deny the presence of much policy representation. But we must remember that the most liberal state electorates do elect legislators who enact the most liberal legislation, even with the absence of any obvious partisan linkage.

Are political parties as irrelevant to the representation process as this analysis suggests? Perhaps political parties do play an important role: It is just that the linkage is more complicated than we have presented so far. But to pursue this possibility, we must have a theory of how partisan elections fit into the representation process in the states. In the next section, we attempt to develop this theory.

A THEORY OF STATE ELECTORAL POLITICS

A theory of state electoral politics must take into account the wide variation in the ideological orientations of state political parties. To take an obvious example, the Democratic Party of Mississippi is far more conservative than the Democratic Party of New York, and perhaps the New York Republican Party as well. With the Democratic and the Republican parties each differing ideologically from one state to the next, the potential exists for serious confounding of our understanding of how parties contribute to the policy representation in the states. This ideological variation of state parties sometimes appears to be chaotic and idiosyncratic to particular state political cultures. But as we have already seen in Chapter 5,

Legislative elections and state policy

Opinion   ⟶   Democratic   ⟶   Policy
Liberalism   Party Control   Liberalism

Figure 6.1 A Simple Model of State Public Opinion and Policy

considerable order and predictability exists, with the ideologies of state party elites a function of the particular party and electoral constituencies.

To develop some propositions about state party ideology, party electoral strength, and state policy, let us take the role of elections in the policy process seriously. Suppose that state electorates actually reward and punish the parties on the basis of their policy positions and specifically on the basis of their placement on the left–right continuum. That is, suppose that state electorates tend to reward the party that best reflects their ideological viewpoints. Suppose also that state parties are motivated (at least in part) to win elections. Then, to the extent parties are electorally motivated, they should respond to state opinion. To the extent parties respond effectively to state opinion, they should achieve electoral success.

Chapter 5 has presented evidence of parties responding to state opinion. Relatively conservative states draw relatively conservative Democratic and Republican elites and relatively liberal states draw relatively liberal Democratic and Republican elites. At the same time, state parties are not driven *entirely* by state opinion. If they were, state parties would always converge to the position of the state's median voter. In actuality state parties, like national parties, are pushed toward the median voter position by electoral considerations and away from the median voter position by the preferences of their activists.

The ideological motivations of state party elites were the focus of the previous chapter. The present chapter focuses on the response of state electorates to the ideological alternatives presented by competing Democratic and Republican elites. To the extent state elections are decided by ideology, state electoral success should go to the party that is ideologically closest to the state electorate. Thus, Republican state parties should be most successful when they move toward the liberalism of the Democratic opposition. Democratic state parties should be most successful when they move toward the conservatism of the Republican opposition. These policies could backfire, but only if the parties move too far, as when the Democrats get so conservative that the Republicans outflank them on the left. But as we saw in Chapter 5, this does not happen with state parties.

To summarize, it is the ideological flexibility of the Democratic and Republican parties in the states that obscures the linkage between party control and public policy in the states. As seen in the previous chapter, ideologically flexible parties respond to state public opinion even as they try to satisfy their own ideological furies. As we will see in this chapter, parties are electorally rewarded and punished based on how well they represent state opinion.[1]

Our argument can be recognized as a continuation from Chapter 5 of the Downsian (Downs, 1957) theme that electoral rewards lie in the political center. Appendix A to this chapter explicates the formal argument in greater detail and, with hypothetical examples, illustrates the propositions described in the following section, where we explore the implications for estimating the role of party control in the representation process in the states.

A model of electoral representation

According to our model, centrist parties are electorally rewarded. This means that the Democrats are rewarded for movement in the conservative direction and the Republicans for movement in the liberal direction.[2] In brief, liberal parties (Democratic or Republican) negatively affect Democratic success. Figure 6.2 introduces party positions to the model of state electoral representation. Let us consider how electorally responsive parties can contribute to representation and at the same time account for the absence of correlations between opinion liberalism and Democratic success and between Democratic success and policy liberalism.

In our model, liberal opinion causes liberal parties. However, when state electorates respond to party positions, liberal parties hinder Democratic success. This makes a negative indirect path from opinion liberalism to Democratic control. At the same time, the model shows a positive direct effect of opinion liberalism on Democratic legislative

1. This argument may apply to cross-national comparisons as well. The U.S. Democratic Party is more ideologically centrist than parties of the Left in Europe and more successful electorally. One may wonder, therefore, whether the relative electoral success of the Left but nonsocialist U.S. Democrats (and also the Canadian Liberals) disturbs the cross-national relationship between leftist party success and policy. However, cross-national studies do not code the nonsocialist U.S. Democrats and Canadian Liberals as parties of the Left. The Left designation is reserved for explicitly Socialist or Social Democratic parties. If cross-national studies were to code the U.S. Democrats and Canadian Liberals as successful leftist parties, cross-national relationships between party control and policy would become seriously attenuated.
2. We speak somewhat loosely about movement to the political "center." Strictly speaking, attempting to observe whether parties are at the political center would require a common metric for parties and the electorate. In actuality, the location of the "center" is irrelevant since each party should be electorally rewarded for moving toward the ideological position of its opposition, whatever side of "center." See Appendix A.

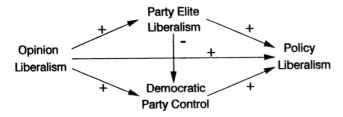

Figure 6.2 Representation Model with Party Elites

strength. The net effect of the combined indirect and direct paths could well be a low bivariate correlation between state opinion and party control.

The model also accounts for the low correlation between party control and policy. According to the model, party ideology suppresses the positive relationship between party control and policy: Liberal parties work against Democratic control but for liberal policies. This source of spurious negative correlation obscures the posited positive effect of Democratic control on liberal policy.

Figure 6.2 also shows how parties' responsiveness to state opinion contributes to representation in a rather straightforward fashion. Liberal state opinion causes liberal state party elites, which result in liberal policies. But also, the combination of state opinion and party elite ideology determine party control, which also determines policy. Finally, the model allows for the direct effect of opinion on policy independent of partisan variables.

The model can be complicated further. Figure 6.3 adds two more variables: state party identification and the liberalism of the state legislature. Figure 6.3 also adds specificity to the meaning of party control by redefining it in terms of Democratic legislative strength.

This new model places party identification as an intervening variable between opinion liberalism and Democratic legislative strength. Partisanship provides a mechanism for translating public opinion into legislative power: Liberal states tend to identify with the Democratic Party, which increases the number of Democratic state legislators. Surprisingly, as previously reported, the correlation between opinion liberalism and Democratic party identification in the states is virtually zero. But the role of party elites can explain this anomaly: Liberal states cause liberal parties, which over time contribute negatively to Democratic partisanship. This effect hides the expected relationship between public opinion and partisanship in which liberals tend to identify with the Democratic Party.

The liberalism of the legislature is introduced as an intervening variable caused by the degree of liberalism among the two major parties' elites and

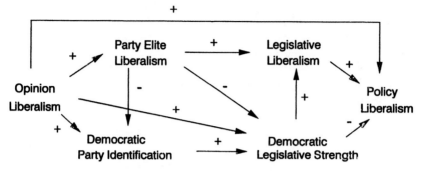

Figure 6.3 Model of the Policy Process

the partisan division of the legislature: The more liberal the parties and the more Democrats in the legislature, the more liberal should be the legislature. The inclusion of legislative liberalism provides an additional subtlety to the model. Electing Democrats should liberalize the legislature, which leads to liberal policies. But as Figure 6.3 suggests, with legislative liberalism and public liberalism held constant, the residual direct effect on policy liberalism of electing Democrats is posited to be negative.

The ceteris paribus condition is crucial for this proposition. We do not seriously speculate that electing Republicans is the way to get liberal policies (although speculation of that sort can be found in the literature, see Goodin, 1983). Rather, under identical political circumstances and with identical ideological values, Republican and Democratic legislators should respond in different directions to electoral motivations: Republicans should find more votes by moving left and Democrats should find more votes by moving right. Of course, Republican and Democratic legislators tend to differ in their ideological values. But conceivably, electoral motivations could be so strong that conservative Republicans and liberal Democrats make ideologically similar decisions when in control of the state legislatures.

In summary, the model of Figure 6.3 shows how state opinion can influence state policy via a variety of indirect electoral pathways. These pathways are based on the assumptions that state parties respond to state opinion and that state electorates respond to party positions. If this theoretical development is correct, electoral politics can be crucial for policy representation in the states, even though party control is statistically uncorrelated with both state opinion and state policy.

One important omission from this model is the governor and his role in state policy. This omission is due largely to measurement considerations rather than disregard for the governor's role in the legislative process. When the dependent variable is a set of policies cumulated from years of legislative decision-making, it makes little sense to include the governor's party affiliation for the short term as an independent variable. And partisan control of governorships over the long term bears little relationship to other indicators of partisanship. Where unusual long-term success for a party is found at the gubernatorial level (e.g., Utah for the Democrats, Michigan for the Republicans), this may result precisely because of gubernatorial leadership that is ideologically atypical for the party. We are far more reluctant to assume that governors share the ideological positions measured for their party's elite than we are that, on the average, state legislators do so.

While we do not include the state's chief executive in our model for measurement reasons, this decision should not significantly distort the model we present. Much has been made in recent years of the increasing formal authority of governors. Yet little evidence exists that demonstrates an empirical link between the powers of the executive and actual policy direction. For instance, state representatives rarely see the governor as playing a significant role in the state legislature. Legislators rank the governor last among 13 potential decision cue sources: Less than 2 percent of all state legislators choose the governor as the principal informant for their decisions (Uslaner and Weber, 1977, 34).

MEASUREMENT

To put the theory to use, it is necessary to operationalize each of the component parts. State opinion (Chapter 2), state party identification (Chapter 2), states' composite policy liberalism (Chapter 4), and party elite ideology (Chapter 5) have all been introduced previously. Of these, only one – party elite ideology – requires additional discussion here.

Party elite ideology was presented as a composite of the ideological positions of county chairpersons, national convention delegates, members of Congress, and state legislative candidates. The former two components tap the ideology of the *activist* party elites, and the latter two the ideology of the *electoral* party elites. As Chapter 5 showed, electoral elite ideology is more responsive to state opinion than is activist elite ideology. For this chapter, we use the composite measure of party elite ideology, thereby combining the views of activists and electoral elites. We do so because as independent variables affecting state elections and state policy, the two cannot be statistically disentangled. That is, based on statistical evidence, state publics view state party positions as a composite of the parties' activist elites and electoral elites. Also, the two components appear to have equal effects on state policy. Here we further reduce the measure of party elite ideology to its essentials, by averaging the Republican and Democratic elite ideology scores as the party midpoint.

Table 6.1. *Correlations among variables for model of state policy process:*
46 *states*

Variables	Opinion liberalism	Party elite liberalism	Democratic party identification	Democratic legislative strength	Legislative liberalism	Policy liberalism
Opinion liberalism	1.00	.76	.06	.01	.82	.83
Party elite liberalism		1.00	-.37	-.42	.79	.85
Democratic party identification			1.00	.87	.15	-.20
Democratic legislative strength				1.00	.19	-.22
Legislative liberalism					1.00	.78
Policy liberalism						1.00

Note: *N*=46. Alaska, Hawaii, Nebraska, and Nevada are excluded.

Two variables that do require introduction in this chapter are Democratic "legislative strength" and "legislative ideology." Democratic state legislative strength is measured as the average of the Democratic strength for each legislative chamber over the 1977–84 period. Upper and lower chambers are weighted equally.

Legislative ideology is a more difficult challenge, requiring indirect measurement. We operationalize legislative liberalism as the weighted average of the Democratic and Republican elite ideology scores, where the weights are determined by the parties' relative legislative strength (weighing the two chambers equally). In other words, we assume that the average liberalism of a state's Democratic legislators is the mean composite liberalism score for the state's Democratic elite; and we assume that the average liberalism of a state's Republican legislators is the mean composite liberalism score for the state's Republican elite. Democratic and Republican composite ideology scores are then combined in proportion to the two parties' average legislative strength.

Table 6.2. *Standardized regressions for path model of policy process: 46 states*

	Dependent variables				
Independent variables	Party elite liberalism	Democratic party identification	Democratic legislative strength	Legislative liberalism	Policy liberalism
Opinion liberalism	0.76* (0.10)	0.83* (0.18)	0.15 (0.14)		0.44* (0.12)
Party elite liberalism		-1.01* (0.18)	-0.24 (0.15)	1.05* (0.04)	
Democratic party identification			0.78* (0.10)		
Democratic legislative strength				0.63* (0.04)	-0.32* (0.07)
Legislative liberalism					0.48* (0.12)
Adjusted R^2	.573	.404	.760	.948	.799

Note: N=46. Alaska, Hawaii, Nebraska, and Nevada are excluded. Standard errors in parentheses.
*Significant at .001.

The following sections report on the empirical fit of the causal model presented in Figure 6.3. For handy reference to these sections, Table 6.1 reports the correlation matrix for the variables; Table 6.2 shows the results of the standardized regression equations; Figure 6.4 shows the causal model with the estimated standardized path coefficients (betas) included.[3] A case can also be made for doing the analysis without the potentially

3. With Nebraska omitted, the opinion–policy correlation rises minisculely from .82 to .83. Certain arrows (e.g., from party identification to legislative liberalism) are deleted from Figure 6.4, on the grounds that the expected direct effect is zero. Technically speaking, therefore, Figure 6.4 presents an *overidentified* model. Inclusion of the omitted effects would be of little consequence other than to clutter the analysis with small theoretically meaningless coefficients.

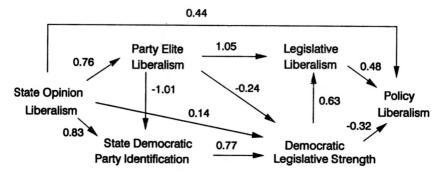

Figure 6.4 Path Model of the State Policy Process (46 states)

confounding (and interactive) effects of southern regionalism. According-ly, we present a brief parallel analysis in Appendix B, with southern states removed.

PUBLIC OPINION AND PARTY ELITES

First, we reprise the relationships between state opinion and the positions of the Democratic and Republican party elites. The correlations are .62 for Democratic elites and .77 for Republican elites. The average of the two party positions (or the midpoint) correlates at .76 with state opinion. These correlations suggest a healthy responsiveness by parties to opinion. As we saw in Chapter 5, much of this responsiveness is merely that state party elites reflect their rank-and-file partisans. A second contributing factor – and for electoral politics a more interesting one – is that state parties deliberately modify their positions in response to state opinion, from fear of electoral sanctions.

But while state parties respond to public opinion, they certainly are not the centrist electoral machines of Anthony Downs's model. State parties clearly represent the ideological predilections of their activists. Figure 6.5 shows how the state parties vary as a function of state opinion but remain ideologically distinct from one another. The unusual dimensions of this figure represents an attempt to scale state parties and state opinion on a common metric. The horizontal axis of this scatterplot is the liberalism of state opinion, scaled as a standardized measure. The vertical axis repre-sents the liberalism of party elites. The scale for the vertical axis is set so that the expected midpoint between the two party positions equals state opinion. In other words, this scaling procedure assumes that on average neither party is more representative than the other and that the relative representativeness of the two parties is unrelated to state opinion. If the

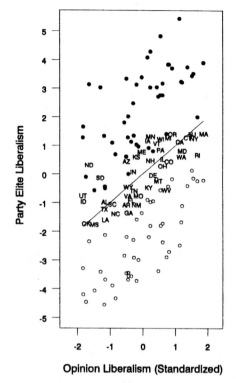

Figure 6.5 Party Elite Liberalism by State
Opinion. *Note:* Solid dots = Democratic
elites; hollow dots = Republican elites;
State labels = party midpoint.

scaling assumptions are correct, we should find the electorate favoring the
party that is depicted as closest to the electorate's mean position.

Figure 6.5 illustrates how state parties position themselves relative to
state opinion and their partisan opposition. In every state, the Democratic
elite is more liberal than the Republican elite. And given the scaling assumptions, each state's Democratic Party is more liberal than state opinion, and each Republican Party is more conservative than state opinion. In
most states, the divergence of the two parties is considerable: Typically,
the divergence between a state's Democratic and Republican positions
exceeds the entire range of mean opinion between the most conservative
and the most liberal states.

Clearly, Figure 6.5 does not present a picture of ideological convergence, with political parties mimicking the ideological stance of the
states' median voters. The considerable within-state divergence of the two
parties' ideological positions suggests a strong ideological pull by the par-

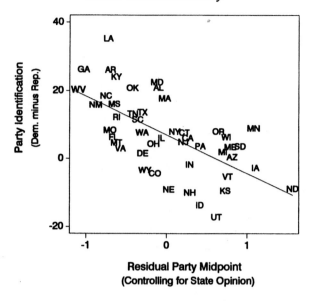

Figure 6.6 Party Identification by Party Elite Liberalism

ties' activists. But this tendency toward ideological extremism is not reason to ignore the responsiveness of the parties to state opinion. Figure 6.5
shows how state party positions vary in response to state opinion: the
more liberal the state, the more liberal the Democratic Party and the more
liberal the Republican Party. On the one hand, activists push state parties
away from the center; on the other hand, electoral considerations push
state parties back toward the center.

STATE OPINION, STATE PARTY POSITIONS, AND PARTY STRENGTH

We argued that party positions should influence state partisanship, with
liberal parties hurting the Democrats. We see in Figure 6.4 that the estimated path coefficient confirms our theoretical expectation. The liberalism of party positions (summarized as the party midpoint) shows a quite
dramatic negative effect on Democratic Party identification (beta =
−1.01). The control for party positions also confirms another important
theoretical expectation: The initial opinion-party identification correlation was only .01, but now, with party positions controlled, we find the
expected positive influence of state opinion on state party identification
(beta = 0.83).

The responsiveness of state party identification to party elite ideology is
shown in Figure 6.6. This figure shows the scatterplot of the relationship

between state party positions, measured as the relative deviation of state party midpoint from the midpoint predicted from state opinion, and state party identification. Clearly, parties that are liberal relative to state public opinion push state electorates toward the Republicans, and parties that are conservative relative to state public opinion push states toward the Democrats.[4]

It may seem dissonant to see state electorates respond to ideological positions of state parties in terms of party identification. This finding conflicts with two supposed axioms of U.S. politics – that party identification is unmoving and that state politics is largely invisible to voters. The pattern that is so clearly observed, however, does not dictate that state electorates frequently change their partisan character in response to short-term ideological maneuvering by state parties. Much more plausibly, it represents the influence of state party positions over the long haul, with the long-term ideological tendencies of state parties accumulating a long-term influence on the party identification of state electorates.

State party identification takes on importance because it is the most important direct cause of state legislative partisanship ($r = .87$; beta = 0.77). In fact, the effects of state opinion and state party elite ideology on Democratic legislative strengths are almost entirely indirect via their influence on state partisanship. The data hint that state opinion and party elite ideology may also directly affect Democratic legislative strength in ways

4. In Chapter 3, we divided state partisanship into its cultural and demographic components. In theory, only the cultural component should be affected by the responsiveness of state party elites to state policy. This presents a test of whether our theoretical interpretation of party identification as a reflection of party representativeness is on the correct track. The cultural component of party identification should respond to state party elites, but the relatively fixed demographic component should not. This expectation is born out nicely.

Party identification =

		Demographic component	Cultural component	All
Ideology	b	0.38*	0.98**	1.27**
	beta	0.65	0.70	0.83
	t	(3.06)	(3.84)	(4.63)
Party elite liberalism	b	−1.85	−10.08**	−11.34**
	beta	−0.43	−0.97	−1.00
	t	(−2.00)	(−5.37)	(−5.61)
Adjusted R²		.145	.375	.398

*significant at .01; ** significant at .001

In effect, over one-third of the variance in the cultural component of state partisanship is accounted for by the relative representativeness of the two state parties.

that bypass state partisanship. According to the coefficients, liberal state opinion directly causes Democratic legislative strength (beta = 0.15), while liberal party ideologies directly lessen Democratic legislative strength (beta = −0.24). Although statistically not significant, these coefficients seemingly reflect small amounts of ideological voting in state legislative elections beyond the long-term component channeled through state party identification.[5]

We see now how public opinion influences legislative party strength even though state opinion does not correlate strongly with legislative party strength as the simplest model would predict. Liberal electorates do cause Democratic legislatures, but liberal state electorates also result in liberal state parties, which works to the electoral advantage of the Republicans. Both processes are surprisingly strong statistically, when the appropriate controls are imposed. But they are not ordinarily visible because they cancel each other out.

STATE OPINION, STATE PARTIES, AND THE LEGISLATURE

Legislative policy preferences should reflect the policy positions of the two state parties and the two parties' relative legislative strength. Indeed that is how we measure legislative preferences: as the sum of state Republican and Democratic elite positions, each weighted according to the party's average legislative strength. Figure 6.4 shows these linkages from state party positions and Democratic legislative strength to legislative liberalism, in the form of large beta coefficients (1.05 and 0.63, respectively). Of course, these coefficients must be interpreted modestly since legislative preferences are defined in terms of party positions and the legislative party division.

Recall that party positions, summarized as the party midpoint, correlates at .76 with state opinion. Now, with the parties reweighted according to their legislative strength, the measure of legislative preferences correlates at an even higher .82 with state opinion. The working of partisan elections accounts for this increase: The more liberal the parties relative to state opinion, the more the electorate will choose the more conservative Republican Party over the more liberal Democratic Party.[6]

5. Somewhat sharper evidence of issue voting can be seen when party elite liberalism is subdivided into its activist and electoral components. With state opinion and state partisanship held constant, the midpoint of party electoral elites presents a near-significant coefficient, with a .07 *p*-value.
6. Testing this proposition directly requires the measurement of state party positions and state opinion on a common scale. Suppose we assume the metric that we used for party positions for the construction of Figure 6.5. Using this scale, we should find

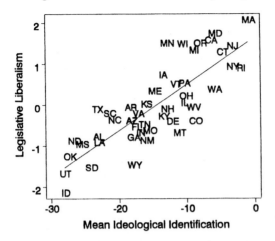

Figure 6.7 Legislative Liberalism by State Opinion

Figure 6.7 presents the scatterplot of the .82 correlation between state opinion and legislative liberalism.

So far, the data show a pattern that comfortably matches our theoretical expectations. State parties select ideological positions that in part are responses to anticipated electoral sanctions. Then, the state electorates' enactment of these sanctions result in a mix of Democratic and Republican

the least Democratic success when the midpoint between the parties is more liberal than state opinion. Indeed, the correlation between the party midpoint–state opinion difference and Democratic legislative strength is strongly negative (-.66). The more proximate the Democratic position to the electorate in comparison with the Republican proximity to the electorate, the greater is the Democratic legislative success.

Of course, the placement of party elites on the same scale with the electorate is arbitrary, based on the assumption that the relative proximity of the parties to the electorate is uncorrelated with state opinion. However, this metric may be uncannily accurate. When state opinion and the party midpoint are calibrated correctly, the separate effects of state opinion and the party midpoint should be represented by coefficients that are equal except for sign. In fact, when (unstandardized) Democratic legislative strength is regressed on state opinion and the party midpoint *using the scaling of Figure 6.5*, the coefficients are nearly identical. The coefficients of 0.15 and –0.15 suggest that either a one standard deviation movement in state opinion or the equivalent movement of the party midpoint results in a 15-percentage-point shift in legislative seats.

Although Figure 6.5 may calibrate equivalent ideological intervals for mass and elite opinion, we can be less sure of the calibration of the zero points that would allow a one-to-one mapping of mass and elite opinion. At stake is the interpretation of why legislative elections generally favor Democrats. Do we attribute the Democrats' greater success at winning legislative elections to the Democratic Party being more representative? Or do we assume that Democrats win more often than they deserve due to some sort of "bias"?

legislators that enhances further the representation of state public opinion. The final task is to observe the translation of legislative preferences into public policy.

LEGISLATIVE ELECTIONS, LEGISLATIVE PREFERENCES, AND STATE POLICY

We posit three variables to directly influence state policy: legislative liberalism, Democratic legislative strength, and state opinion. The coefficients for these variables can be seen in Figure 6.4 and Table 6.2. As Table 6.2 shows, the three independent variables together account for a large 80 percent of the variance in policy liberalism. Figure 6.8 illustrates these effects in terms of scatterplots of the partial regressions and of the multiple correlation between predicted and actual policy liberalism.[7]

As expected, the liberalism of the state legislature helps determine the direction of state policy, but with a beta coefficient of only 0.48, which suggests that other variables also contribute.[8] One of these variables is state public opinion, which exerts a direct effect (0.43) on policy liberalism. This effect presumably represents responsiveness by the state legislature to pressures of public opinion independent of legislative preferences. The most provocative influence is the negative (−0.32) coefficient for the effect of Democratic legislative control on policy liberalism.

A negative coefficient for Democratic legislative strength is not entirely unexpected, given that legislative preferences and state opinion are adequately controlled. As we have observed, even with the evident influence of state opinion, state parties tend to stand quite distant from the center of state opinion. Therefore, we might expect each party to moderate further when translating its positions into policy.

From the coefficients in Figure 6.4, legislative partisanship influences policy in two ways. Obviously, the more Democrats that the voters elect, the more liberals they elect. And liberal legislatures lead to liberal policies. We see this from the indirect path of about 0.30: 0.63 from Democratic strength to legislative liberalism times 0.48 from legislative liberalism to policy liberalism. The second way is the direct negative path (−0.32) from

7. For the illustrations of the partial regressions in Figure 6.8, each independent variable is depicted as the deviation from the value predicted from the other independent (control) variables. The dependent variable (policy liberalism) is also residualized as a deviation from the value predicted by the control variables.

8. For an alternative demonstration that bypasses the measure of legislative liberalism, consider the regression of state policy liberalism on party elite liberalism, state opinion, and Democratic legislative strength. From this equation, the coefficient for Democratic legislative strength is a negligible −0.02. Thus, holding constant both state opinion and the positions of the state parties, Democratic legislative strength does not predict more liberal policies.

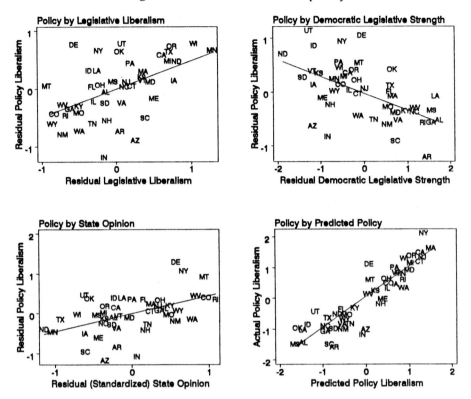

Figure 6.8 Accounting for Policy Liberalism

Democratic legislative strength to policy liberalism. Once again we have two processes that evidently cancel out. The results suggest that the partisan division of the legislature is of little relevance after all, as if, once in office, Democrats and Republicans start acting so much like each other that one cannot tell the difference![9]

Admittedly, some question must remain concerning the accuracy of the estimated negative impact of Democratic legislative strength on policy liberalism. On the one hand, the coefficient for Democratic legislative strength has the strongest t-value (-4.48) of the three predictors of policy liberalism. Assuming correct specification of the model, the negative

9. Just as we have a measure of legislative liberalism, based on weighting state party positions by their legislative strength, so too can we measure the ideological positions of *losing* legislative candidates, weighting party positions by the legislative strength of their opponents. Gratifyingly, when this variable is added to the policy equation, it yields a coefficient of only -0.02. The ideological positions of state parties matter only in proportion to their electoral strengths.

coefficient is highly significant. On the other hand, one can suspect possible bias from misspecification of the model.

Southern regionalism is a natural suspect as a confounding influence. To the extent that the South's history of Democratic success but conservative policies is due to the unique southern culture, it is necessary to control for southern regionalism. Indeed, inclusion of a simple dummy variable for the 11 former Confederate states reduces the coefficient from Democratic legislative strength to policy liberalism from −0.32 to −0.20. (See also Appendix B, for a complete set of coefficients when the 11 former Confederate states are removed.)

Under these and alternative model specifications, the negative path from Democratic legislative strength to policy liberalism can be pushed toward statistical insignificance. Yet the coefficient does not go to zero or change sign. Thus, the net effect of party control on policy remains somewhat ambiguous. The electorate's choice seems to be elect Democrats who are liberal personally but in office trim to the right, or to elect Republicans who are conservative personally but in office trim to the left. The results with the regional control suggest that, on balance, Democrats may make more liberal policies, but the statistical evidence must be viewed with caution.[10]

DIRECT DEMOCRACY

So far, we have ignored the direct effect of state opinion on state policy (beta = 0.44) that is independent of the electoral paths already discussed. Even with the ideological and partisan composition of the state legislature held constant, state opinion exerts an independent influence on state policy. At first glance, this "direct" effect of opinion on policy may seem to reflect sources of representation that are independent of the electoral process. But let us consider how the electoral process may underlie this "direct" effect as well.

---

10. Conceivably, the effect of party control on policy varies across states, with party control being most important in states where parties approximate the ideal of programmatic, disciplined parties. Perhaps in such states, we would find Democratic legislative success with a direct positive effect on policy liberalism. Accordingly, we reexamined the party effect after sorting on several measures of state party characteristics. We sorted on party competition (Ranney, 1971), legislative party cohesion (LeBlanc, 1969), party strength (Cotter et al., 1984), party diversity (Garand, 1985), party elite polarization (our own measure, see Chapter 5), and mass party polarization (our own measure, see Chapter 2). When examining the top-scoring states on each of these variables, we still found in each instance the estimated direct impact of Democratic legislative strength on policy liberalism to be negative. But for an important exception, see Chapter 7.

Legislative elections and state policy

Conceivably, when legislatures follow public opinion over their own collective judgment, they do so because legislators believe that they should play the role of instructed delegates. But a more likely reason for following public opinion is the fear of electoral sanctions when they do otherwise. To some extent, the "direct" effect of state opinion may also reflect the unmeasured role of state governors in the representation process: State electorates presumably tend to elect governors with whom they agree politically and who try to respond to the voice of state opinion. Finally, the "direct" effect of state opinion can reflect direct democracy, in the form of referendum voting.

To a degree that should not be ignored, citizens can participate directly in state policy making. About 300 referenda and initiatives come before state voters during every legislative biennium. Perhaps the best-known recent example of direct citizen input into state government was the 1978 wave of tax and spending limit votes in 15 states following the passage of Proposition 13 in California. But many other issues came before state electorates in the late 1970s and early 1980s (Ranney, 1978; Magleby, 1984; for specific issues and outcomes, consult *Congressional Quarterly Weekly Reports*). In various states, voters made policy decisions on gambling laws (from casinos to horse racing to lotteries), bottle bills, utility regulation (with specific emphasis in many states on nuclear power regulation), public smoking, anticrime measures (death penalty, handgun control, bail reduction, and prison construction), homosexual rights, "right-to-work" laws, state funding of abortion, voluntary prayer in schools, and state equal rights amendments. In sum, state electorates had the opportunity to alter a number of policies, including many that compose our measure of state policy liberalism.

CONCLUSIONS

This chapter has sought to explain why party control of the state legislature is not a particularly good predictor of state policy. The answer is not that electoral politics is unimportant but precisely the opposite. We have seen strong evidence that (1) party positions respond to state opinion, (2) state electorates reward and punish state parties based on their responsiveness to public opinion, and (3) Republican and Democratic legislators moderate their positions when making policy. Ironically, although state Republican and Democratic parties tend to represent ideological extremes, they also respond to state opinion – perhaps even to the point of enacting similar policies when in legislative control. This is, of course, exactly what the Downsian model of the electoral process says that electorally responsive parties should do. It is just that this result is achieved by a circuitous process.

Statehouse democracy

We suggest a new way of thinking about state politics. At the state level, the Democratic and Republican parties offer an ideological choice but also respond to state opinion. How well they respond helps to determine their electoral success at the legislative level and also the content of state policy. "State politics" – in the sense that term is usually understood – does matter.

Appendix A: A model of state elections

Our theoretical approach borrows from the well-known electoral theory of Anthony Downs (1957). Downs showed that an issue-motivated electorate would drive political parties toward the center of the political spectrum, thereby providing policy representation no matter which party would win elections. In a perfectly Downsian world, elections would in fact be ties. As one can readily observe, the pure form of the Downs model does not apply to American state politics. In each state, the Democratic and Republican parties are ideologically distinct–not the Tweedledum and Tweedledee that the Downs model would predict. Moreover, the U.S. electorate is far less ideologically preoccupied than the Downs model supposes.

In its pure form, the Downs model assumes that voters are motivated *solely* by ideology and that parties are motivated *solely* with winning elections. Reality is more complicated. Voters are motivated by ideology plus other considerations. In the language of spatial modeling, voters respond probabilistically, not deterministically, to their relative distances to party positions. Parties (strictly speaking, the candidates who run on the party label) are motivated by the Downsian goal of electoral success, plus other considerations (notably activist opinion) that pull the party toward its ideological extreme.

Here we present a model of state legislative elections that takes into account this mix of Downsian and non-Downsian motives for state electorates and state legislative parties. Figure 6.9 illustrates the model as it might apply to a state where the party midpoint happens to be to the left of state opinion, where

V = state opinion, the electorate's mean (or median) ideological position,
D = the Democratic Party's public ideological position,
R = the Republican Party's public ideological position,

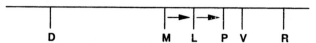

Figure 6.9 Hypothetical State: Party Midpoint to the Left of State Opinion

M = the midpoint between the two parties' ideological positions,
L = the legislature's ideological position, resulting from the electorate's partisan vote, and
P = state policy.

In this example, a party midpoint (M) to the left of state opinion (V) causes the electorate to elect more Republicans, which pushes the legislative position (L) rightward of M toward V. This electoral response may be sluggish, resulting in L only some fraction of the distance between M and V. Public opinion would pressure further movement toward V, so that policy (P) is to the right of the legislature (L) in the direction of V.

This model puts all the variables on one unidimensional ideological scale. In practice, one cannot measure the ideological positions of state parties, legislatures, and policies on such a common scale. Here the common scale is a heuristic device, to generate propositions about the relationships among state electoral variables that do not require one uniform ideological scale.

Suppose, for example, that party positions are constant across states, as in Figure 6.10. Liberal states elect more Democrats, resulting in a legisla-

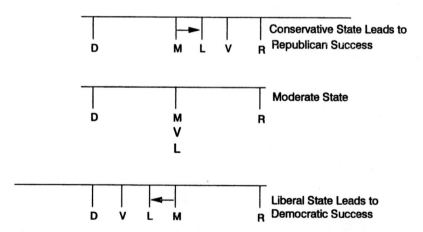

Figure 6.10 With Party Positions Held Constant, Elections Push Legislative Ideology toward State Opinion

Legislative elections and state policy

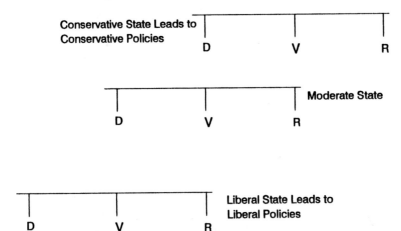

Figure 6.11 Parties Respond to State Opinion

ture to the left of the party midpoint. And conservative states elect more Republicans, resulting in a legislature to the right of the party midpoint.

But state parties can vary their positions in response to state opinion, as illustrated in Figure 6.11. Liberal states get more liberal parties and conservative states get more conservative parties.

State parties will not always move in perfect symmetry with the electorate. Figure 6.12 shows the consequences of different party positions for the same electorate. Relatively liberal parties result in Republican elections and a legislature to the right of the party midpoint. Relatively conservative parties result in Democratic elections and a legislature to the left of the party midpoint.

As in Figure 6.12, the ideological position of the legislature (L) will not necessarily match that of the electorate (state opinion). To the extent the legislature is out of alignment with state opinion, the legislature should

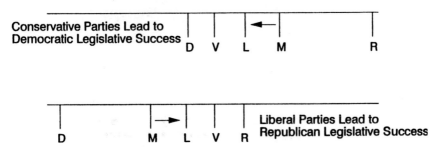

Figure 6.12 With State Opinion Held Constant, Elections Push Legislative Ideology toward State Opinion

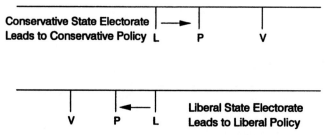

Figure 6.13 With Legislative Ideology Held Constant, Policy Moves in the Direction of State Opinion

respond in the direction of state opinion when making policy. Put another way, with the degree of legislative liberalism held constant, state opinion should influence the policy direction, as in Figure 6.13.

The partisanship of the legislature should make a difference too. With legislative ideology and state opinion held constant, the more Democratic the legislature, the more electorally motivated it would be to shift its policy direction to the right rather than the left. Consider Figure 6.14, which shows two states with the same state opinion (V) and the same legislative ideology (L). In each, the legislature and the party midpoint (M) are (arbitrarily) to the left of state opinion. The legislature in the first example is Democratic (L to the left of M) while that of the second is Republican (L to the right of M).

Since both legislatures are to the left of state opinion, each should move to the right in its policies. But legislative Democrats would be far to the left of state opinion and therefore be motivated to move to the right, while legislative Republicans would be somewhat to the right of state opinion and somewhat motivated to move to the left. Summing these vectors, the Democratic legislature would choose policies farther right (in the direc-

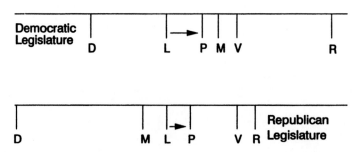

Figure 6.14 With State Opinion and Legislative Postions Held Constant, the More Republican Legislature Is More Liberal

tion of state opinion) than the Republican legislature under similar circumstances.

We emphasize again that we cannot observe the placement of parties, legislatures, policies, and the electorate on a common ideological scale as just depicted. We do not even know, for instance, whether state legislatures generally are to the right or to the left of state opinion. But Figures 6.10 to 6.14 provide the basis for predictions of covariations.

Summary

Figure 6.10 illustrates how ideologically fixed parties should result in liberal electorates electing more Democrats. Figure 6.11 illustrates how, when state parties can be ideologically flexible, their ideologies should correlate with state opinion. Figure 6.12 suggests that with state opinion held constant, liberal parties result in the election of more conservative Republicans and conservative parties result in the election of more liberal Democrats. Figure 6.13 illustrates how state opinion should influence policy direction even with legislative positions held constant. And Figure 6.14 shows how, with legislative positions and electoral preferences held constant, Democratic legislatures should produce more conservative policies than should Republican legislatures.

Appendix B: Taking out the South

Deleting southern states unambiguously removes any complication from the effects of southern culture. Table 6.3 shows the correlation matrix with southern states excluded. Note how better behaved this matrix is, given our usual expectations about electoral politics. Both state party identification and Democratic legislative strength now are correlated positively with both state opinion and state policy. The overall correlation between opinion and policy remains strong at .80.

The nonsouthern standardized regression equations are shown in Table 6.4. The path model is shown graphically in Figure 6.15. In general, the coefficients for 35 nonsouthern states are similar to those for all 46 examined states, but with a few exceptions. The effect of state party positions on party identification and on legislative partisanship are considerably smaller. These coefficients reflect that Democratic and Republican party leaderships do not show as much ideological variation when the South is excluded.

Most important, however, is that with southern states excluded, the direct effect of legislative partisanship on policy is modest (−0.20). As before, this suggests that Democratic and Republican legislators moderate their positions when in office. However the −0.20 coefficient does not override the indirect effect of legislative partisanship on policy via the preferences of the legislature (0.49 × 0.60 = 0.29). Thus, we have some slim evidence that the election of Democrats to the state legislature may lead to more liberal legislation after all.

Table 6.3. *Correlations: 35 non-southern states only*

Variables	Opinion liberalism	Party elite liberalism	Democratic party identification	Democratic legislative strength	Legislative liberalism	Policy liberalism
Opinion liberalism	1.00	.69	.47	.56	.83	.80
Party elite liberalism		1.00	-.01	.10	.86	.78
Democratic party identification			1.00	.87	.42	.22
Democratic legislative strength				1.00	.57	.38
Legislative liberalism					1.00	.83
Policy liberalism						1.00

Table 6.4. *Standardized regressions: 35 non-southern states only*

	Dependent variables				
Independent variables	Party elite liberalism	Democratic party identification	Democratic legislative strength	Legislative liberalism	Policy liberalism
Opinion liberalism	0.69*** (0.13)	0.91*** (0.19)	0.26 (0.15)		0.42* (0.16)
Party elite liberalism		-0.64** (0.18)	-0.08 (0.13)	0.81*** (0.02)	
Democratic party identification			0.75*** (0.11)		
Democratic legislative strength				0.49*** (0.03)	-0.20 (0.11)
Legislative liberalism					0.60*** (0.16)
Adjusted R^2	.465	.392	.771	.980	.734

Note: Standard errors in parentheses.
*Significant at .05; **significant at .01; ***significant at .001.

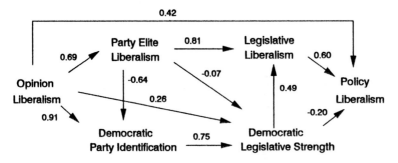

Legislative elections and state policy

Figure 6.15 Path Model of the State Policy Process (Non-South)

7

Political culture and policy representation

In Chapter 3, we accounted for state differences in mass ideology and partisanship in terms of state differences in "political culture." We found that state of residence matters as an influence on political attitudes, although we stopped short of identifying the underlying sources of this state variation. In this chapter, we explore a different usage of the concept "political culture." Here, we examine "state political culture" as a determinant not of mass attitudes but, rather, of the expectations and values that citizens (but mainly elites) share as they conduct the business of governing. We do not attempt to measure this sort of variation directly, but rather turn to Daniel Elazar's (1966, 1972) typology of political subcultures among the American states. This chapter examines whether states classified differently by Elazar in terms of political culture display different styles of representation in terms of the causal pathways from state opinion to state policy.

Elazar's typology undoubtedly is the most prominent contribution to the study of "political culture" in state politics. Elazar divides the U.S. states – and areas within states – according to their dominant political culture: moralistic, individualistic, or traditionalistic (MIT). In capsule form, the moralistic culture emphasizes the concern for the public welfare, the individualistic culture emphasizes politics as a marketplace, and the traditionalistic culture emphasizes the protection of traditional elites. Geographically, Elazar's moralistic states are mainly the northern tier of states settled by New England emigrants; traditionalistic states comprise southern and border states plus those settled by southern emigrants; individualistic states tend to be those geographically in-between.

Here, we explore the relevance of Elazar's typology to the study of representation in the states. From Elazar's discussion, we develop some propositions regarding how various aspects of the representation process might vary by subculture. We test these propositions by examining how certain causal relationships, discussed in Chapters 5 and 6, are conditioned by subculture. These tests offer intriguing support of the Elazar typology as a predictor of how state opinion translates into state policy. They point to significant variations in the opinion–policy linkages that, across the full set of states, we have found to be remarkably strong.

ELAZAR'S THREE SUBCULTURES

Elazar does not classify states according to their dominant subculture by applying some statistical formula. Rather, Elazar's classification reflects his judgment of the shared beliefs about politics, political institutions, and political action within each state. Although impressionistic, Elazar's formulation of three subcultures relies on a rich array of historical materials, particularly on the different migrations of ethnic and religious groups and how they have affected the development of politics in different areas of the country. Political culture in Elazar's formulation offers a way of making some theoretical sense of differences among the states, while at the same time tying together diverse behaviors and fundamental orientations such as political participation, conceptions of the role of government in society, governmental centralization, the role of political parties, and deference to political elites.

In the comparative state policy literature, research using the Elazar classification has been utilized only rarely to predict the *style* of democratic representation in the states. However, Elazar's classification (or Sharkansky's variant, discussed later) has seen extensive service as a predictor of the attitudes and behaviors of state residents and of the content of state policy. As Nardulli (1990, 289) observes, "No self-respecting regression analysis concerned with state politics can ignore the Elazar-Sharkansky scale."

Yet across the many quantitative studies that employ the Elazar framework, considerable ambiguity persists regarding exactly what Elazar's categories stand for. For some scholars, it is just "political culture," with the exact meaning left to the reader's interpretation. For others, the categories are given a particular explanatory role, but not always the same role as Elazar's intent. Some scholars have treated Elazar's MIT classification as a surrogate for state differences in mass attitudes. However, several intensive searches for clusterings of mass attitudes by subculture have produced mixed results (Schiltz and Rainey, 1978; Joslyn, 1980; Savage, 1981; Lowery and Sigelman, 1982; Nardulli, 1990).

Some studies (e.g., Lowery, 1987) have explicitly treated Elazar's classification as a substitute for liberalism–conservatism. In others, the meaning of "culture" is left implicit but seems to stand for mass ideology or something like it. Sharkansky's (1969) formulation of a moralism-to-traditionalism index, for example, has an internal logic closely akin to the liberal–conservative continuum. Anchored at one end are the moralistic states that "welcome the initiative of new programs for the good of the community." The other end is anchored by traditionalistic states that "accept new programs only if they were necessary for the maintenance of the status quo" (Sharkansky 1969, 69). Sharkansky finds that his measure has an independent relationship with a number of policy indicators, controlling for urbanism and state income. Several subsequent studies also report strong effects of some variant of Elazar's subcultures on the liberalism of state policies, thus reinforcing the impression that Elazar's cultural categories stand for something like liberalism–conservatism in the environment of state policy making (Peters and Welch, 1978; Hayes and Stonecash, 1981; Hanson, 1984; Klingman and Lammers, 1984; Fitzpatrick and Hero, 1988). Elazar, however, rejects the equating of political subculture and mass ideology: "The names of the political cultures are not substitutes for the terms 'conservative' and 'liberal' and should not be taken as such" (1972, 126).

This confusion about the meaning of Elazar's subcultures parallels the division into two different general usages of the term "political culture" in the political science literature. Following the lead of *The Civic Culture* (Almond and Verba, 1963), some studies reference political culture in terms of individual attitudes and behavior. From this perspective, sample surveys of citizens are a natural tool for measuring political culture. This was our usage in Chapter 3, where we reported major state differences in mass ideology and partisanship that remain after controlling for state demographics. We equated these residual "state effects" with state-to-state variation in political culture. That meaning of "political culture" is as a local climate of opinion that influences political attitudes independent of peoples' demographically induced predispositions.

Elazar's intent has more in common with the second, more encompassing view of political culture. This second usage is an extension of anthropologists' conception of culture as sets of perceptions, values, and expectations that help to constitute the rules of social and political life within communities. *Political* culture, in this view, represents commonly held assumptions about the proper roles of the citizenry and elites and about the appropriate goals of governmental action. Thus, political culture may influence how demands by different groups are articulated and received in the political system. In this formulation, political culture does not connote only (or even necessarily) differences in mass attitudes, but rather general expectations and practices about how different needs and preferences are treated in the political arena. Viewed in this way, political culture is an attribute of the political community more than it is a characteristic of any specific individuals or institutions.

Political culture and policy

As Elazar describes the three subcultures, each one represents a distinct understanding about the nature of politics, public participation in politics, and the relationship between citizens and public officials. As such, the three subcultures represent alternative ways that the representation of citizen demands can be achieved (or not achieved) in a democratic political (sub)system. The emphasis is not so much on the content of public policies as on the process by which states transform political demands into public policy. From this perspective, let us examine Elazar's intent for the MIT typology.

The moralistic subculture

Consider first the seemingly more "liberal" moralistic subculture, concentrated in the states settled by New England emigrants. According to Elazar, the moralistic subculture reflects the belief that government should be an active agent for the public good. It includes the moral obligation to participate in government affairs by ordinary citizens and by elites. In the moralistic subculture, political competition is over issues, and political parties are seen as vehicles for achieving goals perceived to be in the public interest. The importance placed on issues and principles suggests that the moralistic subculture is the ideal habitat for ideological activists. Relatedly, the moralistic culture includes a sense of obligation for community welfare. This obligation extends to a general readiness for policy initiatives in the "public interest" on the part of the political leadership even when such action is not demanded by state electorates. These activities are "to achieve the 'good community' through positive action" (1972, 100). Thus, we would expect to find active governments even without widespread support for liberal policies. From this description of the moralistic subculture, one can readily understand the frequent inference of a cultural predisposition for liberal policies.

The traditionalistic subculture

The largely southern traditionalistic subculture offers a very different model for the role of democratic institutions. It includes a general presumption against government action to solve peoples' problems and an overall assumption that the chief end of politics is to serve the interest of traditional elites. As described by Elazar, the traditionalistic subculture promotes government principally "as a means of maintaining the existing order" (1972, 100). This belief should act as a brake on policy initiatives, yielding, first, an overall bias toward conservative policies and, second, a sluggish response to mass preferences for policy change.

Statehouse democracy

The individualistic subculture

Elazar's discussion of the individualistic subculture presents a third model for democratic representation. In individualistic states, politics tends to be viewed as a marketplace with few preconceptions about the goals of government. Politics is an (often dirty) means of brokering public demands into public policy. Government initiatives are neither encouraged (as in the moralistic states) nor discouraged (as in the traditionalistic states) but instead are the natural response to citizen demands. Politicians tend to be political "professionals," driven not so much to protect public or elite interests as they are by the pragmatic political concerns of getting and staying elected.

SUBCULTURE AND REPRESENTATION: SOME PROPOSITIONS

So how can we expect Elazar's subcultures to differentiate between paths to policy representation? Clearly, as others have, we would expect traditionalistic states to reflect a cultural predisposition to conservatism and moralistic states to reflect a cultural disposition to liberalism. (Individualistic states presumably would be in-between.) We would expect to see these dispositions manifested in the ideological directions of state policies, especially after other causal variables are taken into account. We might also expect these ideological predispositions to be measurable in the attitudes of political elites, even after the preferences of public opinion are taken into account.

Just as interesting as the possible effects of different subcultures on policy *direction* are the possible effects of subculture on the *process* of representation. By the "process of representation" we mean the various intermediate causal relationships that connect state opinion and policy, which were discussed in Chapters 5 and 6. For instance, political culture may affect the responsiveness of political elites to state opinion. It may affect how state opinion results in state party control and in the policy views of state officeholders. Or political culture may affect the manner in which elected officials respond to the demands of state public opinion.

In generating specific hypotheses about the conditional effects of subculture on the democratic process, an easy starting point is to propose that the various causal relationships should be most sluggish for the more elite-dominated traditionalistic states. We should be careful about the seemingly symmetrical proposition, however, that democratic responsiveness is greatest in the public interest–oriented moralistic states. While the moralistic subculture includes the norm of general political participation, we are reminded of Elazar's assertion that the moralistic norm for political leaders is to legislate for the public good rather than to satisfy public desires.

The most interesting distinction is between Elazar's descriptions of moralistic and individualistic states in terms of the way democratic politics is played. In Chapter 5, we distinguished between two models of the representational process. One is the familiar Downsian model of representation, which relies on pragmatic politicians seeking reelection. According to the Downs model, electorally driven candidates should converge toward the moderate ideological position in the center of the political spectrum. The second model is that of responsible party government, which posits two parties that are ideologically distinguished from one another, driven by politicians more concerned with policy (or ideology in our version) than with electoral success. Reality is in fact a hybrid of these two models, with politicians responding to both the ideological concerns of activists, including themselves, and the necessity of getting elected to accomplish one's goals.

We expect to find the strongest approximation of the Downsian model in the individualistic states. In these states, the subculture supposedly contains no particular disposition to act in an ideologically liberal or conservative fashion. In these states, we expect to see the strongest evidence of pragmatic politics. While it is not clear the *electorate* should be more ideologically sensitive in the individualistic states than elsewhere, we expect to see evidence that political parties and elected officials are more responsive to state opinion than their elitist counterparts in traditionalistic subcultures or their public interest–driven counterparts in the moralistic subcultures.

Elazar posits a greater concern for the interpretation of the public interest among political actors of moralistic subcultures. It is an easy translation to say that politicians of moralistic states should be our ideologues, with politics in the moralistic states offering the closest approximation to responsible party politics. This means we should find greater party differences on issues, party control playing a more central role in the policy process and ballot behavior from the electorate that reflects a greater partisan polarization.[1]

---

1. Elazar (e.g., 1970, 260–5) contends that "party regularity" is more strongly rooted in the individualistic culture than the moralistic culture. To the extent "regularity" or discipline goes with party "responsibility," it may seem that our hypothesis of pragmatic parties in moralistic states and responsible parties in individualistic states has been reversed of what it should be. However, the individualistic "regularity" to which Elazar refers is that of a patronage-driven party organization. We explicate the pragmatic vs. responsible distinction in terms of ideological polarization, not regularity or discipline.

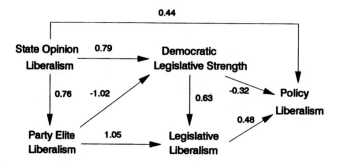

Figure 7.1 Path Model of the State Policy Process (46 States)

Evidence of these interaction effects would come from inserting state culture dummy variables, both additively and interactively, in the equations of our causal model of state representation. To review, Figure 7.1 presents a condensed version of our causal model of policy representation in the states, as reported in Chapter 6. As before, the coefficients are based on standardized measures. This is identical to the Chapter 6 model, except that the intervening variable of state partisanship is omitted for simplicity. State opinion is measured as the state-level means on ideological self-ratings from CBS/NYT surveys, 1976–88. Party elite liberalism in the states is our composite of four indicators, as described in Chapter 5. Democrats and Republicans weigh equally for this measure. Legislative liberalism is the composite of Republican and Democratic elite liberalism, with each party's score weighted by the party's state legislative strength. Democratic legislative strength is a composite for 1977–84. State policy liberalism is our composite of eight policy indicators.

The coefficients reported in Figure 7.1 reveal a strong role for electoral politics in providing the connection between state opinion and state policy. First, the ideologies of state party elites vary predictably with state opinion. Second, parties' legislative success is determined by state opinion (liberals vote Democratic) plus the party elites' responsiveness to state opinion. The negative coefficient from party elite liberalism to Democratic legislative strength reflects electoral rewards for centrist positions. Third, policy is a function of legislative preferences, legislative partisanship, and state opinion. The negative coefficient for Democratic legislative strength represents legislatures practicing centrist politics. Everything else being equal, Democrats will trim to the right and Republicans to the left, each toward the center. The residual effect of state opinion, remaining after legislative preferences and partisanship are controlled, represents the direct responsiveness of legislatures to mass preferences.

Political culture and policy

In our reanalysis of this model with subculture included, measurement of all continuous variables is in standardized units. (In all instances, scores are standardized in terms of the means and standard deviations for the full set of 46 states and not states of a particular subculture.) We measure the three subcultures by means of dummy variables for the traditionalistic and the moralistic states, with individualistic states serving as the base category.[2] The influence of political culture as a conditioning factor in the representational process is assessed from so-called interaction terms in the regression model. Interaction terms are additional variables, created as the product of the particular measure of interest (say, Democratic legislative strength) and the relevant subculture dummy variable. Interaction terms yield coefficients as changes in the slopes for the moralistic and the traditionalistic subcultures from the base slope for the individualistic states (Wright, 1976).

Our strategy is to incorporate the possible effects of state political culture on the the nature of policy representation in the states. For each of three dependent variables in the model – party elite ideology, legislative partisanship, and policy liberalism – we start with the base causal model shown in Figure 7.1. Then we bring in the subculture dummy variables for moralism and traditionalism, to see if subculture has an additive effect independent of the other variables. Then we introduce the interaction terms to see if subculture affects the magnitudes of the various causal relationships that connect state opinion with state policy.

ANALYSIS

As a preliminary step, we assess the relationship between subculture and the ideological direction of state opinion. This is to determine the extent to which Elazar's typology operates as a proxy for public liberalism–conservatism. With state opinion measured in standardized form, the equation is

$$\widehat{\text{State opinion}} = .70 - 1.35 \times \text{Traditionalistic} - 0.70 \times \text{Moralistic}$$
$$(t\text{-value}) \qquad\qquad (-4.33) \qquad\qquad\qquad (-2.28)$$
$$\text{Adjusted } R^2 = .267$$

The coefficient for traditionalism is negative, reflecting the conservatism of traditionalistic southern states. A more revealing test is whether the

2. Our dummy variable coding represents Elazar's classification of "dominant" subcultures for the states. Elazar acknowledges minor strains competing with dominant subcultures. For example, Arizona reflects a dominant traditionalistic subculture combined with a lesser moralistic strain. We consider only the dominant traditionalistic subculture.

supposedly more liberal moralistic states actually are more ideologically liberal than the base category of individualistic states. This test "fails" spectacularly, as the moralistic state electorates are actually significantly more conservative than are individualistic ones. Thus, when arranged as a traditionalistic-to-moralistic continuum, Elazar's subculture typology definitely is not a simple surrogate for mass ideology. Elazar's three cultural categories do statistically "explain" 27 percent of the variance in state opinion, but this reflects the liberal–conservative difference between the North and the "traditionalistic" South, and little more.

Subculture and policy: A first look

Although Elazar's subcultures do not represent mass ideology, do they affect the ideological direction of state policy independent of state opinion? Table 7.1 presents the evidence. First, Column 1 shows that Elazar's categories account for only 46 percent of the variation in policy, with the sole distinction that the southern traditionalistic states have more conservative policies than the others. Meanwhile (Column 2), state opinion by itself predicts policy with a coefficient (beta or, in the bivariate case, an "r") of 0.83, accounting for 67 percent of the variance. Add subculture (Column 3), and this coefficient drops only slightly, although the two subculture dummies help to predict policy. But again only the traditionalism coefficient is significant. With the control for state opinion, a traditionalistic subculture continues to predict policy conservatism while a moralistic subculture now predicts liberal policies, albeit with a nonsignificant coefficient.

An even more interesting set of questions is whether subculture shows "interactive" effects with the strength of the opinion–policy connection varying by subculture. Column 4 presents the appropriate equation. The coefficients in Column 4 offer a hint that traditionalism and moralism dampen the effect of state opinion on policy. The state opinion coefficients are 0.91 for individualistic states, 0.63 (or 0.91 − 0.28) for moralistic states, and 0.48 (or 0.91 − 0.43) for traditionalistic states. These different slopes are shown in Figure 7.2. These results are not strong enough on their own to claim a meaningful net difference in representation for the different subcultures, however, since they fall just short of statistical significance.[3]

3. To see how marginal the answer to the question of statistical significance is here, consider the following. The equations of Table 7.1 are based on 47 states, including Nebraska. (Although Nebraska is excluded from most regressions because of missing data on its nonpartisan legislature, there is no reason to exclude it from the equation predicting policy from state opinion and culture.) If we exclude Nebraska,

Table 7.1. *State policy liberalism by state opinion and state subculture*

Variable	(1)	(2)	(3)	(4)
		State Policy Liberalism		
State opinion (standardized)		0.83 (9.94)***	0.70 (8.44)***	0.91 (6.27)***
Traditionalism	-1.54 (-5.73)***		-0.58 (-2.78)**	-0.59 (-2.62)**
Moralism	-0.25 (0.96)		0.26 (1.44)	0.39 (2.04)*
Traditionalism x Opinion				-0.43 (-1.83)
Moralism x Opinion				-0.28 (-1.53)
Adjusted R^2	.448	.680	.794	.800
Significance of R^2 increment:			(3)>(2) .000	(4)>(3) .16

Note: N = 47; Alaska, Hawaii, and Nevada are excluded. *t*-values in parentheses.
*Significant at .05; **significant at .01; ***significant at .001.

This first examination of the data would seem to show that subculture is of little consequence for the study of political representation in the states. However, the same degree of overall representation can be achieved in several ways. When we examine the specific causal pathways of the representation process, we will see evidence of real and significant differences across subcultures.

the coefficients for traditionalism and moralism approach collective significance with a *p*-value at .072. Alternatively, suppose we restore Nebraska and replace the two culture-opinion interaction terms with one individualism–state opinion interaction term. This term approaches significance, with a *p*-value of .072. Finally, if we substitute the truncated version of state opinion, measured for the period 1976–82 only, the interaction terms are significant.

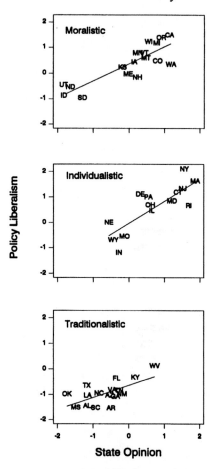

Figure 7.2 Policy Liberalism and State
Opinion by Political Subculture

We will also see that individualistic states show the strongest evidence
of pragmatic Downsian representation, with flexible electorally driven
parties. The strong statistical evidence of pragmatic Downsian state politics shown in Chapters 5 and 6 is even stronger when individualistic states
are isolated. Moralistic states approximate the opposite extreme of responsible party government. When moralistic states are isolated, we see
parties that appear more ideological than electorally driven, with the legislative partisan division being more decisive at the policy stage. Traditionalistic states are not as easy to classify. In terms of the representation
process, traditionalistic states are in some ways in between the individualistic and moralistic states.

Political culture and policy

Political subculture and party elite liberalism

A starting point is to explore how subculture affects the response of party elites to state opinion. In preceding chapters, we have recognized the strong relationship between state opinion and party elite liberalism. This is because elites are drawn from their mass constituencies and because party positions must reflect public opinion if the party is to prosper electorally. Suppose we include the effects of political culture in our analysis of the relationship between mass and elite ideologies. Table 7.2 shows what happens.

The simple equation represented in Column 1 accounts for party elite liberalism in terms of subculture alone. The culture dummies account for considerable variance in party elite liberalism. Meanwhile, Column 2 shows that state opinion (alone) also predicts party elite liberalism, but (perhaps surprisingly) with an only slightly higher R^2 than from the combined culture dummies alone. Note that the predictive power of culture is almost entirely the work of the traditionalistic dummy variable, reflecting the conservatism of southern political culture. Moralistic states and individualistic states on average have virtually identical degrees of party elite liberalism. For party elites, as for state opinion and for state policy, we fail to find a simple moralism–liberalism association.

We next combine state opinion and culture to predict party elite liberalism. Column 3 shows the additive equation. With the control for state opinion, we continue to find that the traditionalistic states' party elites are significantly more conservative. Most interestingly, with the control for state opinion, we now also find that moralism is significantly related to elite liberalism. One aspect of the moralistic subculture therefore is that the partisan elites are more liberal than would be expected from state opinion.

Next, Column 4 shows the conditional (interaction) effects of subculture on the opinion–elite relationship. With negative coefficients for the interaction terms, the result is as if the liberalism of state party elites is most responsive to mass ideological sentiment in the (base) individualistic states. However, since these two interaction terms are not statistically significant (either individually or collectively) these possible interaction effects are too fragile to pursue seriously.

In summary, we do find a strong statistical tie between Elazar's moralistic states and party elite liberalism, but only after controlling for state opinion. This result is impressive evidence for the distinctiveness of Elazar's subcultures. In terms of mass opinion or even policy, moralistic states are not particularly liberal. The readily inferred connection between moralistic subculture and liberalism emerges only when the dependent variable is the ideological preferences of state political elites. This is a

Table 7.2. *Party elite liberalism by state opinion and state subculture*

Variable	(1)	(2)	(3)	(4)
		Party Elite Liberalism		
State opinion (standardized)		0.76 (7.83)***	0.61 (7.50)***	0.81 (5.05)***
Traditionalism	-1.56 (-6.25)***		-0.69 (-3.41)**	-0.55 (-2.32)*
Moralism	0.02 (0.07)		0.51 (2.86)**	0.67 (3.22)**
Traditionalism x State opinion				-0.26 (-1.07)
Moralism x State opinion				-0.28 (-1.46)
Adjusted R^2	.553	.573	.804	.806
Significance of R^2 increment:			(3)>(2) .000	(4)>(3) .33

Note: $N = 46$; Alaska, Hawaii, Nebraska, and Nevada are excluded. *t*-values in parentheses. *Significant at .05; **significant at .01; ***significant at .001.

satisfying result because, if political culture actually molds political attitudes, the strongest influence would be on political elites.

Political subculture and party elite polarization

Since the moralistic cultural climate purportedly nurtures ideological activists, it should contribute to the *polarization* of the Democratic and Republican party elites. Table 7.3 shows a series of regressions predicting party elite polarization from subculture dummies and other relevant variables. Party elite polarization, recall from Chapter 5, is the simple difference between the composite liberalism score for a state's Democratic and Republican elites. Apart from mass-level party polarization (see

Table 7.3. *Party elite polarization by state opinion and state subculture*

Variable	Party Elite Polarization			
	(1)	(2)	(3)	(4)
State opinion (standardized)		-0.02 (-0.30)	-0.01 (-0.17)	-0.06 (-0.92)
Traditionalism	0.05 (0.36)		0.03 (0.19)	0.16 (0.95)
Moralism	0.44 (3.22)**		0.43 (2.90)**	0.36 (2.56)*
Mass party polarization (standardized)				0.18 (2.63)*
Intercept	1.41 (13.83)		1.42 (12.19)	1.40 (12.83)
Adjusted R^2	.202	-.021	.184	.285

Note: N = 46; Alaska, Hawaii, Nebraska, and Nevada are excluded. *t*-values in parentheses.
*Significant at .05; **significant at .01; ***significant at .001.

Chapter 2), moralistic subculture is the sole variable that consistently predicts party elite polarization. Thus, party elites are more liberal but also more ideologically polarized than in other states.

This result presents a certain irony. Earlier (Chapter 5), we noted that several categorizations of states that scholars had posited to predict polarized parties in fact did not; but they did in each case predict party elite liberalism. Elazar's classification is an exception to this rule. Elazar's moralistic states produce party elites that are more polarized but not (in the absence of controls) noticeably more liberal. With state opinion controlled, however, the party elites of the moralistic states are both more polarized and more liberal.

How can moralist party elites be more liberal *and* more polarized ideologically? Figure 7.3 presents Democratic and Republican party elite liberalism scores as a function of state opinion, separately for each subculture.

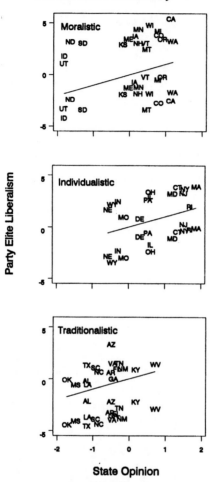

Figure 7.3 Party Ideology and State
Opinion by Political Subculture. Note:
Democrats above the diagonal;
Republicans below.

We scale this figure like we did Figure 6.5, forcing state opinion and party
elite liberalism onto a common metric based on the assumption that,
nationally, the party midpoint is uncorrelated with state opinion. Note
that parties are farther apart in moralistic states, with the key difference
being that Democratic elites in moralistic states are unusually liberal –
more liberal, that is, than their counterparts in individualistic or tradi-

tionalistic states with the identical degree of liberalism among the mass public.[4]

Figure 7.3 also presents a hint of how the relative proximity of the parties to the electorate may vary by subculture. Presented with liberal party elites, the electorates of moralistic states appear ideologically closer to their local Republican parties. Meanwhile, given conservative party elites, the electorates of traditionalistic states appear closer to their local Democratic parties. These differences suggest some subcultural variation in partisan voting – a subject that we turn to next.

Political subculture and legislative partisanship

When state party elites diverge ideologically from the preference of state opinion, the electorate can make the ideological correction at the ballot box. Electorates in traditionalistic states, with elites more conservative than projected from state opinion, can correct by leaning toward their relatively conservative Democratic parties over their seemingly too conservative Republican parties. Similarly, electorates in moralistic states, with elites more liberal than projected from state opinion, can correct by leaning toward their relatively liberal Republican parties over their seemingly too liberal Democratic parties.

Table 7.4 shows a series of equations predicting Democratic legislative strength from state opinion, party elite liberalism, and the additive and interaction effects of the culture dummies. Column 1 shows the simple prediction from culture alone. As expected, the traditionalistic states tend to have strongly Democratic legislatures. Moralistic states have legislatures that are far more Republican than average. Column 2 presents the representation equation without the culture dummies. Democratic legislative success is greatest when state opinion is most liberal and when party elites are most conservative. This is consistent with Downsian logic, since Democrats are closer to the electorate when both parties are more conservative than their norm, and Republicans are closer to the electorate when both parties are more liberal than their norm (see Chapter 6).

Column 3 shows the result with culture dummies combined additively with state opinion and party elite liberalism as predictors of Democratic legislative strength. The moralistic pro-Republican "effect" almost vanishes, as if it is accounted for by moralistic electorates adjusting for their seemingly overly liberal party elites. However, even with the controls, the traditionalistic subculture still shows a positive effect on Democratic legis-

---

4. As an alternative, we can repeat this analysis by subdividing party elite liberalism into scores for activists and electoral elites, as done in Chapter 5. The greater polarization of the parties in moralistic states is present for both groups of elites, but stronger for activist elites than for electoral elites.

Table 7.4. *Accounting for democratic legislative success*

Variable	Democratic legislative success			
	(1)	(2)	(3)	(4)
State opinion (standardized)		0.79 (4.44)***	0.57 (3.07)**	1.62 (4.25)***
Party elite liberalism (standardized)		-1.02 (-5.75)***	-0.37 (-1.59)	-1.16 (-2.77)**
Traditionalism	0.97 (3.55)***		1.22 (3.54)***	0.54 (1.65)
Moralism	-0.66 (2.47)*		0.20 (0.70)	-0.17 (0.53)
Traditionalism x State opinion				-1.38 (-3.03)**
Moralism x State opinion				-1.31 (-3.14)**
Traditionalism x Party elite liberalism				-0.08 (-0.15)
Moralism x Party elite liberalism				1.48 (3.05)**
Adjusted R^2	.467	.409	.557	.776
Significance of R^2 increment:			(3)>(2) .001	(4)>(3) .000

Note: *t*-values in parentheses.
*Significant at .05; **significant at .01; ***significant at .001.

lative strength. Traditionalism is a marker for the once one-party politics of the southern political culture (Key, 1949).

Column 4 shows the interaction effects involving culture. These are the subculture-to-subculture differences in the effects of state opinion and party elite liberalism on Democratic legislative strength. Here, for the first time, we find strong evidence that effects of other variables depend on

subculture. Both traditionalistic and moralistic subcultures appear to se-
verely dampen the gradient by which a state's electorate translates its
ideological preferences into the partisan division of legislative seats.
Effects of state opinion on Democratic legislative strength are 1.62 for
individualistic states (the base), 0.31 (or 1.62 − 1.31) for moralistic states,
and 0.24 (or 1.62 − 1.38) for traditionalistic states. Meanwhile, moralism
(but not traditionalism) appears to dampen the coefficient for party elite
liberalism − as if electorates in moralistic states give little regard to their
parties' ideological nuances. The party elite liberalism coefficient changes
from −1.16 (the base, for individualistic states) to 0.32 (or −1.16 + 1.48)
for a sign reversal in moralistic states. These patterns are highly significant
statistically. How do we account for them?

For traditionalistic states, the seemingly less responsive electorate may
be a by-product of the supposed elite domination of the electoral process.
For moralistic states, we need a different explanation because their partisan legislative divisions are less responsive to both state opinion and elite
ideology. Our speculation is that the seemingly sluggish electoral response
in moralistic states is actually a response to the more programmatic parties. With polarized parties that approximate the national party positions
ideologically, minor differences in our measure of party positions should
have little impact on partisan voting. Party polarization, however, magni-
fies the policy impact of each increment of Democratic legislative control
(discussed ahead). Thus, provided with more programmatic divergent
parties, electorates in moralistic states can employ a smaller partisan adjustment to achieve a given ideological result. The statistical result is the
smaller regression coefficients in moralistic states for the effect of state
ideology on legislative party strength.[5]

The interaction effect of moralism on the effect of party elite liberalism
on Democratic legislative strength suggests that moralistic electorates ignore nuances of each party's ideology. This makes sense for the same
reason that a low coefficient for state opinion makes sense when the parties are polarized. With ideologically diverse parties, electorates in moralistic states properly respond by fine-tuning the correct electoral mix of
conservative Republicans and liberal Democrats, rather than selectively

5. It may seem counterintuitive that polarized parties produce *lesser* coefficients for
   state opinion predicting a partisan response. Consider, however, the following hypothetical examples. In Set A of states, the Democratic and Republican positions are
   0.5 and −0.5, respectively. In Set B, the Democratic and Republican parties are
   farther apart, at 1.0 and −1.0. Suppose, in each set, the state electorates chose the
   partisan mix that matches its mean ideological preference on the same scale. A state
   at −0.5 would choose all Republicans if in Set A but only 75 percent Republicans if
   in Set B (0.75 × (−1) + 0.25 × (+1) = −0.5). Similarly, a state at +0.5 would choose all
   Democrats if in Set A but only 75 percent Democrats if in Set B. For Set A, the slope
   is 2.0, or 1.0 − (−1.0). For Set B, the slope is 1.5, or 0.75 − (−0.75).

rewarding parties for their ideological moderation, as electorates in individualistic and traditionalistic states can do.

Political subculture and legislative liberalism

We measure legislative liberalism as the combination of Democratic and Republican party elite liberalism, rescaled so that the two party elites are weighted in accordance with their legislative strength. Since legislative liberalism is defined in terms of party elite liberalism and Democratic legislative strength, there is little to be gained by pursuing the direct effects of subculture on legislative liberalism. Instead, we examine how subculture might alter the net (direct plus indirect) effect of state opinion on legislative liberalism. Following our usual procedure, we examine first the simple additive models and then the conditional impact of state culture on the net state opinion–legislative liberalism relationship. Table 7.5 shows the details.

Column 1 shows the simple differences in legislative liberalism across subcultures. Without controls, there is not much of a relationship, but we do see the greater conservatism among the legislators of traditionalistic states. Column 2 shows the strong ($r = .79$) bivariate relationship between state opinion and legislative ideology. Column 3 shows the joint additive effects of culture and state opinion. With interaction effects not yet included, the additive effects of culture on legislative ideology are not significant.

Column 4 adds the interaction effects. The net responsiveness of legislative liberalism to state opinion is very strong (1.22) in individualistic states, slightly (and insignificantly) less (0.94 = 1.22 – 0.28) in the moralistic states, and almost invisible (0.34 = 1.22 – 0.88) states. Thus, if we gauge the quality of representation by the responsiveness of legislative preferences to opinion in the state, the traditionalistic subculture gets low marks.

Traditionalism by itself, however, does not seem to breed legislative conservatism. An ideologically middle-of-the-road state would have about the same kind of legislature ideologically, whether the state embraced the traditionalist or individualist culture. We also see that with the interaction terms included, a significant, positive coefficient emerges for moralistic states. A moralistic subculture appears to provide the state with a more liberal legislature than otherwise, even after the electoral process is allowed to do its work.

The policy equation

The story does not end with the determination of the ideological leanings of state legislatures. State policies are not an exact function of the legisla-

Table 7.5. *State opinion, state subculture, and legislative liberalism*

Variable	Legislative liberalism		
	(1)	(2)	(3)
State opinion (standardized)	0.82 (9.62)***	0.90 (8.67)***	1.22 (6.39)***
Traditionalism		0.33 (1.27)	0.24 (.83)
Moralism		0.37 (1.64)	0.63 (2.56)*
Traditionalism x State opinion			-0.88 (-3.03)**
Moralism x State opinion			-0.28 (-1.20)
Adjusted R^2	.670	.676	.725
Significance of R^2 increment:		(2)>(1) .26	(3)>(2) .014

Note: $N = 46$; Alaska, Hawaii, Nebraska, and Nevada are excluded. *t*-values in parentheses.
*Significant at .05; **significant at .01; ***significant at .001.

tors' collective preferences. The partisan division of the legislature can make a difference. Also, legislatures sometimes allow public opinion to override their own preferences (Miller and Stokes, 1963). Our final statistical task is to see how these processes are affected by subculture.

Table 7.1 showed the additive and interaction effects involving state opinion and political subculture as predictors of state policy liberalism. Table 7.6 shows the policy equations that also include additive and interaction effects involving Democratic legislative strength and legislative liberalism. We focus mainly on the "best" equation shown in Column 3, which includes terms for the interactions of culture with state opinion and Democratic legislative strength but excludes those involving legislative liberalism. Several features of the results warrant attention.

First, note the additive moralistic effect in the conditional models of

Table 7.6. *Accounting for state policy liberalism*

Variable	State policy liberalism			
	(1)	(2)	(3)	(4)
State opinion (standardized)	0.44 (3.59)***	0.40 (3.08)**	1.14 (4.47)***	1.11 (2.77)**
Legislative liberalism (standardized)	0.48 (3.88)***	0.36 (2.72)**	0.14 (0.93)	0.16 (0.51)
Democratic legislative strength (standardized)	-0.32 (-4.48)***	-0.09 (-0.41)	-0.44 (2.28)*	-0.44 (-2.15)*
Traditionalism		-0.56 (-2.29)*	-0.18 (-0.71)	-0.25 (-0.42)
Moralism		0.09 (0.47)	1.08 (2.92)**	1.00 (2.51)*
Traditional x State opinion			-0.73 (-2.60)*	-0.63 (-1.38)
Moralism x State opinion			-0.88 (-3.23)**	-0.88 (-2.01)
Traditionalism x Democratic legislative strength			0.37 (1.57)	0.39 (1.55)
Moralism x Democratic legislative strength			0.95 (2.65)*	0.87 (2.00)
Traditionalism x Legislative liberalism				-0.22 (-0.46)
Moralism x Legislative liberalism				0.04 (0.11)
Adjusted R^2	.799	.819	.846	.839
Significance of R^2 increment:		(2)>(1) .047	(3)>(2) .040	(4)>(3) .809

Note: *t*-values in parentheses.
*Significant at .05; **significant at .01; ***significant at .001.

Columns 3 and 4. Even apart from legislative liberalism, Democratic legislative strength, and state opinion, something about the moralistic culture makes moralistic states enact policies that are far more liberal than in other states. For a middle-of-the-road state (at zero – the national mean on state opinion and Democratic legislative strength), a moralistic (instead of individualistic) culture is worth about a 1.08 standard deviation increment in policy liberalism. This is the residual effect of the moralistic subculture apart from the direct working of the electoral process. No more than a trace (−0.18) of a mirror-image "conservative" policy effect appears for the traditionalistic subculture.

Second, in the full model (Column 4, see also Column 3), the combined additive and interactive effects of legislative liberalism become nonsignificant and virtually nonexistent. The strong effect of state legislative liberalism seen when culture is absent from the model gets absorbed by culture and its interactions. Quite arguably this result could be no more than an adverse response of the data to multicolinearity. But a possibility that cannot be ruled out is that what appears to be evidence of legislatures responding to their own preferences could really be the by-product of political culture.

Third, especially, for the equation reported in Column 3, we observe a major interaction effect involving moralism and Democratic legislative strength. Whereas in individualistic (and to a lesser degree traditionalistic) states the sign for Democratic legislative strength is negative, for moralistic states the sign is clearly positive ($0.51 = −0.44 + 0.95$). In individualistic states where a more politically pragmatic politics reigns, Democratic legislators trim to the right and Republicans trim to the left when making state policy. In fact, working through the equations suggests that parties overcompensate, so that the best way to enact liberal policies in an individualist state might be to elect Republicans, and the best way to enact conservative policies might be to elect Democrats. But in moralistic states where parties are supposedly more programmatic and clearly more polarized in ideological tone, partisanship accentuates policy differences. In moralistic states, the best way to enact liberal policies would clearly be to elect programmatic Democrats, and the best way to enact conservative policies would clearly be to elect programmatic Republicans.

The variation in the functioning of legislative partisanship in the policy process can be seen dramatically from Figure 7.4. Here, the simple correlation between (unstandardized) Democratic legislative strength and state policy liberalism is shown separately for the three subcultures. For traditionalistic states, the legislative strength–policy correlation is actually somewhat negative (−.32), with Democratic legislatures manufacturing the most conservative policies. For individualistic states, the correlation is positive but slim (.37). But for moralistic states, a sharp .89

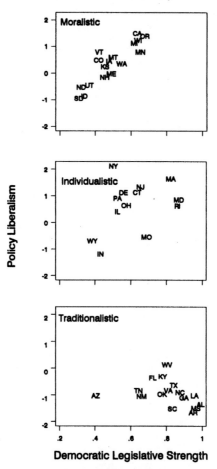

Figure 7.4 Policy Liberalism and
Democratic Legislative Strength by
Political Subculture

correlation exists, as if policy liberalism is almost solely a direct function
of Democratic legislative strength.

This last result might suggest that the moralistic subculture enhances
responsiveness of policy to public opinion. But consider the fourth and
perhaps most important observation to be made from Table 7.6. Apart
from all legislative responses we have been considering, the *direct* effect of
state opinion is strongly conditioned by political culture. From Column 3,
for the reference base of individualistic states, the direct effect of opinion
on policy is a major coefficient of 1.14. Meanwhile, the direct effects of

public opinion in the other two cultures are negligible: only 0.26 (1.14 − 0.88) in moralistic states and only 0.41 (1.14 − 0.73) in traditionalistic states. State legislatures are much less responsive to state opinion in the moralistic and traditionalistic states.

The startlingly large differences in the coefficients for moralistic and individualistic states can be attributed to the difference between pragmatic politicians in individualistic states and the programmatic politicians in moralistic states. In moralistic states, the relative partisan division of legislatures has important policy consequences, while legislatures are less responsive to the direct input of public opinion. In individualistic states, the party division has less easily discernible policy consequences, but the pragmatic legislatures respond strongly to state opinion.

Summary: Three state subcultures

Let us summarize the features of democratic representation, as it varies across the three subcultures. As a statistical guide, Figure 7.5 summarizes the representative processes across the three subcultures in terms of separate causal models. The continuous variables are measured in units that are standardized at the national level rather than the subculture level, thus making the coefficients comparable across subcultures.

The traditionalistic subculture, representing mainly southern states, presents few surprises. For traditionalistic states, most coefficients are muted versions of what is found when all states are considered together. The exception is a strong negative coefficient from party elite liberalism to Democratic legislative strength. This coefficient represents the strong sensitivity to parties' ideological nuance on the part of southern electorates. Overall, the degree of representation is relatively low in the traditionalistic subculture.

The comparison between the moralistic culture and the individualistic culture is particularly interesting. For individualistic states, the pattern of coefficients presents a hyper version of the model when all states are considered together. For individualistic states, we can paint a portrait of pragmatic democratic politics, as if politicians respond to public opinion out of a desire to get and stay elected: Democratic legislative strength is a strong positive function of mass liberalism and a strong negative function of the liberalism of party positions. Due to electoral considerations, legislatures push policy toward the center, away from the dominant party's ideological beliefs, and respond strongly to state opinion in anticipation of electoral sanctions.

For moralistic states, the coefficients portray a system where ideological parties play a major role: With ideologically distinct parties, a given level

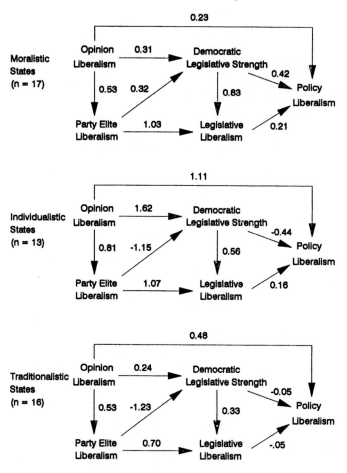

Figure 7.5 Variations in the Policy Model by Political Culture

of change in the party division in the legislature has larger policy consequences. State electorates need only move in modest partisan increments
to achieve noticeable policy changes.

Is either the pragmatic individualistic system or the responsible parties
moralistic system noticeably "better" from the standpoint of policy representation? Based on our information, we cannot choose a winner. The net
slope predicting policy from opinion is slightly larger in individualistic
states, but not significantly so. In any case, opinion and policy are measured in different metrics, so we possess no direct knowledge of the ideal
slope for comparison. Only with the same, correct, metric for opinion and

policy could we assess whether any of the opinion–policy slopes are too strong (hyper-representation) or too weak (hyporepresentation).[6]

CONCLUSIONS

In this chapter, we have applied Elazar's categorization of the states into three subcultures to the task of differentiating among styles of representation. Our results offer strong support – sometimes startlingly strong support – for Elazar's formulation. In almost all instances where we find interaction effects or additive effects involving the subculture categories, the results are consistent with what we would expect from Elazar's discussion. Similarly, in almost all instances where an additive or interaction effect is posited, one is found. Due to the impressionistic origin of Elazar's typology, our conclusions must include a note of ambiguity regarding its exact contribution to the study of representation. Elazar based his classifications on a host of variables. Although the main defining characteristic clearly was immigration flows, the contemporary style of representation also swayed his classification decisions. States were described as traditionalistic in part because their elites tended to ignore public opinion. States were described as individualistic in part because their politicians were pragmatic. States were described as moralistic in part because their politicians tended to impose their version of the public interest on their citizenries. The contribution of Elazar's categories to the study of representation may not be "causal" in the usual sense. Culture, as Elazar defines it, may not be a cause of representational variation. Instead, perhaps Elazar's categories should be considered as the *defining* characteristics of different styles of representation. If so, our usage (and many others) of Elazar's categories may be more of a validation exercise than a positing and testing of causal relations.

This observation is not a criticism of Elazar's formulation. It is more of a comment on the overriding breadth of Elazar's conceptualization. Perhaps it took no great insight to classify the southern states and some of their neighbors as traditionalistic states where cultural expectations enhance the insulation of the political elites from their masses. More remarkable is how the distinction between moralistic and individualistic states separates two different modes of representation. The individualistic states present the archetypal models of Downsian pragmatic politics as described in Chapters 5 and 6. Moralistic states present an important variation, where party positions are more distinct and offer greater predic-

6. We could also compare the net fits of the regression lines in the different subcultures. These correlation coefficients are a similar .85 and .84 for moralistic and individualistic subcultures. Although these numbers provide no grounds for choosing a winner, they do beat the slightly lesser .66 found for traditionalistic subcultures.

tion of what politicians do in office. Thus, Elazar's categories present more than a theoretical distinction among styles of representation. His classifications enable the spotlight to be pointed at different states with real variation in how the game of politics is played. That is an important contribution.

8

Partisanship, ideology, and state elections

Among state political analysts, a common pastime is classifying the states according to their degree of Republican or Democratic partisanship. The most frequently cited is Ranney's (1976) classic measure of interparty competition. The Ranney index is a combination of the two parties' relative legislative strength and the two-party vote for governor. Used as a directional measure, the Ranney index arrays the states on a continuum from safely Democratic to safely Republican. "Folded," the index measures the distinction between "competitive" states and "one-party" states. Others, notably David (1972), have developed indexes of state partisanship based on the vote for a wide variety of state offices. The rationale for classifying the states on the basis of partisanship is the measurement of meaningful differences in the two parties' relative chances of winning elections. Presumably, some states almost always elect Democrats and others almost always elect Republicans, with others in the middle enjoying the presumed ideal condition of "competitive" elections.

To what extent are statewide election outcomes determined by state levels of Democratic versus Republican partisanship? Our measure of state party identification can help to answer this question. In Chapter 6, we saw that the correlation between state party identification and legislative partisanship was a quite high .87. This strong correlation was to be expected, because the measure of legislative partisanship is the net balance of all legislative races, averaged for each chamber over eight election years.

But when we turn to the vote for major state-level offices (governor or U.S. senator) or for president, state partisanship is a less certain electoral predictor. For instance, by all historically based measures of party competition, as well as our measure of state partisanship, southern states are decidedly Democratic. But as everybody knows, southern states are no longer Democratic at the presidential level and quite often vote Republican for major state offices. Meanwhile, traditionally Republican states have been the source of many Democratic electoral victories. The best contemporary example is the traditionally Republican state of North Dakota. In the late 1980s, "Republican" North Dakota was the only state with a Democratic governor, two Democratic U.S. senators, and a solidly Democratic U.S. House delegation (admittedly, with an N of 1). North Dakota's clustering of major offices in the hands of one party is rare enough, but for the clustering to favor the party seemingly disfavored by the state's underlying partisanship presents a particularly strong anomaly. Given recently observable levels of partisan unpredictability in state elections, it would seem that (to borrow a sports cliche) in any given state, each party has a solid chance of winning major state office. The reason, we will see, is that state electoral outcomes depend on the relative strengths of the competing candidates as well as the strengths of the state parties.

This chapter explores state-level elections. We examine state-level voting for three offices: governor, U.S. senator, and U.S. president. We set our focus on the contribution of the two central variables of this project – state electorates' mean levels of party identification and ideological identification.

In order to explore the micro-/macrolevel electoral connection in the states, we also exploit CBS/NYT Election Day exit polls. Between 1982 and 1988, CBS/NYT conducted 73 separate state-level exit polls in which respondent ideological and partisan identifications were asked. States were selected on the basis of general interest in their senatorial and gubernatorial contests, so that, when applicable, vote choices for governor and U.S. senator were ascertained. For 1984 and 1988, these exit poll surveys ascertained the respondents' presidential votes as well. Since each state exit poll includes about a thousand respondents, such polls provide the best measure of mean partisanship and ideology for voters in specific state elections.

As a guide for our investigation of state-level election outcomes, we borrow some old but useful conceptual language that was introduced by the *American Voter* authors in their second book together, *Elections and the Political Order* (Campbell, Converse, Miller, and Stokes, 1966). In *Elections and the Political Order* (hereafter referred to as *EPO*), Campbell et al. presented election outcomes as a composition of the "normal vote" for the particular constituency (states in our investigation) plus deviations from the normal vote, which they termed "short-term partisan forces" (Campbell, 1966; Converse, 1966).

The "normal vote" is the two-party vote division that would result from an election in which the "balance of partisan forces are equal" (Converse, 1966). Roughly speaking, this would be the neutral electoral outcome in which Democratic and Republican partisans defect at equal rates and voters who are Independent split their votes 50–50 between Republican and Democratic candidates. In *EPO* terminology, deviations from the normal vote are due to "short-term partisan forces." Writing a quarter century ago, Campbell (1966) posited "short-term" forces to be strongest in "high stimulus" national presidential elections, when turnout, interest, and information peak. Campbell theorized that short-term forces would be weak for nonpresidential offices – particularly when the election is conducted at midterm.

As Campbell saw it, elections below the presidential level were "low stimulus" affairs that were decided by little more than partisans voting for their party. (The one clear exception would be when election outcomes are influenced by the short-term forces of higher-level elections conducted at the same time – what are usually termed "coattail" effects.) This rather static view of subpresidential election outcomes, however, was not based on any analysis of actual election outcomes, at least none that Campbell et al. presented to the reader. It was instead an inference from individual-level survey data. The survey data available to Campbell et al. showed a strongly partisan U.S. electorate and a relatively uninvolved and uninformed U.S. electorate, particularly when it came to elections below the presidential level. (See Stokes and Miller, 1966, in addition to the previously mentioned *EPO* references.) It is easy to see how the national electorate, considered from the perspective of the 1950s through the mid-1960s would lead to the view that elections below the presidential level were basically predictable partisan affairs. Indeed, based on a casual reading of the political science literature of this earlier era, one might think that the way to forecast an election for U.S. senator or governor would be simply to consult one's favorite index of party competition in the states and extrapolate the election outcome from the states' partisan natures.

To political scientists steeped in the voting literature of the 1970s, 1980s, and 1990s, the *EPO* expectation of weak short-term forces in elections below the presidential level appears curiously in error. The literature on congressional elections, which once emphasized constituency partisanship, now emphasizes the candidates and their campaigns (e.g., Mann, 1978; Jacobson, 1990; Erikson and Wright, 1993). This new emphasis has spread from U.S. House campaigns to include statewide U.S. Senate elections as well (e.g., Wright and Berkman, 1986; Abramowitz, 1988; Squire, 1989). Even gubernatorial elections are being discovered (Kenney, 1983; Kenney and Rice, 1983; Patterson and Caldiera, 1983; Tompkins, 1984; Holbrook-Provow, 1987; see also Wright, 1974). Below the presidential level, campaign stimuli – and not just constituency partisanship – matter. So, let us take a fresh statistical look at state-level election results. Our major concern is the state vote for governor and U.S. senator. We start, however, with a more familiar data set – state voting patterns for the office of president.

STATE VOTING IN PRESIDENTIAL ELECTIONS

It is widely known that national presidential election outcomes cannot be projected from the national distribution of party identification. Given the usual Democratic edge in party identification, the normal vote prediction for national elections is a margin of about 54 percent Democratic and 46 percent Republican. This prediction of a 54–46 Democratic edge approximates the national average vote division in recent House elections. Recent presidential elections, however, have decidedly favored the Republican Party. Table 8.1 presents the evidence. Over 11 elections, the record is 7 Republican victories and 4 Democratic victories. The mean national vote division for president over this span is 52.5 percent Republican, 47.5 percent Democratic. Clearly, the usual division of Democrats and Republicans is a poor expectation for national presidential election outcomes. Instead, let us substitute the mean 1952–92 presidential vote division (47.5 percent Democratic) as the best estimate of the normal national *presidential* vote. We can more reasonably estimate short-term forces of presidential campaigns as departures from this electorally based norm than as departures from the 54 percent Democratic normal vote.

Note that the standard deviation of the national vote is a relatively large 6.5 percentage points. This standard deviation serves as a rough index of the general magnitude of national short-term forces for president, 1952–92. As a measure of short-term forces, the 6.5 standard deviation reflects a sampling distribution in which outlier landslide elections such as 1964 (Johnson vs. Goldwater) and 1972 (McGovern vs. Nixon) are almost two standard deviations from the mean. Later we will use this 6.5 estimate of short-term forces in national presidential elections as a standard of comparison for our estimates of the magnitude of short-term forces in senate and gubernatorial elections.[1]

The macro-level: Party, ideology, and the presidential vote

In this section, we bring to bear some unusual resources to explore state-level differences in presidential voting. To what extent does state variation

1. Of course, other methods could be used to estimate the national-level short-term forces. We could, for instance, control for a linear time trend, which would lower the estimate of short-term forces. We could alternatively assume as correct the baseline of a 54 percent Democratic normal vote. Deviations of the presidential vote from this baseline would of course increase the estimate of the short-term forces. If we do an ordinary *t*-test of the hypothesis that the mean outcome is 54.0 percent Democratic, using the 11-year distribution of the two-party vote, the hypothesis can be rejected at the .05 level.

Table 8.1. *Democratic presidential vote, 1952-92*

Year	National Vote	State Vote Mean	State Vote S. D.
1952	44.6	45.0	11.2
1956	42.2	43.2	8.6
1960	50.1	49.4	5.9
1964	61.3	57.8	13.2
1968	49.6	47.7	7.1
1972	38.2	35.9	6.9
1976	51.1	50.1	6.1
1980	44.4	42.9	8.1
1984	40.8	38.9	5.8
1988	46.2	44.8	5.5
1992	53.5	51.8	6.2
Mean	47.5	46.2	7.7
S. D.	6.5		

Note: Based on 48 contiguous states. All computations in terms of the Democratic share of the two-party vote.

in presidential voting depend on state-level party identification and state-level ideological identification?

Table 8.1 summarizes the univariate statistics of not only national-level but also state-level presidential voting. Of particular interest is the state-level standard deviation for each election year. The median value of this statistic is 7.7 percent, or about the same as the national-level standard deviation. We can summarize this comparison in the following way. To predict how a state will vote in a presidential election, it is virtually of the same importance to know which state is referenced as to know the particular election year.

It has long been recognized that state-level presidential outcomes reflect state differences in partisanship and ideology. In the mid-1980s, Rabinowitz, Gurian, and McDonald (1984) presented an innovative factor analysis of state presidential voting. They found two factors, which they labeled partisanship and ideology. The partisan factor strongly correlated with state partisanship in voting below the presidential level. The ideological factor strongly correlated with ideological voting by the states' congressional delegations. Rabinowitz et al. found a growing importance of the ideological factor at the expense of the partisan factor.

Our data show a similar pattern: State-level voting in recent presidential elections is more a function of state ideological identification than of state party identification. In past elections, however, state party identification used to dominate. Table 8.2 presents the regressions of presidential voting in specific elections, 1952–92, on our CBS/NYT measures of state ideology and partisanship. Note the growing importance of ideology at the expense of partisanship. In terms of our survey measures obtained over two decades later, partisanship determined the two Eisenhower elections (1952, 1956) at the expense of ideology. Ideology did not become important until the contests of 1964 (Johnson–Goldwater) and 1972 (Nixon–McGovern). In 1976, partisanship rebounded for the Carter–Ford contest. The 1984 and 1988 contests saw a strong return of ideological identification as a determinant of the state-level presidential vote.

All this conforms with most observers' interpretations of recent presidential elections. One might even think that the task is complete – that there is very little more beyond Table 8.2 that can be said statistically about state presidential voting. But one interesting puzzle remains: We have seen that in recent presidential elections, ideology has dominated partisanship as a predictor of state-level voting. Yet when we study individual voters instead of states, voter partisanship is a decisively better predictor of presidential choice than is voter ideology. What accounts for this discrepancy? We will spend some effort trying to solve this puzzle. Finding a solution requires that we identify the linkages in the seemingly contradictory macro-/microlevel relationships.

1984 and 1988 exit poll data

To better understand the micro/macrolevel connection for presidential voting at the state level, we simulated state election outcomes from the Election Day state exit polls conducted by CBS News/NYT on election day in 1984 and 1988 – 18 in 1984 and 24 in 1988. Each exit poll contains from 652 to 2,778 voters, each interviewed as they left their polling place. Given exit poll methodology, it is essential that the data be "weighted" rather than used in raw form. The weights were furnished by CBS/NYT. Among other considerations, each state's Bush and Dukakis voters are reweighted in the necessary fashion to generate the correct proportions of Bush and Dukakis voters in the voting electorate. In other words, the weighted marginals for the state samples equal the actual vote. This is a strong convenience, as it allows one to make forecasts of state voting from sample distributions without worrying about adjusting for sampling error in the dependent variable.

Table 8.2. *Predicting the state presidential vote from state partisanship and ideology*

| | 47 States | | | | | 36 Nonsouthern states | | | | |
| | Partisanship | | Ideology | | | Partisanship | | Ideology | | |
	b	Beta	b	Beta	Adjusted R^2	b	Beta	b	Beta	Adjusted R^2
1952	0.62**	.63	-0.26	-.17	.384	0.37*	.61	0.14	.16	.470
1956	0.45**	.60	-0.41**	-.34	.420	0.30**	.62	-0.15	-.22	.264
1960	0.36**	.68	0.14	.17	.484	0.15	.28	0.40**	.54	.493
1964	-0.27**	-.23	1.17**	.64	.413	0.12	.19	0.60**	.67	.577
1968	0.30**	.48	0.43**	.43	.424	0.20	.28*	0.61**	.61	.590
1972	-0.08	-.14	0.70**	.73	.518	0.07	.11	0.51**	.61	.410
1976	0.43**	.80	0.10	.11	.646	0.35**	.68	0.18*	.25	.662
1980	0.49**	.70	0.41**	.37	.662	0.38**	.48	0.56**	.51	.698
1984	0.20**	.41	0.52**	.66	.632	0.23**	.36	0.51**	.58	.640
1988	0.09*	.19	0.51**	.68	.496	0.19*	.35	0.38**	.50	.508
1992	0.18**	.34	0.64**	.76	.718	0.18*	.28	0.62**	.69	.725

Note: N=47. Nevada, Alaska, and Hawaii are omitted.
*Significant at .05 level; **significant at .01 level.

To begin, we explore a model that forecasts exit poll presidential votes solely from trichotomous partisanship and ideology. With a dichotomous dependent variable (Republican vote = 0; Democratic vote = 1), the appropriate multivariate technology is probit analysis rather than our usual OLS regression. These probit equations, for 1984 and 1988, are shown in Table 8.3, Columns 1 and 4. In both contests, partisanship is clearly the stronger of the two vote predictors, but with ideology a respectable sec-

Table 8.3. *Probit equation of presidential vote in 1984 and 1988 CBS/NYT exit polls*

	1984 (N = 26,638)			1988 (N = 30,414)		
	(1)	(2)	(3)	(4)	(5)	(6)
Party identification	1.02** (84.0)	1.04** (84.2)	1.04** (84.2)	1.03** (90.4)	1.05** (90.1)	1.04** (90.2)
Ideological identification	0.52** (39.0)	0.51** (37.4)	0.51** (37.4)	0.67** (48.4)	0.66** (47.3)	0.66** (47.3)
State party ideological midpoint			0.12** (13.6)			0.11** (13.1)
Intercept	-0.30** (-30.2)		-0.36** (-32.8)	-0.06** (-6.2)		-0.10** (-10.2)
AL		-0.52**				
CA		-0.29**			0.04	
CT					-0.07	
FL					-0.28**	
IL		-0.28**			-0.01	
IN					-0.23**	
IA		-0.09*			0.29**	
MD					-0.20**	
MA		-0.30**			-0.08	
MI		-0.26**			-0.03	
MN		0.01			0.14**	
MS		-0.54**			-0.43**	
NV						
NH		-0.41**				
NJ		-0.36**			-0.13**	
NM					-0.15**	
NY		-0.25**			0.04	
NC		-0.58**			-0.26**	
OH		-0.40**			-0.15**	
OR		-0.17**			0.19**	
PA		-0.18**			-0.06	
TX		-0.52**			-0.19**	
VT		-0.16**			0.12*	
WA					0.14**	
WV		-0.31**				
WI		0.12**				
Estimated R^2	.529	.540	.536	.572	.578	.582

Note: *t*-values in parentheses.
*Significant at .05; **significant at .01.

ond, especially in 1988. The two intercepts reflect the tilt of the vote among voters at "zero" – that is, among moderate Independents. Both intercepts are negative, reflecting the Republican short-term forces of the two presidential contests.

To convert these equations into state-level predictions, we first convert each voter's probit prediction into the probability of a Democratic vote. Then, we averaged these probabilities for each state's (weighted) exit poll respondents to obtain state-level percentage point predictions.

The result of our simulation exercise is a set of state projections based on the individual-level equations and the marginal distributions on the independent variables (partisanship, ideology) in the CBS/NYT exit polls. These estimates represent a forecast for the state assuming (1) the (weighted) marginal distributions of party and ideological identification for the state in the 1984 and 1988 exit polls, plus (2) the probit coefficients for the effects of party and ideological identification on presidential voting found in the 1984 and 1988 exit polls.

How well these projections predict the actual 1984 and 1988 vote can be seen in Figure 8.1. The remarkable aspect of the two graphs is the degree to which the state presidential projections are off the mark. The forecasts correlate at only .58 (1984) and .70 (1988) with the state vote. Under the circumstances, these are not strong correlations. Our post hoc simulations of the state vote from state-level marginal distributions of partisanship and ideology cannot even explain half the variance in state voting.

Our exit poll data contain sufficiently large state samples to allow us to estimate the effect of state context as an additional source of presidential voting. Columns 2 and 5 of Table 8.3 show the individual-level equations with state effects added. State effects reflect state-to-state differences in the intercept of the equation and contribute only modestly to the prediction of individual votes, but they are of major importance at the state level. By definition, each state's observed partisan and ideological composition plus the state effect fully accounts for the state presidential vote.[2]

In part, state effects can reflect the influence of omitted individual-level variables that change from state to state. More important, state effects represent the contextual effects of residence in the state. But what are these contextual effects? Inspection of the 1984 and 1988 state coefficients reveals that positive (pro-Democratic) coefficients tend to cluster in liberal and Republican states – as if state Democratic strength retards Democratic voting while state liberalism encourages Democratic voting,

2. Technically speaking, the sum of the products of the state mean and coefficient for each variable plus the intercept exactly predicts the state mean score on the underlying probit model. The state vote is a modestly curvilinear function of the underlying mean score.

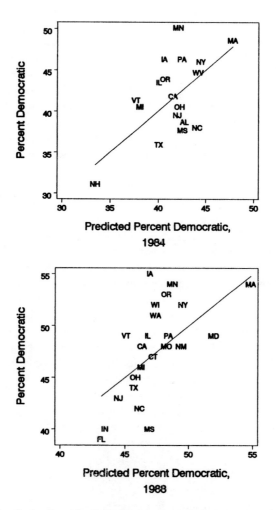

Figure 8.1 Simulating Presidential Vote from Exit Poll Party Identification and Ideology

each over and above what the individual's partisanship and ideology would indicate.[3]

From a purely statistical standpoint, this result properly accounts for why the role of ideology appears exaggerated and the role of partisanship appears muted in state-level presidential election returns. The macrolevel regression coefficients for partisanship and ideology reflect both the individual-level effects and state-level contextual effects. Our next task is to make theoretical sense of the state-level contextual effects on the presidential vote.

State partisanship in presidential elections

The seeming unimportance of state partisanship in presidential elections has its roots in the fact that state partisanship is shaped by state as well as national politics. In Chapter 6, we saw that state partisanship is shaped by the electorate's own ideological leanings but also by its reaction to the ideological tilt of the state's party elites. Where the party elite midpoint is to the left of the electorate's mean position, the electorate will tilt toward the Republicans in its party identification. Where the midpoint is to the right of the electorate's, the electorate will tilt toward the Democrats. In this way, state partisanship is an indicator of whether the parties collectively are too liberal or too conservative for their state-level constituencies.

Theoretically, to a rational electorate this "state politics" component of partisanship would be of little relevance to presidential voting, but empirically, its actual importance depends on the degree of "stickiness" of state partisanship when people vote for president. At one possible extreme, the state politics component could "irrationally" govern how state electorates vote for president, with citizens unable to shake the influence of those aspects of their partisanship that are irrelevant to the voting task at hand. At the other extreme, we can imagine state electorates responding to the task of choosing a president as if that portion of their partisanship induced by state politics did not matter.

We will show that the reality of presidential voting is closer to the latter of these two extremes. Two relatively liberal parties make state electorates more Republican than otherwise, and two relatively conservative parties make state electorates more Democratic than otherwise. The "extra" Democrats or Republicans recruited by the ideological division of state parties are the most likely to defect in presidential politics. Restated, state

---

3. The state coefficients correlate at −.61 (1984) and −.49 (1988) with state partisanship and .49 (1984) and .48 (1988) with state ideology. The comparable correlations with exit poll partisanship and ideology are −.11 (1984) and −.22 (1988) for partisanship and .58 (1984) and .71 (1988) for ideology.

party ideology exerts an independent effect on presidential voting. Controlling for party identification, party elite liberalism "causes" Democratic presidential voting.

Figure 8.2 demonstrates the effect of party elite ideology on state presidential voting. It shows the relationship between the state ideological midpoint on the one hand and the 1984 and 1988 state coefficients (from Table 8.3) on the other. As presented in Chapter 5, net party elite ideology is a standardized measure, calibrated as the average (or midpoint) of the two parties' scores on a composite index of four components – based on the ideologies of the parties' congressional candidates, state legislators, national convention delegates, and county chairs.

As Figure 8.2 illustrates, the party midpoint correlates with the state probit coefficients at .81 in 1984 and .73 in 1988. With a bit over half of the variance in the state coefficients explained by state party ideology, it is no overstatement to claim that state party ideology accounts for most of the variance in recent state-level presidential voting that cannot be accounted for by state partisanship and ideology.

We can also insert state party ideology directly into the exit poll equations, as a contextual variable in place of the state dummy variables. These equations are shown in Table 8.3, Columns 3 and 6. Simulations of the state vote from these equations offer considerable improvement in predicting the vote over simulations from state partisanship and ideology alone from Figure 8.2. Figure 8.3 shows that our new simulations based on exit poll respondents' partisanship and ideology, plus party elite ideology, correlate impressively – at .83 (1984) and .85 (1988) – with the actual state vote. The peculiar contribution of party elite ideology solves the earlier puzzle of why it seemed there existed state-level contextual effects that retarded Democratic voting in Democratic states but encouraged Democratic voting in liberal states. These are spurious patterns, generated by the correlations of state partisanship and ideology with the ideological tendencies of the state parties. For reasons we have explored, liberal state parties are associated positively with liberal electorates but negatively with Democratic electorates. Once we control for state party ideology, no correlation remains between either state partisanship or state ideology and the state coefficients.[4]

For a broader demonstration of the role of state party ideology in predicting state presidential voting, let us return to the 46-state analysis and our familiar CBS/NYT aggregations of state partisanship and ideology for

---

4. With state party ideology included in the model, all evidence of a partisan or ideological contextual effect vanishes. For instance, if mean state partisanship and mean state ideology are added to the individual-level probit equations that include party ideology, neither mean partisanship nor mean ideology achieves statistical significance – even with the many thousands of cases.

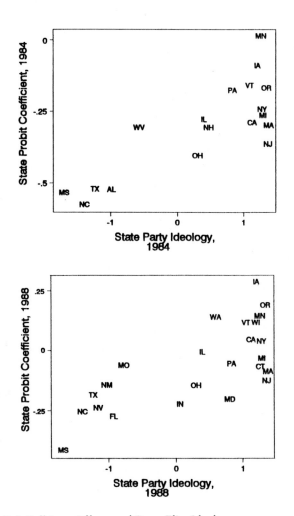

Figure 8.2 Exit Poll State Effects and Party Elite Ideology

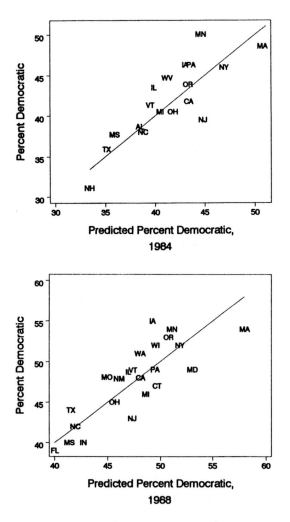

Figure 8.3 Including Party Elite Ideology in Presidential Vote Simulations

the 1976–88 electorate. Table 8.4 shows a series of equations for 1984 and 1988. In Columns 1 and 4, the vote is predicted from the state electorate's ideology plus state party ideology but not from state partisanship. In these equations, the electorate's ideology is quite significant, while state party ideology makes no significant contribution. This makes sense, because party elite ideology matters only as a correction to the omitted variable of state partisanship. The set of equations in Columns 2 and 5 repeat from Table 8.3, including partisanship and the electorate's ideology only. These equations merely present our initial puzzle, as ideology dominates partisanship.

In Columns 3 and 6, all three independent variables are included. Now, everything changes. The electorate's ideology, previously dominant, ceases to be statistically significant. Meanwhile, the previously dormant variables of state partisanship and party elite ideology dominate the full equation. With the party midpoint in the equation, party identification now is restored to the place of importance it holds at the individual level. But while state ideological identification is no longer significant, the fall from significance is partially due to the relatively high standard error for ideology. Statistically, this results from the lesser state-level variance for ideology than for partisanship. Actually, the two coefficients for ideological identification are about what they should be – about one-half (1984) or two-thirds (1988) the comparable coefficients for partisanship. These are the same ratios as found in the individual-level exit poll probit equations. This makes a satisfactory match between the microlevel and macrolevel equations.[5]

Presidential approval

Even with the exit poll simulations that include state party ideology, the best reported correlation between the predicted and actual presidential vote is .85. Squaring this number, it would appear that we can account for no more than about two-thirds of the variance in state presidential voting. Most of the seemingly unexplainable variance represents differential state reactions to administration policies. State presidential verdicts are referenda on all aspects of the president's performance, not simply a reaction based on partisanship and ideology.

To see this, we can return to the 1988 exit polls, which (unlike 1984) asked respondents whether they approved of President Reagan's perfor-

---

5. The pattern shown in Table 8.4 holds for both 1984 and 1988 when southern states are excluded. The pattern is replicated weakly at best for other years, but with the powerful exception of 1972. For 1972, the seemingly powerful effect of ideology on the vote (Table 8.2) is reduced to insignificance when the state midpoint is included in the equation (with a beta coefficient of .74).

Table 8.4. *Predicting the 1984 and 1988 state-level presidential vote from state-level party and ideological identification, and from state party ideology*

Variable		1984			1988		
		(1)	(2)	(3)	(4)	(5)	(6)
State ideological	b	0.56***	0.52***	0.16	0.37**	0.50**	0.11
identification	Std.err.	(0.12)	(0.07)	(0.12)	(0.13)	(0.08)	(0.14)
	Beta	.73	.68	.19	.50	.68	.15
State party	b		0.19***	0.32***		0.07	0.22**
identification	Std.err.		(0.04)	(0.05)		(0.05)	(0.06)
	Beta		.39	.64		.14	.43
State parties'	b	-0.25		3.37***	1.04		3.50**
ideological	Std.err.	(0.95)		(0.93)	(0.92)		(1.07)
midpoint[a]	Beta	-.04		.60	.24		.67
Intercept		47.4	45.3	39.1	50.6	51.9	45.2
Adjusted R^2		.468	.623	.707	.469	.466	.568
Standard error of estimate		4.1	3.5	3.1	4.0	4.0	3.6

Note: N=46. Nebraska, Nevada, Alaska, and Hawaii omitted.
*Significant at .05 level; **significant at .01 level.
[a]Party ideological midpoint is calibrated in standard deviation units.

mance. Among individual voters, presidential approval is strongly colored by partisanship and ideology. The state party ideology also contributes as a corrective for the state politics component of party identification. When presidential approval is added to the presidential vote equation, it competes strongly with party identification and ideological identification as a predictor of the presidential vote. This is true even for 1988, with President Reagan unable to seek reelection. Reagan approval was a strong predictor of Bush and Dukakis votes. Table 8.5 shows the details of the exit poll equations using presidential approval.

When the 1988 state results are simulated from exit poll probit equations that include presidential approval, prediction improves enormously, with a correlation of .96! The scatterplot is shown in Figure 8.4. Clearly,

Table 8.5. *Exit poll probit equations with presidential approval, 1988*

Independent variable	Presidential approval	Democratic vote
Party identification	-0.86 (-78.6)	0.76 (55.2)
Ideological identification	-0.53 (-40.9)	0.49 (29.5)
State party ideological midpoint	-0.09 (-10.4)	0.09 (8.9)
Reagan approval		-1.71 (-77.4)
Intercept	0.24 (26.0)	0.90 (50.5)
Estimated R^2	.700	.480

Note: *t*-values in parentheses. All coefficients are significant at .001 or greater.

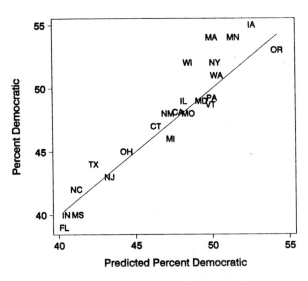

Figure 8.4 Including Presidential Approval in the Vote Simulation for the 1988 Presidential Election

193

presidential approval fills out the rough edges of our state predictions. Where a state votes more Democratic or Republican for president than one would expect from its partisanship, ideology, and the ideologies of the state parties, short-term presidential approval or disapproval may be responsible.[6]

STATE ELECTIONS FOR U.S. SENATOR AND GOVERNOR

For state-level presidential voting, we told a complicated story in which state partisanship matters, but only when its "state politics" component is unmasked. For state office, the story is more straightforward. In elections for governor or senator, partisanship provides the simple "normal vote" base from which to forecast elections. State partisanship reflects the relative ideological proximities of the two parties vis-à-vis state opinion. (See the discussion of Chapter 6.) Elections for state office are also determined by the localized state-level issues – or short-term forces – of the particular state-level campaign. As we will see, these short-term forces in elections for governor and U.S. senator are surprisingly large. In fact, they are larger than the short-term forces of presidential campaigns.

For the gubernatorial and senatorial analysis, we can pool election results across years and across states. Table 8.6 shows the results of a series of regressions predicting outcomes of the 151 contested gubernatorial elections for the period 1976 to 1988, the span during which we obtained our measures of partisanship and ideology. Table 8.7 shows the comparable regressions for the 213 contested Senate elections, 1976–88. Independent variables include partisan and ideological identification, the party elite midpoint, incumbency, plus the national House vote in the election year, as a control for the national partisan trend.[7]

Predicting gubernatorial elections

Gubernatorial contests are not easily predicted from the combination of state partisanship, state ideology, the state party ideological midpoints,

6. Adding presidential approval to the 1988 probit equations in no way detracts from the contribution of state party elites. Party elite ideology is clearly significant in both equations of Table 8.5. Alternatively, state party ideology can be replaced by state dummies in the equations. When this is done, the resultant state coefficients of the approval equations correlate at .58 with state party ideology. The resultant state coefficients of the vote equation correlate at .71 with state party ideology. State "effects" here clearly reflect party elite ideology.
7. We also included a southern dummy variable to the equations predicting the gubernatorial and senatorial vote. In no instance does the southern dummy become significant or alter the coefficients for the remaining variables. Consequently, southern dummies are omitted from the equations shown in Tables 8.6 and 8.7.

Table 8.6. *Predicting gubernatorial elections, 1976-88*

Independent variable	All contested races			Nonincumbent races only	
	(1)	(2)	(3)	(4)	(5)
Ideology	0.13 (0.17)		0.40** (0.14)		
Partisanship	0.21* (0.09)	0.25*** (0.06)		0.32** (0.09)	0.34** (0.09)
Incumbency	7.30*** (0.91)	7.17*** (0.91)	7.63*** (0.92)		
Party midpoint	-0.85 (1.14)		-3.19** (1.08)		
National Democratic. House vote[a]	0.78 (0.43)	0.78 (0.42)	0.91* (0.44)	1.34 (0.69)	
Intercept	52.7	50.6	57.9	4.9	5.0
Adjusted R^2	.389	.381	.367	.205	.170
Standard error of estimate	8.3	8.3	8.4	7.6	7.8
N	148	151	148	65	65

Note: N=47. Alaska, Hawaii, and Nevada are excluded. Standard errors are in parentheses.
*Significant at .05; **significant at .01; ***significant at .001 level.
[a]As deviation from 7-election mean: 54.4 per cent.

the election year, plus incumbency (Table 8.6). Incumbency appears to be the best predictor, with state partisanship second. Both are quite significant statistically. State ideology and the state parties' ideological midpoint, however, are decidedly not significant. To summarize, knowing the partisanship of the state and which party (if any) enjoys an incumbency advantage are both modestly helpful for forecasting gubernatorial elections; but the ideological leanings of neither the state electorate nor the state parties adds any further increment to our forecasting ability.

Table 8.7. *Predicting U.S. Senate elections, 1976-88*

Independent variable	All contested races			Nonincumbent races only	
	(1)	(2)	(3)	(4)	(5)
Ideology	0.05		0.54***		
	(0.16)		(0.14)		
Partisanship	0.40***	0.34***		0.38**	0.36*
	(0.08)	(0.06)		(0.14)	(0.14)
Incumbency	7.72***	7.97***	8.20***		
	(0.72)	(0.72)	(0.75)		
Party midpoint	0.88		-3.05**		
	(1.24)		(1.03)		
National Democratic House vote[a]	1.20***	1.30***	1.10**	1.00	
	(0.34)	(0.34)	(0.35)	(0.75)	
Intercept	48.6	48.5	58.3	47.9	48.1
Adjusted R^2	.471	.470	.430	.114	.100
Standard error of estimate	9.0	9.0	9.4	10.1	10.2
N	208	213	213	51	51

Note: Standard errors are in parentheses.
*Significant at .05; **significant at .01; ***significant at .001.
[a]As deviation from 7-election mean: 54.4 per cent.

However, it does not follow that the electorate's and the parties' ideologies are electorally insignificant in state contests. We can manipulate the equation to get both to emerge as significant contributors to the vote – by omitting state partisanship from the equation. See Table 8.6, Column 3. Ideology does matter, at least indirectly. Note also that the .13 coefficient for ideology in the equation from Column 1 is about two-thirds the size of the partisanship coefficient. The estimate of the ideology coefficient is wobbly, however, as reflected by its larger standard error.

Next, we turn to the estimation of short-term forces. For each equation in Table 8.6, the standard error of estimate is a measure of the standard deviation of the election forecast based on the equation at hand. Thus, except for the influence of incumbency, the standard error of estimate is a rough index of the short-term forces of the campaign. In the gubernatorial equations, the standard error is in the range of 8 percentage points. This is slightly larger than the 6.5 standard deviation for the national presidential vote. What can be concluded from this comparison? Suppose one knows the incumbency status of a gubernatorial election, plus the state's partisan makeup and the partisan trend for the particular election year. Although that is a lot of information, it still is not a good predictor of the gubernatorial election. In fact, the forecasting error is greater than predicting a presidential election outcome based on no information other than the long-term mean of presidential vote outcomes.

Counting incumbency effects as part of the short-term forces makes these forces loom even larger. Suppose we sum each gubernatorial contest's residual vote and incumbency effect (each from the equation in Column 2). The resultant standard deviation is 9.7, for a considerable increase in the estimate of short-term forces.

We might expect the weakest short-term forces in nonincumbent races, where incumbency is no factor and candidates are presumably less well known. We should pay special attention, therefore, to the two equations for nonincumbent gubernatorial races, of which there were 65, 1976–88. For nonincumbent races, the best fit is the equation predicting the vote from partisanship plus House vote control for the electoral trend, shown in Column 4. Note that the standard error for even this equation, 7.6, slightly exceeds the observed standard deviation of national presidential vote outcomes. Comparing the two as estimates of short-term forces, we arrive at a provocative conclusion: Open-seat elections for governor are more unpredictable than national presidential contests.

To summarize, state-level party identification does influence the outcomes of elections for governor. But, although state partisanship directly matters while state ideology does not, this effect of partisanship is small relative to the short-term forces of the gubernatorial campaign. Even counting only "open" races without an incumbent, and controlling for the national trend, a state's vote divisions for governor will generally vary more than will the national division of the two-party vote for president.

Predicting Senate elections

Next we consider the results for Senate elections, 1976–88, shown in Table 8.7. For Senate elections, we can account for almost half of the variance in the vote. This "improvement" is largely due to the fact that senatorial elections produce more variance to explain.

In other respects, the pattern for Senate elections closely parallels that for gubernatorial elections. State ideology and party elite ideology do not seem to matter, except when state partisanship is omitted from the equation. Party identification clearly matters, to a slightly greater degree than for governor. Incumbency matters too, at about the same magnitude as for governor. Incumbency is worth about 8 percentage points to the advantaged party.

We estimate the short-term forces for senator to be greater than those for governor. As estimated by the standard error of estimate, the short-term forces for senator are about 9.0. As estimated by the standard deviation of the incumbency effect plus the residual vote (from the equation in Column 2), the short term forces rise to to 11.3. Finally, even Senate elections for open seats appear quite immune from easy prediction, showing a 10.1 standard error of estimate.

To summarize, for Senate elections (as for gubernatorial elections), state party identification summarizes all that is relevant about the electorate's and the parties' relative ideological leanings. For Senate elections (as for gubernatorial elections), omitted variables account for much of the variance in outcomes. Clearly, "short-term forces" – the stimuli of the specific contest – matter.[8]

8. The importance of short-term forces in state elections can be appreciated even without a direct measure of state partisanship. Consider the state-level correlations between the votes for senator and for governor in the same election year. To the extent that elections are decided by state partisanship (or any state-level variables), the vote divisions for the two offices should be correlated. To the extent that elections are decided by short-term forces unique to the specific campaigns, the vote divisions for the two offices should be uncorrelated. In actuality, the two sets of votes are remarkably uncorrelated. Over the five midterm election years, 1966–86, the average correlation between the gubernatorial and senatorial vote divisions is a feeble .14. Details follow:

1966	.24 ($N = 23$)
1970	−.12 ($N = 22$)
1974	.15 ($N = 22$)
1978	.48 ($N = 26$)
1982	.05 ($N = 23$)
1986	.06 ($N = 23$)

A similar test is to examine the correlation between the state votes for U.S. Senate in successive elections. (Short-term forces in the two elections should be independent because they represent the votes for two different Senate seats.) These correlations are as follows:

1966–8	.22 ($N = 14$)		1978–80	.09 ($N = 14$)
1968–70	.13 ($N = 18$)		1980–2	−.09 ($N = 15$)
1970–2	.59 ($N = 18$)		1982–4	.09 ($N = 17$)
1972–4	.26 ($N = 16$)		1984–6	.17 ($N = 16$)
1974–6	.06 ($N = 16$)		1986–8	.25 ($N = 15$)
1976–8	−.11 ($N = 14$)			

Partisanship, ideology, and elections

Ideology and partisanship in individual state elections

So far we have examined state contests solely at the aggregate level. As we did for presidential contests, we can also examine individual-level voting data from exit polls of state-level gubernatorial and senatorial contests. Between 1982 and 1988, CBS/NYT conducted 41 exit polls of gubernatorial elections and 69 exit polls of senatorial elections that ascertained respondents' partisan and ideological identifications. For each exit poll survey, we conducted a probit equation predicting the vote from partisan and ideological identification. The results of these 110 equations are shown in Tables 8.8 (for governor) and 8.9 (for senator). For a reference point, these equations can be compared to the comparable presidential 1984 and 1988 equations, presented in Table 8.3.

The first thing to note from these tables is the dominant role of party identification at the individual level. In *all* 110 equations, the probit coefficient for party identification exceeds the coefficient for ideology. The mean party identification coefficient is 0.84 (0.80 for governor, 0.87 for senator), somewhat below the 1.03 coefficient for the presidential vote in the 1988 exit poll. Variation in the partisanship coefficient tracks the degree to which the specific contest taps traditional partisan issues. The highest coefficient is a 1.26 in the Bond–Woods 1988 Missouri Senate contest, in which Harriet Woods conducted a strongly populist campaign. The weakest is for the Weicker–Lieberman 1988 Connecticut Senate contest in which the Democrat was arguably to the right of his Republican opponent.

Although overshadowed by partisanship, ideological identification also influences votes for senator and governor. Just because state ideology does not forecast aggregate state election outcomes (once party identification is controlled), we should not be surprised to find that individual voters' ideologies predict their votes in state elections. In 108 of the 110 equations, the ideology coefficient is positive. The average coefficient is 0.37, somewhat less than the 0.52 and 0.67 found for the 1984 and 1988 presidential races. One could make the plausible argument that since gubernatorial campaigns deal with state issues, they should be less ideological than senatorial campaigns, which necessarily involve national issues. However, such a pattern is not found for the ideology coefficients. On average, the ideology coefficient is 0.35 for governor, and 0.38 for senator.

The ideology coefficient varies across contests, with a standard deviation of 0.16, which is identical to the standard deviation of the partisanship coefficient. The size of the ideology coefficient reflects the degree of ideological division in the particular campaign. The strongest ideology co fficient for a gubernatorial contest is 0.62, found for two campaigns

Table 8.8. *Probit equations of CBS/NYT governor exit polls, 1982–88*

| State | Year | Republican Candidate | Democratic Candidate | Democratic Vote | Probit Coefficients | | | |
					Party Identification	Ideological Identification	Constant	N
AL	1982	Fulmar	Wallace	.60	0.99	0.25	-0.01[b]	1,695
AZ	1986	Mecham	Warner	.47	0.83	0.62	0.06[b]	750
AR	1982	White[a]	Clinton	.55	0.67	0.50	-0.07[b]	777
CA	1982	Deukmejian	Bradley	.49	0.76	0.44	-0.07	2,933
CA	1986	Deukmejian[a]	Bradley	.38	0.87	0.54	-0.29	2,445
CO	1986	Strickland	Romer	.59	0.82	0.32	0.41	1,198
CN	1982	Rome	O'Neill	.54	0.72	0.23	0.03	1,949
FL	1986	Martinez	Pajcic	.45	0.97	0.42	-0.07[b]	1,411
GA	1986	Davis	Harris[a]	.71	0.50	0.27	0.75	599
IL	1982	Thompson[a]	Stevenson	.50-	0.88	0.22	-0.13	1,485
IL	1986	Thompson[a]	Stevenson	.43	1.05	0.18	-0.13	1,018
IN	1988	Mutz	Bayh	.53	0.84	0.47	0.41	1,073
IA	1982	Branstad	Conlin	.47	0.76	0.45	-0.05[b]	1,074

ME	1982	Craggin	Brennan[a]	.62	0.73	0.28	0.31	1,475
MA	1982	Sears	Dukakis	.62	0.88	0.58	0.21	2,750
MI	1982	Headlee	Blanchard	.53	1.00	0.35	0.03[b]	813
MN	1982	Whitney	Perpich	.59	0.99	0.16	0.20	1,129
MO	1988	Ashcroft[a]	Hearnes	.35	0.79	0.34	-0.46	867
NE	1982	Thone[a]	Kerrey	.51	0.73	0.42	0.20	1,166
NV	1982	List[a]	Bryan	.56	0.65	0.26	0.13	1,077
NV	1986	Caffarata	Bryan[a]	.74	0.59	0.19	0.86	977
NH	1984	Sununu[a]	Spirou	.33	0.84	0.18	-0.36	560
NM	1982	Irick	Anaya	.53	0.68	0.44	0.05[b]	1,124
NY	1982	Lehrman	Cuomo	.52	0.70	0.44	-0.01[b]	2,306
NY	1986	O'Rourke	Cuomo[a]	.67	0.57	0.36	0.57	1,363
NC	1984	Martin	Edniston	.46	0.77	0.54	-0.21	1,632
NC	1988	Martin[a]	Jordon	.44	0.92	0.39	-0.21	1,325
OH	1982	Brown	Celeste	.60	1.00	0.41	0.36	922
OR	1986	Paulus	Goldschmidt	.52	0.56	0.34	0.13	763
PA	1986	Scranton	Casey	.51	0.80	0.02[b]	0.04[b]	1,346

Table 8.8. (continued)

State	Year	Republican Candidate	Democratic Candidate	Democratic Vote	Party Identification	Ideological Identification	Constant	N
					Probit Coefficients			
RI	1982	Marzullo	Garrahy[a]	.76	0.76	0.19	0.72	1,147
SD	1986	Mickelson	Herseth	.48	0.80	0.08[b]	-0.02[b]	917
TN	1982	Alexander[a]	Tyree	.40	1.07	0.41	-0.41	826
TX	1982	Clements[a]	White	.54	1.02	0.52	-0.07[b]	1,980
TX	1986	Clements	White[a]	.47	0.94	0.36	-0.14	1,435
VT	1982	Snelling[a]	Kunen	.44	0.82	0.38	0.03[b]	1,056
VT	1984	Easton	Kunen	.51	0.71	0.51	0.12	826
VT	1988	Bernhardt	Kunen[a]	.55	0.62	0.47	0.31	680
WA	1988	Williams	Gardner[a]	.62	0.71	0.62	0.48	780
WV	1984	Moore	See	.47	0.80	0.08[b]	-0.35	989
WY	1982	Morton	Herschler[a]	.63	0.81	0.18	0.62	872

Note: [a]Incumbent.   [b]not significant at .05.

with unusually strong infusions of ideology. One is Arizona's 1986 contest, won by archconservative and ideologically contentious Edward Mechem. The other is Washington's 1988 contest, in which the Republican primary produced a follower of Evangelist Pat Robertson to oppose Democratic Governor Booth Gardner. The strongest ideological coefficient for a senatorial contest is found for the ideologically polarized 1984 Helms–Hunt North Carolina contest. The 0.73 ideology coefficient for the Helms–Hunt race is the only one that exceeds the ideology coefficient of the 1988 presidential contest (0.67 – see Table 8.3.)

At the other extreme, particularly weak ideological coefficients are found for those campaigns either devoid of ideological content or where traditional partisan–ideological battle lines were confused. For governor, the weakest coefficient (.02) is for Pennsylvania's 1986 Casey–Scranton contest, in which Democrat Casey posed as the more culturally conservative candidate. For senator, we find the two negative coefficients, in the aforementioned Weicker–Lieberman race and for Packwood of Oregon's 1986 reelection. Both contests featured a moderate-to-liberal Republican incumbent. Low positive coefficients are found for other Senate contests involving moderate incumbents, for instance, Chafee, Hatfield, Heinz, and Spector among Republicans and Dixon, Stennis, and Zorinski among Democrats.

That ideologically polarized candidates generate a more ideological electorate can be demonstrated statistically, following Wright and Berkman (1986). For one set of contests, we have a numerical measure of the ideological division of the candidates, which can be related to the ideology coefficient. For all 1982 Senate candidates, CBS/NYT ascertained opinions on a set of 10 ideologically relevant issues. We combined the responses to create a 10-item scale. Then we computed an ideological polarization score as the difference between the ideological position of the states' Democratic and Republican candidates. For the 23 Senate contests in 1982 for which we have exit poll data, we computed the correlation between this measure of ideological polarization and the ideology coefficient from the exit poll equation. This correlation is a healthy .64. Ideology matters more in elections that offer a choice to state voters.

Because Democrats outnumber Republicans and conservatives outnumber liberals, a plausible line of reasoning is that highly partisan contests work to the Democrats' advantage while highly ideological contests favor the Republicans. Thus, one might expect that Democratic candidates gain from a strong partisanship coefficient and Republicans gain from a strong ideology coefficient. But neither tendency is evident from the data. The Democratic vote correlates at −.18 (wrong sign) with the partisan coefficient and −.01 with the ideology coefficient. Clearly, elections are not won or lost based on candidates' ability to manufacture

Table 8.9. *Probit equations of CBS/NYT Senate exit polls, 1982-88*

State	Year	Republican Candidate	Democratic Candidate	Democratic Vote	Probit Coefficients			N
					Party Identification	Ideological Identification	Constant	
AL	1984	Smith	Heflin[a]	.63	0.69	0.29	0.33	1,330
AZ	1986	McCain	Kimball	.40	0.95	0.47	-0.11	1,083
CA	1982	Wilson	Brown	.47	0.86	0.52	-0.23	2,882
CA	1986	Zchau	Cranston[a]	.51	1.05	0.50	0.07	2,437
CA	1988	Wilson[a]	McCarthy	.47	1.01	0.56	-0.05[b]	2,031
CO	1986	Kramer	Wirth	.51	0.95	0.58	0.14	1,196
CN	1982	Weicker[a]	Moffett	.48	0.64	0.07[b]	-0.15	1,915
CN	1988	Weicker[a]	Lieberman	.50	0.35	-0.06[b]	-0.03[b]	1,125
FL	1986	Hawkins	Graham	.55	0.69	0.34	0.19	1,427
GA	1986	Mattingly[a]	Fowler	.51	1.07	0.47	-0.09[b]	624
IL	1984	Percy[a]	Simon	.51	0.94	0.39	0.06[b]	1,714
IL	1986	Koehler	Dixon[a]	.66	0.92	0.18	0.44	1,034
IN	1988	Lugar[a]	Wicks	.32	1.01	0.49	-0.68	840
IA	1984	Jepson[a]	Harkin	.56	1.06	0.30	0.31	1,623
LA	1988	Moore	Breaux	.53	0.89	0.39	-0.09[b]	1,132

State	Year							
ME	1982	Emery	Mitchell	.61	0.87	0.30	0.28	1,516
MD	1988	Keyes	Sarbanes[a]	.62	0.82	0.49	0.24	1,019
MA	1982	Shamie	Kennedy[a]	.61	0.86	0.62	0.12	2,822
MA	1984	Shamie	Kerry	.55	0.90	0.56	-0.11	1,356
MA	1988	Malone	Kennedy[a]	.66	0.74	0.63	0.32	1,061
MI	1982	Ruppe	Riegle[a]	.59	0.87	0.15[b]	0.15	828
MI	1984	Lousma	Levin[a]	.52	1.02	0.39	0.21	1,053
MI	1988	Dunn	Riegle[a]	.61	0.83	0.42	0.58	1,280
MN	1982	Durenberger[a]	Dayton	.47	0.94	0.42	-0.27	1,175
MN	1984	Boschwitz[a]	Growe	.42	1.17	0.39	-0.39	1,276
MN	1988	Durenberger[a]	Humphrey	.42	0.98	0.33	-0.26	1,001
MS	1982	Barbour	Stennis[a]	.64	0.54	0.21	0.28	956
MS	1984	Cochran[a]	Winter	.39	0.91	0.47	-0.43	1,139
MS	1988	Lott	Dowdy	.46	0.83	0.37	-0.20	976
MO	1982	Danforth[a]	Woods	.49	0.92	0.37	-0.15	2,034
MO	1986	Bond	Woods	.47	1.26	0.46	-0.07[b]	1,189
MT	1982	Williams	Melcher[a]	.57	0.84	0.40	0.25	1,327
NE	1982	Keck	Zorinsky[a]	.70	0.71	0.10[b]	0.75	1,120
NV	1982	Hecht	Cannon[a]	.49	0.79	0.38	-0.07[b]	1,117
NV	1986	Santini	Reid	.53	1.09	0.31	0.15	973
NV	1988	Hecht[a]	Bryan	.52	0.70	0.46	0.14	767
NH	1984	Humphrey[a]	D'Amours	.41	0.83	0.46	-0.11	602

Table 8.9. (continued)

State	Year	Republican Candidate	Democratic Candidate	Democratic Vote	Probit Coefficients			N
					Party Identification	Ideological Identification	Constant	
NJ	1982	Fenwick	Lautenberg	.51	0.87	0.11	0.01[b]	1,996
NJ	1984	Mochary	Bradley[a]	.65	0.92	0.38	0.56	1,380
NJ	1988	Dawkins	Lautenberg[a]	.54	0.94	0.32	0.14	1,193
NM	1988	Schmidt[a]	Bingaman	.54	0.81	0.39	-0.02	1,996
NM	1988	Valentine	Bingaman[a]	.63	0.71	0.35	0.45	1,132
NY	1982	Sullivan	Moynihan[a]	.66	0.65	0.40	0.70	1,121
NY	1986	D'Amato[a]	Green	.42	0.72	0.47	-0.36	1,343
NY	1988	McMillan	Moynihan[a]	.68	0.67	0.66	0.78	1,502
NC	1984	Helms[a]	Hunt	.48	0.74	0.73	-0.03[b]	1,745
NC	1986	Broyhill	Sanford	.52	1.09	0.61	0.00[b]	1,148
ND	1986	Andrews[a]	Conrad	.50	1.10	0.32	0.13	957
OH	1982	Pfeifer	Metzenbaum[a]	.58	0.90	0.54	0.28	933
OH	1988	Voinovich	Metzenbaum[a]	.57	0.88	0.43	0.26	1,353
OR	1984	Hatfield[a]	Hendriksen	.33	0.62	0.25	-0.53	1,331
OR	1986	Packwood[a]	Bauman	.36	0.61	-0.02[b]	-0.39	753
PA	1986	Specter[a]	Edgar	.43	0.90	0.27	-0.27	1,367
PA	1988	Heinz[a]	Vignola	.33	0.76	0.25	-0.66	1,356

State	Year							
RI	1982	Chafee[a]	Michaelson	.49	0.90	0.15	-0.18	1,262
SD	1986	Abnor[a]	Daschle	.52	0.98	0.44	0.23	934
TN	1982	Beard	Sasser[a]	.62	1.01	0.28	0.19	1,262
TX	1982	Collins	Bentsen[a]	.59	0.82	0.49	0.21	1,973
TX	1984	Gramm	Doggett	.41	1.07	0.64	-0.23	1,800
TX	1988	Boulter	Bentsen[a]	.60	0.93	0.47	0.46	1,720
UT	1982	Hatc[a]	Wilson	.42	1.06	0.51	0.10	1,534
VT	1982	Stafford[a]	Guest	.48	0.82	0.17	0.04[b]	1,056
VT	1988	Jeffords	Gray	.31	0.39	0.18	-0.56	651
VA	1982	Trible	Davis	.49	1.10	0.36	-0.07[b]	939
WA	1988	Gorton	Lowry	.48	0.93	0.62	-0.03[b]	966
WV	1982	Benedict	Byrd[a]	.69	0.98	0.36	0.45	632
WV	1984	Reese	Rockefeller	.52	0.79	0.18	-0.14	971
WI	1988	Engeleiter	Kohl	.52	0.73	0.31	0.06[b]	1,239
WY	1982	Wallop[a]	McDaniel	.43	0.83	0.29	-0.05[b]	873

Note: [a]Incumbent. [b]not significant at .05.

partisan or ideological heat. Instead, as we will see, it is the relative ideological placement of the candidates that matters.

A crucial statistic in Tables 8.8 and 8.9 is the intercept. Each intercept reflects the behavior of voters at "zero" on both partisanship and ideology – in other words, given our scoring procedure, the behavior of "moderate Independents." Where the coefficient is positive, most of these "neutral" voters voted Democratic. Negative coefficients indicate that most moderate Independents voted Republican. The standard deviation of the 110 intercepts is 0.32, with a range from −0.68 to 0.86. For comparison, the intercept of the 1988 presidential race is only −0.06. More tellingly, the intercept for Reagan's 1984 landslide was only −0.30. Intercepts with absolute values greater than 0.30 are found for 35 of the 110 state exit poll equations. By this test, the short-term forces of gubernatorial and senatorial contests exceed those of the 1984 Reagan landslide about one-third of the time.

For all practical purposes, the intercept predicts the election outcome. It correlates at .91 with the Democratic vote. In the overwhelming proportion of the contests (97 of 110), the direction of the intercept predicts the election winner. Thus, the collective decisions of moderate Independents is almost always electorally decisive. An interesting implication is, once again, that state ratio of Democrats to Republicans (or of conservatives to liberals) is of lesser electoral significance. It is short-term forces generated by the candidates that matter most.

Candidate appeal is determined by many factors. Incumbents usually obtain positive coefficients (56 out of 67), but incumbency may be an effect as well as a cause of candidate popularity. Other factors such as candidates' charisma, cash, and possible taint of scandal also contribute to short-term forces (Abramowitz, 1988). Among these other factors we also find the ideological positions of the candidates. Careful perusal of Tables 8.8 and 8.9 suggests that moderate candidates tend to obtain favorable intercepts and win elections.

Following our usual logic, our expectation is that the more liberal the two candidates are, the better the Republican candidate should do. We can test this notion empirically using the liberal–conservative scores of 1982 Senate candidates. For the 23 races for which we have relevant data, the correlation between the candidate midpoint on the 10-point ideological scale and the intercept of the state's individual voter equation is a healthy .51. This correlation holds up for the subsample of Republican incumbents ($r = .56; N = 8$) but dissipates for Democrats ($r = .17; N = 11$). Within each party, sitting senators tend to be more moderate than senatorial challengers. A suspicion is that their moderation allows Senators to stay elected.

CONCLUSIONS

The partisan division of a state is electorally important. Recall, for instance, that state partisanship is a strong predictor of the relative strength of the two parties in the state legislature. Over time, a strongly Democratic or strongly Republican state will find its state legislature almost always controlled by the dominant party. The reason is that short-term forces in individual legislative races cancel out, while state-level issues only modestly affect legislative election outcomes. All this leaves state party identification as the natural predictor of legislative control. If state partisanship determines legislative control, it might seem to follow that state partisanship works to retard the process of representation in the states. We offer a quite different interpretation. The relative strengths of the Democratic and Republican parties within a state electorate reflect their relative success at representing state opinion.

This chapter has examined state elections by focusing on state-level voting for president, governor, and senator. Our investigation has highlighted both the importance and the limitations of state partisanship as a predictor of state election outcomes. State partisanship takes on special importance because it reflects the relative ideological proximity of the state electorate to the two major political parties. In presidential elections, however, state electorates appear to discount that portion of their partisanship that is traceable to the ideological locations of their state parties.

Although important, state partisanship leaves vast amounts of the unexplained variance in state outcomes, particularly in elections below the presidential level. State elections for senator and governor are largely the result of short-term forces independent of state partisanship. Setting knowledge of the candidates aside, state elections are more difficult to forecast from partisanship alone than national presidential elections are from knowing only the post–World War II partisan track record.

We illustrate this important point with one final set of electoral scatterplots. Figure 8.5 shows the statistically significant but weak relationships between state partisanship and the vote in nonincumbent races for governor and the U.S. Senate. The regression lines are borrowed from Column 5 of Tables 8.6 and 8.7. Since these are all races without an incumbent candidate, we might expect that candidate-generated short-term forces would be weak, and the election would be relatively safe for the dominant party where one party holds a clear edge in party identification. Note, instead, the wide variation around the regression lines. Given

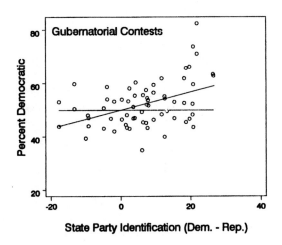

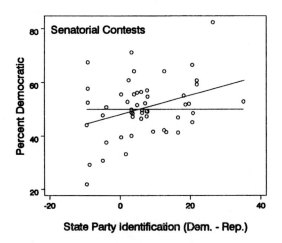

Figure 8.5 Predicting Open Seat Electoral Outcomes for Governor and U.S. Senator from State Party Identification, 1976–88

the positive regression lines for party identification, we can certainly conclude that owning a lead in party identification helps a party in state elections. But the benefit is marginal. Throughout the U.S. states, voters' party loyalties are sufficiently weak to allow both parties to achieve competitive stature in major state elections.

9

State opinion over time

So far, our discussion has focused solely on political life in the states as it is quantified for the late 1970s and the 1980s. The present chapter expands the focus backward in time, in order to place our findings in historical perspective. For this task, we assemble measures of state ideology and partisanship from earlier eras. These measures, drawn from Gallup polls from 1936 to 1963, are far noisier than the contemporary measures of state ideology and partisanship that have dominated our discussion so far.

Measurement error demands that our indicators of "historical" ideology and partisanship be analyzed with considerable care. Still, Gallup-based measures of early ideology and partisanship provide helpful leverage for understanding the historical continuity of state-level public opinion and its consequences – from the times of the New Deal to the Reagan presidency. In the following pages, we will see that earlier state-level ideological sentiment may have been less stable than we found for the more recent period, 1976–1988. We will also see evidence that even for the 1930s to the 1960s, state ideology was an important influence on state policy.

HISTORICAL MEASURES OF STATE OPINION

Chapter 2 demonstrated that for the 13 years from which our CBS/NYT survey data were collected, states moved very little in terms of their relative positions on the scales of net ideological identification and partisan identification. The stability of the states was particularly evident in the case of ideology. We might imagine that our measure of the ideological preferences of state electorates captures a cleavage in state-level public opinion so enduring that it has been present for decades. Still, we must consider the possibility that the ideological ordering of the states has not always been stable. Thus, we expand our time horizon backward more than 50 years in a search of an evolutionary change in the way state publics orient themselves ideologically.

State opinion over time

Gallup polls: 1937–64

Because it has regularly monitored Americans' political beliefs since the mid 1930s, the Gallup poll is the obvious data source to estimate the partisanship and ideology of state electorates prior to 1976. With the aid of the Roper Center for Public Opinion Research, we were able to identify 19 national Gallup polls conducted between 1937 and 1964 that contained questions about the ideological preferences of respondents. The irregularity with which Gallup (and other pollsters) probed ideological preferences during this earlier era is far different from current practice. Indeed, for the eventful period from 1964 to 1969, Gallup evidently did not ask an ideological question once. This drought is the reason why our sporadic series of historical ideological observations stops in 1964.

Almost half of the long-term "sample" for our historical readings of ideology come from seven surveys from the prewar 1937–39 period. We aggregate these seven surveys, with 19,119 usable ideological responses, to construct a measure of pre–World War II state opinion. We also aggregate the post–World War II portion of our historical sample, composed of 29,465 usable ideological responses from 12 Gallup surveys between 1947 and 1964. Thus, we have measures of ideology for three periods:

pre–World War II (1937–9),
post–World War II (1947–64), and
contemporary (1976–88).

The ideological questions that Gallup asked were not today's standard question regarding ideological identification as a liberal, moderate, or conservative. In some variant, 7 of the surveys asked respondents whether their political views were liberal or conservative, without encouraging a moderate or middle-of-the-road response. The remaining 12 surveys, again with variation in question wording, offered respondents a hypothetical choice of two ideological parties in place of the standard Democrats and Republicans. Respondents were asked whether they would join or prefer the party for liberals or the party for conservatives. Survey dates and exact question wordings are presented in the appendix to this chapter. For the prewar surveys, party identification was not regularly asked. Consequently, we offer no measure of state partisanship from the 1930s here. After World War II, however, Gallup monitored party identification regularly. Thus, from the 12 surveys from which we drew estimates of postwar state ideology, we also obtained estimates of postwar state partisanship.

For our historical samples we measured ideological and partisan identification in our customary way. Counting liberal responses as +100, in-between or neutral responses as 0, and conservative responses as –100, we computed state means, which can also be interpreted as percentage point

Statehouse democracy

Statehouse democracy

differences – percent liberals minus percent conservatives. Similarly, we computed state party identification in the usual way as the state mean of Democratic (+100), Independent (0), and Republican (–100) responses.

Methodological problems

Comparing state means from contemporary CBS/NYT polls with state means from earlier Gallup polls presents certain hazards. We must consider differences due to ordinary house effects, differences in question wording, and differences in sampling procedure. In addition, we must be sensitive to the much lower Ns from the pooled Gallup series. The most serious pitfall, however, from the standpoint of estimating state means, is the greater geographic clustering of respondents for in-person surveys of the earlier era.

House effects. Studying historical trends based on polling data from different survey research organizations presents a hazard of uncertain magnitude. Even when different organizations attempt to measure the same public sentiment at exactly the same point in time, their estimates often diverge. These differences are usually attributed to "house effects," or the marginal variation in response achieved by different survey teams. House effects include not only variation in exact question wording and in sampling procedure (discussed separately in upcoming sections), but also such details as differing approaches to handling nonresponses, contextual (question-order) effects, interviewer training and supervision, and coding decisions. Historical trend analysis that requires use of data collected by more than one survey firm runs the risk of mistaking house effects for true change (Smith, 1978, 1982, 1987; Converse and Schuman, 1984; Turner, 1984).

Question wording. Survey researchers now recognize that even seemingly minor variations in how questions are worded can have surprisingly large effects on survey answers. Thus, differences in question wording over the time span of our historical analysis deserve special consideration. To consider the mildest example first, Gallup and CBS/NYT preface their "party identification" question differently. Gallup asks respondents whether "in politics as of today" they consider themselves to be Democrats, Independents, or Republicans. CBS/NYT asks respondents whether "generally speaking" they regard themselves as Democrats, Independents, or Republicans. Fortunately, it turns out that the Gallup and the CBS/NYT variants produce virtually identical distributions of partisanship over time (MacKuen, Erikson, and Stimson, 1992). This result only reinforces our confidence that the two variants of the party identification question should order the states similarly on the partisan continuum.

But what about the crucial variable of ideological preference? In recent years, Gallup and CBS/NYT have asked similar questions concerning respondent identification as liberal, moderate, or conservative. The contemporary menu of "liberal," "moderate," or "conservative" was not the choice offered by Gallup in our historical samples. As mentioned, some were asked whether they considered themselves a liberal or conservative, with no clear middle alternative. Others were asked whether they would prefer a liberal or a conservative party.

Conceivably, the national division of ideological sentiment depends in some important way on the exact question asked. In terms of state mean scores, Gallup's earlier questions should generate greater variance because of their discouragement of the middle position. For our purposes, however, the most crucial question concerns not the metric but whether states' *relative positions* on the ideological continuum vary with exact question wording. That sort of contamination strikes us as relatively improbable. Although differences in wording may affect the percentage, say, of both New Yorkers and Indianans who call themselves liberal or conservative, the relative rankings should hold constant across minor question format differences. New York ought to score considerably more liberal than Indiana as long as the questions tap the same underlying dimension of liberal–conservative ideology. Consequently we see little risk in comparing state means from different surveys that measure ideological sentiment with different questions.

Sampling. Changes over time in standard survey procedure present an additional reason for caution. Changes over time in the pattern of survey responses may actually be artifacts of sampling methodology. Like other polls of the era, early Gallup polls relied on "quota" sampling techniques (Gallup, 1948, 1972; Frankel and Frankel, 1987). In the aftermath of the miscall of the 1948 election, many firms removed the power to choose subjects from their interviewers and adopted strategies designed to ensure random selection of interviewees within tightly drawn population clusters. The 1970s saw a second revolution in sampling strategies as interviewers were pulled off the street and assigned to call randomly selected telephone numbers. Random digit dialing, while incorporating the clustering approach, permitted contact with a greater number of geographically dispersed clusters (Waksberg, 1978). Each of these shifts in sampling strategy has the potential to distort inferences about true change over time.

One special source of sampling change over time is the shift of the universe that the sample is supposed to represent. Early Gallup polls, designed to reflect the composition of the electorate, underrepresented women and minorities relative to their proportion of the population (Glenn, 1975; Glenn and Frisbie, 1977). Yet these early polls reasonably reflect the composition of the voting electorate at the time. We must be careful to understand just what we are measuring and what comparisons may be made with these data. Our early state-level estimates will reflect the states' voting electorates of the time. Our later CBS/NYT state samples more closely reflect the general population.

Sample sizes. A serious concern regarding the state- level prewar and postwar Gallup estimates is the "small" sample sizes involved. Aggregated national samples of 19,169 and 29,465 would not normally be called small, except in comparison to our mammoth aggregation of over 150,000 respondents for our contemporary measures of state ideology and partisanship. Quite obviously, the statistical reliability of the historical estimates is much lower than for the contemporary measures.

Clustering. More than sample size affects the statistical reliabilities of our Gallup-based state estimates. The reliabilities of the historical estimates are further compromised because of the practice by Gallup (and other pollsters) of clustering respondents geographically for in-person interviews. Survey organizations typically cluster respondents for a national survey in as few as 80 primary sampling units or PSUs (counties or SMSAs), and even by specific neighborhoods within PSUs. For reasons of cost, survey researchers will often maintain the identical clusters for years on end. As a result, even when aggregated over years, state subsamples are clustered by geography.

The potential consequences of this sampling procedure include severe distortion of state-level estimates. For any state, it is conceivable that all respondents for a decade or more may reside in a small number of arbitrarily selected counties – and perhaps even from a small number of neighborhoods within those counties. Thus, a procedure that is sensible for interviewing a national sample of respondents in their homes offers the uncertainty of some unknown bias when used for what it is not designed for – estimating the breakdown of opinion by state. Put simply, Gallup's state-level mean estimates are even less reliable than the number of respondents per state would indicate.

This problem of severe clustering separates the Gallup-based measures of historical opinion from our contemporary CBS/NYT measures. As discussed in Chapter 2, sample clustering is a lesser problem for the contemporary telephone surveys conducted by CBS/NYT. With sampling from repeated draws of a large number of telephone exchanges, over-time aggregations of CBS/NYT telephone surveys offer reasonable approximations of representative samples within states.

From this discussion, it should be clear that the earlier Gallup-based measures of state opinion are considerably inferior to the CBS/NYT–based measures that we use for our contemporary analysis. As we will see, however, this caveat certainly does not mean that the historical measures are of little value. In the following pages, we use the historical opinion measures to gather clues about the stability of state opinion over time and about the stability of the representational process.

LONG-TERM STABILITY OF STATE IDEOLOGY AND PARTISANSHIP

Correlations representing the long-run relative stability of ideology and partisanship are presented in Table 9.1. These correlations are presented for three sets of states. The first set is all 47 (Nevada excluded) continental states. The second set includes only the 30 (Nevada excluded) northern (nonsouthern, nonborder) states only. The third includes only the 12 largest northern states, which each contain a combined prewar and postwar sample of a thousand or more respondents.[1] The culling of first southern and border states and then small states serves two obvious purposes. Deleting southern states (and border states as well) controls for the interesting sectional evolution of the South toward both conservatism and competitive political parties. Deleting small states helps to reduce the sampling error for our historical measures of state ideology and partisanship.

The stability of state partisanship, 1947–88

Consider first the relatively simple matter of following state partisanship over time. We have only two measures of state partisanship – postwar (1947–64) and contemporary (1976–88). As the correlations indicate, state-level partisanship is fairly stable over the long haul. This conclusion remains when we control for southern sectionalism and for state sample size. The basic stability of state partisanship can be seen by comparing the postwar map of state partisanship with the contemporary version (Figure 9.1).

Relative stability does not imply absolute stability. Figure 9.2 displays the scatterplot of the two temporal readings of state partisanship. This figure reveals a certain compression of the distribution of state partisanship, mainly from the declining Democratic strength of southern states. Between the postwar and contemporary periods, the range of state means on party identification compressed to the point that the standard deviation of the distribution declined by almost one-half from its former magni-

---

1. The "large" northern states are California, Illinois, Indiana, Iowa, Michigan, Minnesota, Ohio, New Jersey, New York, Pennsylvania, and Wisconsin. By the 1970s and 1980s, Iowa would have dropped off this list of largest northern states. Nevada is omitted from the correlation base for comparability with our contemporary analysis.

Table 9.1. *Over-time correlations of state partisanship and ideology*

Variable	Ideology			Partisanship	
	Prewar (1937-39)	Postwar (1947-64)	Contemporary (1976-88)	Postwar (1947-64)	Contemporary (1976-88)
47 states					
Ideology					
Prewar	1.00				
Postwar	.11	1.00			
Contemporary	.03	.56	1.00		
Partisanship					
Postwar	.43	.11	-.19	1.00	
Contemporary	.34	.16	.08	.77	1.00
Mean	-1.7	-3.9	-14.6	15.1	7.0
S.D.	11.3	11.7	7.3	21.5	11.4
30 northern states					
Ideology					
Prewar	1.00				
Postwar	.39	1.00			
Contemporary	.35	.57	1.00		
Partisanship					
Postwar	.18	.61	.44	1.00	
Contemporary	.05	.51	.73	.63	1.00
Mean	-4.7	-4.0	-12.6	4.0	1.4
S.D.	11.2	11.6	7.4	15.6	6.5
12 large northern states					
Ideology					
Prewar	1.00				
Postwar	.71	1.00			
Contemporary	.46	.60	1.00		
Partisanship					
Postwar	.16	.37	.37	1.00	
Contemporary	.34	.50	.70	.73	1.00
Mean	-1.7	-5.3	-8.9	8.0	5.4
S.D.	6.0	8.6	4.7	9.9	5.5

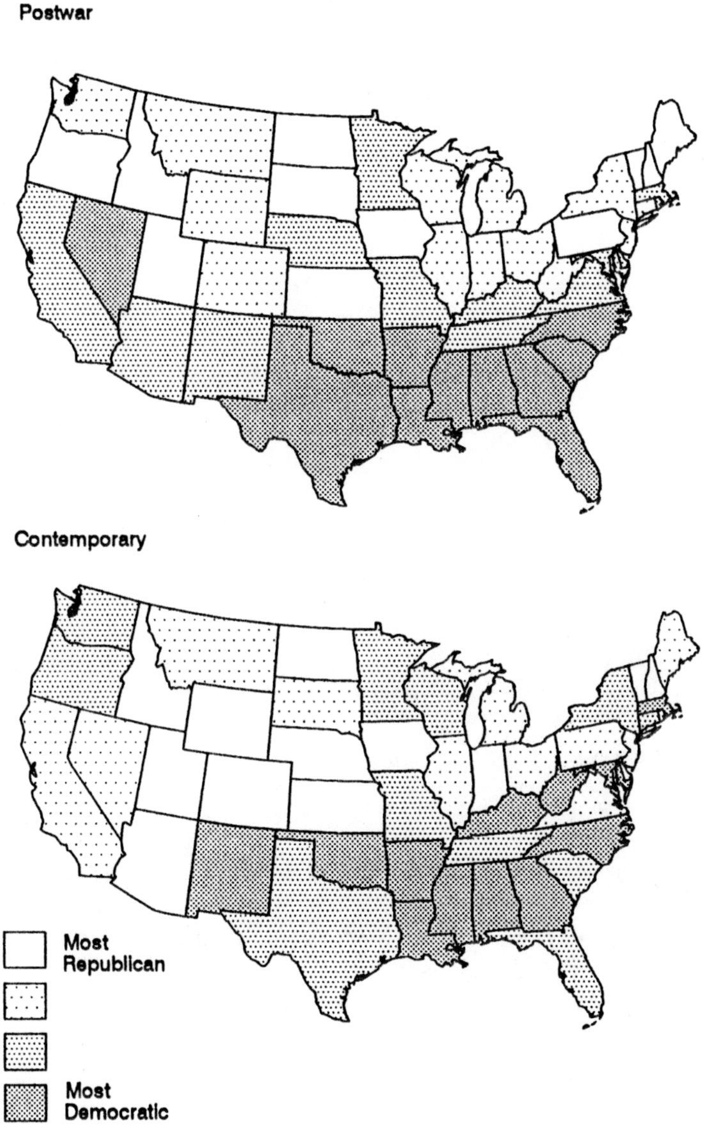

State opinion over time

Postwar

Contemporary

Most
Republican

Most
Democratic

Figure 9.1 Maps of State Partisanship Over Time

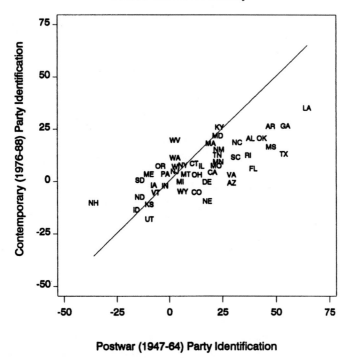

Figure 9.2 Plot of State Partisanship Over Time. Note: Higher Scores Indicate Greater Democratic identification.

tude. See Table 9.1. In part this compression of the variation in state partisanship scores may be a trick of measurement error, which exaggerates the observed variance of a variable. Based on sampling considerations, we know that the postwar measure of state partisanship should be somewhat contaminated from measurement error. Meanwhile, from Chapter 2 we also know that the contemporary measure of state partisanship is relatively free of measurement error. The decline in measurement error from the postwar to the contemporary readings of state partisanship could by itself produce the illusion of a compression of state differences in mass partisanship.

But another likely source of this compression is that the actual differences in state party preference did indeed get smaller. In the immediate postwar era, state electoral outcomes favored the dominant party to an extent that would not be imaginable today. Such instances are found almost entirely in the once one-party (Democratic) South. To an extent not found today, states were divisible into those with meaningful party competition and those without.

State opinion over time

The stability of state ideology, 1937–88

Chapter 2 showed that within the relatively narrow time range from 1976 to 1988, state electorates were quite stable in their ideological positions. Each state held a certain position on the ideological continuum and stayed there – at least for the 13 years examined. When we look backward over a fifty-year span, however, we observe evidence that a remarkable amount of ideological movement occurred.

To appreciate the amount of movement on the ideological scale, one need only observe the changes in the ideological map from prewar to postwar to contemporary times, shown in Figure 9.3. Note that the most liberal states included a strong concentration in the South, while conservatism prevailed mainly in rural western and midwestern states. Most New England states also were on the right, living up to their reputations as bastions of crusty Yankee conservatism. By the postwar reading, these regional stereotypes had largely faded. By the contemporary reading, a new pattern had emerged: southern and western conservatism versus bi-coastal liberalism.

Figure 9.4 shows this ideological movement via a series of scatterplots. As the figure shows, there is virtually no statistical relationship ($r = .11$) between the states' prewar and postwar ideological means. Similarly, virtually no correlation exists between the prewar configuration of the states and the ideology of state electorates in the 1980s ($r = .03$). Even between the postwar measure, 1947–64, and our contemporary measure (1976–88), the correlation is a mere .56.

Even if the true over-time correlations were perfectly stable, we would expect some slippage in the observed correlation due to measurement error. But appealing on the grounds of bad measurement is an inadequate defense when observed correlations are near zero. Although the details may be foggy due to inadequacies of measurement, the general contours are clear: The positions of the states on the liberal–conservative continuum have undergone major shifts, particularly from before to after World War II. To understand these shifts, we should first consider how the ideological terms "liberal" and "conservative" were popularly used in the 1930s. By the late 1930s, liberalism had already evolved from its classic meaning of belief in limited government and laissez-faire economics into its quite different current meaning: a willingness to use government as a positive instrument, particularly to help the disadvantaged. The transformation followed the 1932 presidential election. Both candidates, Hoover and Roosevelt, championed the cause of liberalism and limited government. Once Roosevelt was elected, the term "liberal" was commandeered to become a pro–New Deal pro-government action label. Slowly, the opposition rallied to the conservative label (see Rotunda, 1986).

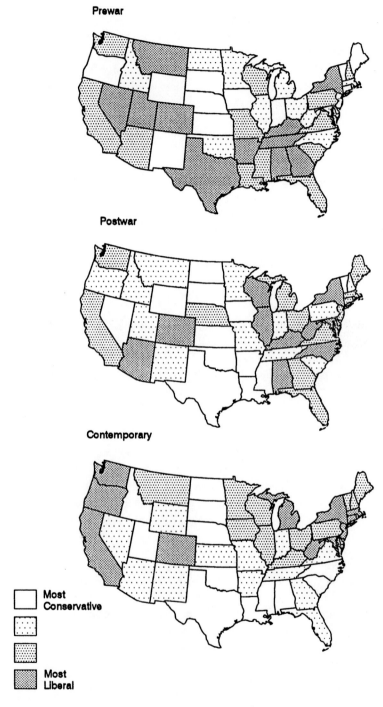

Figure 9.3 Maps of State Liberalism Over Time

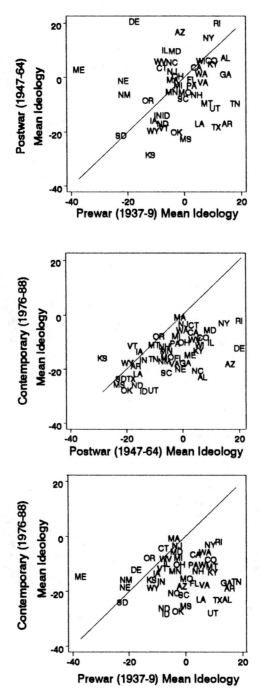

Figure 9.4 State Ideology Over Time. Note: Higher scores indicate greater liberalism.

By the late 1930s, the liberal–conservative distinction had become almost synonymous with the pro– or anti–New Deal distinction. Thus, for our prewar 1937–9 sample, we find Democratic states, including those of the South, calling themselves liberal. In fact, the most liberal of the prewar states were found incongruously (by current standards) in the Democratic South.

At first glance, the liberal characterization of prewar southern (mainly white) electorates may appear suspicious. The history of the KKK, religious fundamentalism, and the civil rights battles of the 1950s and 1960s color historical assessments of the region. But our depiction of the 1930s South as liberal is not revisionist history. Consider how V. O. Key's *Southern Politics* summarizes the political leanings of the region:

> Southern liberalism is not to be underestimated. Though southern conservatism is not entirely a myth . . . fundamentally within southern politics there is a powerful strain of agrarian liberalism, now reinforced by the growing unions of the cities. It is not always perceptible to outsiders – or even to the southerner – because of the capacity of the one-party system to conceal factional differences. (1949, 670)

One can see this earlier southern liberalism by examining responses to some of the issue questions asked by the Gallup polls of the late 1930s. Cantril (1951) reports state breakdowns for several polls conducted during the late 1930s. In comparison with the rest of the country, the states of the Old South were more supportive of loans to farmers, a national welfare system, and the idea of reducing the workweek in an attempt to reduce unemployment. Similarly, Ladd and Hadley (1978) examine regional distributions of public opinion during the late 1930s and early 1940s: More southerners supported compulsory old age insurance, federal regulation of business, and FDR's court packing plan than did residents of the Northeast, Midwest, or West. Hero (1969) also documents this earlier southern liberalism.[2]

---

2. An earlier southern liberalism can be seen by focusing on Congress as well as the public. In his definitive history of the South during the first half of the twentieth century, Tindall (1967) documents the extent to which FDR relied on southern leadership in the House and Senate to ensure passage of the principal legislation of the New Deal. Southerners Joseph Byrns (D.-Tenn), William Bankhead (D.-Ala.), Sam Rayburn (D.-Tex.), and Robert Doughton (D.-N.C.) among others led the fight to pass Roosevelt's legislative proposals in the House. Senate support was mustered by Majority Leaders Joseph Robinson (D.-Ark., 1933–6), Alben Barkley (D.-Ky., 1937–40) with key committee leadership provided by southerners such as Pat Harrison (D.-Miss.) and Joseph Byrnes (D.-S.C.). Similarly in 1940 and 1941 as the war in Europe grew closer, southern congressmen quickly abandoned neutrality. Thus, it appears that the congressional delegations in southern states were very sensitive to the expectations of the folks back home. A populace that supported federal programs and an interventionist foreign policy were well represented in both House and Senate.

State opinion over time

The depiction of the South as liberal, however, certainly is no longer valid. Since the 1930s, the common meanings of political liberalism and conservatism expanded to include the dimensions of law and order versus permissiveness, cultural liberalism versus fundamentalism, and the like. Most important from the standpoint of state-level positioning, the terms began to apply to civil rights and racial policies. As desegregation and civil rights for blacks came to the forefront of national politics, southern ideological preferences underwent a strong conversion, as white southerners embraced the ideology of conservatism to rationalize their resistance to federal action to advance the cause of civil rights (Black and Black, 1988).

Not all of the ideological movement of the U.S. states over the past half century can be attributed to the movement of the South. But the South's sectional shift certainly is a major factor. Because of the South's unique political history, our historical analysis yields crisper results if we eliminate states with a southern exposure. For much of the analyses that follow, we separate out not only the 11 former Confederate states, but also the border states, defined broadly here to include all states with compulsory school segregation prior to the 1954 *Brown v. Board of Education* Supreme Court decision (Delaware, Kentucky, Maryland, Missouri, Oklahoma, and West Virginia). Separating out the South – and the border states for good measure – helps to restore some historical stability to the states' ideological positioning. For the North (N = 30 states), we find an outline of a positive relationship (r = .35) between prewar liberalism and contemporary liberalism. For southern and border states, we see the reverse pattern (r = −.28) with hitherto liberal states marching to the front of the conservative line.

Even for the northern states alone, the over-time correlations are weak: prewar–postwar = .39, postwar–contemporary = .57, and prewar–contemporary = .35. These low correlations signify the reality of actual historical change in the ordering of states' ideological preferences. Of that there can be little doubt. But to the extent we can adjust for the measurement error of the historical ideological readings, an underlying stability also becomes manifest.

We can see an improved stability if we isolate a smaller set of states – the 12 large northern states with a combined prewar and postwar sample size that exceeds a thousand. These are the states for which measurement problems should be relatively minimal. Among these states, the prewar–postwar correlation rises to a respectable .71; the postwar–contemporary correlation rises slightly to .60; and the prewar–contemporary correlation improves to .46.

Following our procedure of Chapter 2 for sorting out the stability over time of state ideology for the 13-year period of contemporary readings, it might seem that our obvious next step would be to adjust our observed over-time correlations for the statistical "reliabilities" of the various measures. We can conduct such an exercise for the prewar and postwar readings, using the "sampling theory" derivation, to obtain reliability estimates near .80.[3] Adjusting for these reliability estimates would push the correlation estimates upward by about 25 percent from their observed values.

The difficulty with this procedure is that the reliability estimates depend on the assumption of representative state samples. Gallup's clustering procedure violates this assumption. We can at best take the reliability estimates as only an upper bound–violation of representativeness makes the true reliabilities worse. The observed correlations probably should be inflated by *more* than 25 percent, but how much is difficult to gauge.

So far, we have learned that state ideological positions have moved, largely on a regional basis. At the same time, apart from this regional movement, the relative positions of states may be much more stable than the literal reading of the observed scores would suggest. Measurement error is of a sufficient presence to cast suspicion on the observed ideological movement of specific states. It is difficult to disentangle the residue of measurement error from real change due to such factors as population movement and mass responses to national political events.

The ideology-partisanship relationship

One persistent finding is the lack of a statistical relationship between state ideology and state partisanship, particularly before controlling for region. As we saw in Chapter 2 for the full set of 46 states, the contemporary readings of the two variables correlate at only .08. Here (Table 9.1) we can see a similar result with a mere .11 correlation for the postwar era. The strongest ideology–partisanship correlations turn out to be across years: between prewar ideology on the one hand and postwar partisanship (.43) or contemporary partisanship (.34) on the other.

The reason for these somewhat larger correlations between prewar ideology and later partisanship is not difficult to figure out: The prewar South held a somewhat liberal ideological preference to match its Democratic Party preference. The latter survived longer than the former. The combination of conservatism and Democratic identification in the

---

3. The estimated reliabilities *assuming the equivalent of simple random sampling* of state ideology are .78 (prewar) and .80 (postwar) for the 30 northern states and .76 (prewar) and .91 (postwar) for the 12 largest states. While the reliabilities for the 12 largest states were aided by the enlarged state samples, this leverage is somewhat undercut by the smaller range of observed ideology.

South is the source of the low ideology–partisanship correlation in recent times. If we control for southern regionalism by culling southern and border states, the two variables do correlate. For northern states only, the observed ideology–partisanship correlations are .61 for the postwar era and .73 for the contemporary era. Still, although these correlations are reasonably high, the two variables, state ideology and state partisanship, represent decidedly different political phenomena.

STATE PRESIDENTIAL VOTING AND THE GALLUP MEASURES

In Chapter 8, we investigated the roles of ideology and partisanship in the prediction of state voting. Here we offer a modest historical extension, simply exploring how earlier measures of state ideology and partisanship correlate with presidential voting at the time.

Table 9.2 displays the correlations between state presidential election returns, 1932–88 and estimates of state ideology and partisanship from the same era. Results are shown for 47 states and for 30 northern states. Correlations are generally lower for the prewar and postwar eras than for the contemporary period. This is to be expected if for no other reason than that the earlier measures are suspect due to measurement era. Viewed from this perspective, many of the prewar and postwar correlations reach impressive size.

The coefficients for northern states and those for all (47) states often take contrasting paths, the latter responding to southern ideology. When the South was liberal (the 1930s), for example, state liberalism predicted Democratic voting. Later, when the South was conservative but still voted Democratic, state liberalism weakened as an electoral predictor. Later still, when the conservative South began voting Republican for president, state ideology once again correlated with the vote. Partisanship, meanwhile, began to slide as a predictor when the South, still Democratic, began to vote Republican for president.

Because of the regional divergence between the North and South, the correlations for the North alone are of special interest. It is for northern states that the ideology–partisanship comparison is particularly revealing; the coefficients for partisanship and (especially) ideology show considerable strength. Except for 1932 (an election that actually preceded the current partisan alignment) and 1956 (that atypically nonideological contest so carefully analyzed in *The American Voter*), northern state ideology predicts northern state voting rather well. Two elections in which state ideology at the time correlates with the presidential vote at a particularly

227

Table 9.2. *Correlations between state ideology, state partisanship, and the
presidential vote, 1932-88*

Presidential Vote	47 States		30 Northern States	
	Ideology	Partisanship	Ideology	Partisanship
Prewar (1937-39) measures				
1932	.40		.07	
1936	.51		.45	
1940	.51		.53	
1944	.49		.56	
Postwar (1947-64) measures				
1948	.13	.75	.36	.58
1952	.19	.62	.65	.56
1956	-.05	.61	.11	.39
1960	.32	.59	.57	.51
1964	.22	-.38	.42	.24
1968	.32	.29	.52	.38
1972	.33	-.37	.33	.34
Contemporary (1976-92) measures				
1976	.18	.81	.66	.82
1980	.43	.73	.78	.78
1984	.69	.46	.73	.81
1988	.69	.24	.67	.76
1992	.78	.40	.83	.80

impressive level are those in 1952 and 1960. Our postwar ideology measure taps a surprisingly rich vein of ideological division for the 1950s era
that previously had been largely uncharted.[4]

Of special interest is the degree of decay to the correlations between

4. The 1960 election is the only one in which, for northern states, the observed correlation of the vote with ideology exceeds the correlation of the vote with the previous
presidential vote. For predictions of the 1952 northern state presidential vote, postwar ideology loses the correlation battle to the 1948 vote, but only by .66 to .65.
Note that by the "ideological" 1972 election, postwar ideology fades as an electoral
predictor.

measures of state ideology and partisanship at one time period and the presidential vote at either the same time or another. For northern states, Table 9.3 presents the correlations between the measures of ideology/ partisanship for all time periods and those for presidential voting in all elections, 1932–88. This table clearly shows that each measure predicts the vote best for elections that were nearby in time but does not predict well for those that were temporally distant. Contemporary measures of ideology and partisanship, for example, are excellent predictors of recent state voting but correlate poorly with the vote in the 1930s. Similarly, prewar ideology predicts the presidential vote reasonably well from 1936 as far forward as 1952, but it is virtually uncorrelated with the vote in recent elections. This pattern of temporal decay in the correlation between ideology or partisanship and the vote is unmistakable, but what does it mean? Some might argue that it represents state electorates rationalizing their attitudes into alignment with their vote decisions. But almost surely this pattern can be traced to evolutionary change in state ideology and partisanship over the decades. Ever so slowly, state electorates change their ideological and partisan preferences. And as they do, state voting patterns also change. After half a century or so, the ordering of states may be completely reshuffled, even without the intervention of a single sharp electoral realignment.

State socioeconomic variables and state ideology

In Chapter 3, we asked where state ideology came from. We were partially able to account for contemporary ideology in terms of a number of traits of the individual voters within the states. When predicting state ideology solely from aggregate (macrolevel) characteristics of the state citizenry, however, two variables were particularly powerful: state urbanism (percent residing in SMSAs) and religious fundamentalism. The urban (or SMSA) population is a marker in general for the kinds of voters who identify with liberalism. Religious fundamentalists tend to be political conservatives.

Here, in a simple fashion, we extend this demographic analysis backward to predict prewar and postwar state ideology from the states' population characteristics. By noting changes in the variables that predict state liberalism or changes in the magnitudes or even the signs of their relationships to state ideology, we can obtain further clues regarding the sources of ideological change in the states. Toward this end we set up a series of regression equations predicting state ideology from several state-level variables. We started with our familiar measures of state income, urbanism, and education (see Chapter 4). To these we added three religious

Table 9.3. *Over-time correlations between ideology, partisanship, and the presidential vote, 1932-92: northern states only*

Presidential vote	Ideology			Partisanship	
	Prewar (1937-39)	Postwar (1947-64)	Contemporary (1976-88)	Postwar (1947-64)	Contemporary (1976-88)
1932	.07	.00	-.38	.23	-.01
1936	.45	.15	-.17	.29	.05
1940	.53	.45	.16	.35	.25
1944	.56	.55	.26	.39	.34
1948	.45	.36	.15	.58	.43
1952	.52	.65	.63	.56	.65
1956	.30	.11	.18	.39	.46
1960	.47	.57	.66	.51	.72
1964	.20	.42	.76	.24	.62
1968	.22	.52	.74	.38	.75
1972	.13	.33	.63	.34	.81
1976	.06	.32	.66	.35	.82
1980	.08	.45	.78	.40	.78
1984	.18	.39	.73	.40	.81
1988	.13	.31	.67	.40	.76
1992	.17	.47	.83	.39	.80

variables – percent fundamentalist, percent Catholic, and percent Jewish – and also included two regional dummies for southern and border states.

These are a lot of variables for the task, and the full set of equations presents a cluttered analysis that we spare our readers. Our initial equations showed that several variables never approached a statistically significant contribution in any relevant specification and were therefore dropped from the presentation. Rejected variables include state income, border state, percent Catholic, and percent Jewish. Results based on the surviving four variables (urbanism, education, fundamentalism, and South) are shown, in standardized form, in the equations of Table 9.4.

Table 9.4 reveals the substantive basis of ideological change. For all three ideological measures, state urbanism is an important predictor of state liberalism. To a much lesser extent, education consistently predicts conservatism. The shifts are in the effects of the variables fundamentalism

Table 9.4. *Regressions predicting state ideology from state characteristics*

Independent variable	Prewar ideology (1937-39)	Postwar ideology (1947-64)	Contemporary ideology (1976-88)
Education	-.17 (-1.20)	-.50 (-2.71)**	-.14 (-1.12)
Urbanism	.51 (3.62)***	.59 (4.00)***	.42 (4.82)***
The South	.40 (2.52)*	-.27 (-1.43)	-.29 (-2.25)*
Religious fundamentalism	.37 (2.57)*	-.05 (-.37)	-.53 (-5.38)***
Adjusted R^2	.362	.300	.660

Note: Coefficients are standardized regression coefficients, with *t*-values in parentheses. Urbanism is percent SMSA for 1980; census-defined percent "urban" for 1940 and 1960. Education is percent high school graduates for 1940, 1950, and 1980, respectively. Religious fundamentalism is derived from Johnson, Picard, and Quinn (1974), as explained in Chapter 3. South is the 11 former Confederate states.
*Significant at .05; **significant at .01; ***significant at .001.

and South. Prewar liberalism was a *positive* function of both variables; postwar liberalism was unaffected by them; and contemporary liberalism is a negative function of fundamentalism and (at a barely significant level) the South.

This progression of regression coefficients clearly highlights the source of ideological change. Liberalism as "economic liberalism" attracted residents of both the cities and the Bible Belt. It was in these groups, after all, that Roosevelt's votes were concentrated. Conservatism, following a familiar stereotype of the day, was the ideology of the contented, prosperous, mainstream Protestant establishment. In recent years, ideological polarization on New Deal issues has been partially displaced by a new division along "cultural" lines, between the largely southern culture of Protestant fundamentalism and the culture represented by big-city urbanism. The data are unmistakable: Protestant fundamentalism is the pivotal variable for ideological change of the states over the past 50 years.

Statehouse democracy

STATE IDEOLOGY AND STATE POLICY IN HISTORICAL CONTEXT

Our resurrection of state ideology from earlier eras would not be complete without trying to correlate it to policy measures from the same eras. Simply put, does ideological liberalism correlate with policy liberalism in earlier times as it has recently? To answer this question, we need to identify acceptable measures of policy liberalism for earlier decades.

Measuring policy liberalism historically

In Chapter 4, we presented a general measure of state policy liberalism for the late 1970s and early 1980s, with components drawn from the contemporary debate among liberals and conservatives. The eight components of policy liberalism, circa 1980, concerned taxation, education, criminal justice, welfare, health care, gambling, consumerism, and women's rights. Ideally, we would simply replicate these measures for earlier eras. Not all of these contemporary policies were the subject of controversy during earlier historical periods. For example, little variation exists historically in state policies regarding gambling, consumerism, and women's rights.

Given the limited variations of some policies (and the limited historical information about others), we generate a new state policy measure based on policies that exhibit some readily identifiable variation and comparability over the past 50 years. This new measure is our index of welfare/education spending, constructed from the following four items:

per pupil spending for education,
mean teacher salaries,
per recipient monthly AFDC [ADC] payment, and
per recipient monthly general assistance.

Measures of each were collected for each census year, 1940 to 1990.[5] Factor analyses of these four items yield a dominant first factor that explains about 50 percent of the variance in these items for each census year. For each year, we construct the composite index by summing the standardized scores for the four items for that year.

Table 9.5 summarizes the stability of our state spending measure over time. As we expect from earlier literature (Sharkansky, 1968), we obtain very high over-time correlations, meaning that the relative positions of the states on this spending index have changed little over the decades. Note that these correlations are not indicators of absolute stability – substantial changes have occurred as a function of inflation and federal government

5. For 1990, the latest available data is actually for 1988 or 1989. For 1990, per capita general assistance spending was unavailable. We replaced it by doubling the weight of the mean AFDC payment.

Table 9.5. *Over-time correlations for the index of welfare/education spending*

Welfare/ education spending	1940	1950	1960	1970	1980	1990
1940	1.00					
1950	.92	1.00				
1960	.92	.96	1.00			
1970	.88	.87	.93	1.00		
1980	.88	.90	.94	.94	1.00	
1990	.83	.79	.85	.92	.90	1.00

Note: N =47 states; Alaska, Hawaii, and Nevada are excluded.

intervention if nothing else. But the policy positions of the states relative to one another have changed very little over the passage of half a century. We can validate the index of welfare/education spending from the correlation between the 1980 version of this measure and our original composite measure of policy liberalism, for the period centered around 1980. This correlation is a rather satisfactory .84. (Of course, a high correlation should be expected if for no other reason than that the two indices share one item – per pupil spending – in common.) A second validation is that the 1980 index of welfare/education spending correlates at .73 with the contemporary measure of state ideology.

The opinion–policy correlation historically

Table 9.6 shows the simple correlation coefficients between welfare/education spending for each of six decades, on the one hand, and all three readings of state ideology, on the other. The numbers are presented three ways. The top set represents the correlations for 47 states. The middle set is for 30 northern states. The bottom set is for the 12 largest northern states. Looking at the top set, we find that contemporary ideology is about as strongly related to welfare/education spending going back to 1940 as it

Table 9.6. *Correlations between state ideology and welfare/education spending, 1940-90*

Welfare/ education spending	State ideology		
	Prewar	Postwar	Contemporary
47 states			
1940	-.05	.41	.66
1950	-.14	.37	.62
1960	-.13	.37	.67
1970	-.06	.41	.76
1980	-.04	.42	.73
1990	-.07	.44	.81
30 northern states			
1940	.62	.61	.60
1950	.58	.51	.58
1960	.53	.56	.69
1970	.47	.52	.78
1980	.55	.55	.72
1990	.42	.51	.83
12 largest northern states			
1940	.71	.73	.77
1950	.61	.81	.81
1960	.72	.89	.70
1970	.64	.82	.74
1980	.75	.80	.74
1990	.70	.57	.78

is to recent 1980–90 spending. This is the pattern one would expect if both state ideology and policy were stable (although we know ideology is not). Postwar liberalism is also related to welfare/education spending throughout the time span – but less strongly, a plausible result given its greater measurement error. Prewar liberalism presents a different result. As measured for the late 1930s, liberal sentiment does not correlate at all with liberal spending, even for 1940. This result, certainly not attributable to measurement error, goes against our theoretical expectations about representative democracy. Did something go wrong?

Actually, there is a ready explanation in terms of the one-time political uniqueness in the U.S. South. Figure 9.5 displays the scatterplots of the ideology–spending correlations for 1940, 1960, and 1980, in each instance using the temporally closest measure of state ideology. Southern and border states are highlighted as solid dots in the graphs. Over time, the southern scatterplot has begun to approximate the North's. For 1940, however, the North and South diverged dramatically. The dominant feature of the 1940 graph is the clustering of southern states in the lower right corner, a location indicating relatively conservative spending policies combined with a plurality of liberals over conservatives in the electorate. This mismatch of ideology and policy in the South easily accounts for the noncorrelation for 1940 between prewar ideology and policy nationally.

But if southern opinion was so "liberal," why was southern policy more conservative?[6] Again, we turn to V. O. Key. Key believed that the liberalism of the southern electorate was thwarted by the structure of the political system that permitted economic conservatives to prevail over other interests by fanning the flames of racial antagonism. Economic conservatives, in control of policy making in the states of the Old South, restrained the expansion of state governments. The task was eased by an unresponsive one-party system. In Key's words, "An underlying liberal drive . . . is held in check in part by the one-party system which almost inevitably operates to weaken the political strength of those disposed by temperament and interest to follow a progressive line" (1949, 670).

With time, the South discovered the two-party system and accepted black suffrage. Along the way, state ideology and state policy became more congruent, but not – as Key had predicted – by the adopting of liberal policies. Instead, ideology became conservative to match policy. The impetus, of course, was the new urgency in the 1950s of racial policy as the defining issue of southern politics. The white South rediscovered "states rights" and the virtues of "limited government." In more recent years, the dominance of conservatism as the preferred label in the South has been aided by the new ideological polarization along cultural lines. The dominance of conservatism in the South became complete. (See Black and Black, 1988, for a thorough discussion.)

For northern states, the analysis of the ideology–spending relationship is not so complicated. Compared to southern and border states, northern states were less affected by changing meanings of "liberal" and "conservative" in terms of race and culture. Northern states were not preoccupied

6. Actually, prewar ideology and 1940 spending are correlated for the South and border states, but in the wrong direction, –.65.

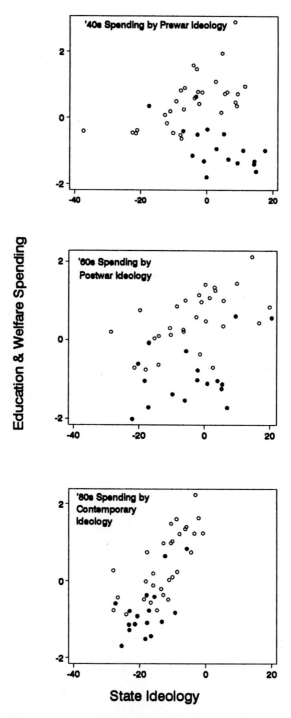

Figure 9.5 Ideology-Spending Relationship Over
Time. Note: Solid dots = southern and border states.

by battles over voting rights and desegregation, nor did they undergo a transformation from one-party to two-party politics. For the remainder of our analysis of the ideology–policy connection, we will concentrate on our set of 30 northern states.

The Table 9.6 correlations for 30 northern states are all positive, with opinion liberalism at each of three periods predicting policy at all five readings. The same is true of correlations for the 12 largest northern states, with the correlations involving the pre- and postwar measures improving considerably. This is because restricting the sample to large states diminishes the threat of measurement error.

State income

So far we have ignored one important complication. Since our historical policy measure represents the degree of liberal *spending,* this variable is influenced by state wealth as well as ideology. Although state wealth may not have much of an independent effect on policy liberalism in general (see Chapter 4), rich states do spend more than poor states, in part for the reason that they can afford it. Indeed, for our 30 northern states, the average decennial state spending–state income correlation is a rather imposing .80. For complex reasons, state income also correlates with opinion liberalism.[7] Clearly we should check whether the observed ideology–spending correlations are "spurious" due to both variables correlating with income. Therefore, controlling for state income is in order. However, when both state ideology and state wealth compete within the same equation, state ideology is disadvantaged by its measurement error. One does not know for sure how much the independent "effect" of state income actually reflects an income effect and how much it represents state ideology.[8]

Table 9.7 presents the multivariate welfare/education spending equations, 1940 to 1990, for 30 northern states. Spending is predicted as a function of per capita income at the time plus each measure of state opinion liberalism, entered separately.[9] Look first at the equations predicting 1980 and 1990 spending from 1980 income and *contemporary* state ide-

---

7. Wealthy states are liberal largely because urbanism makes a state wealthy and urbanism attracts liberals. See Chapter 3. Urbanism does not show an independent effect on state spending, once state income is taken into account.

8. One bit of evidence that income stands for liberalism is that the contemporary measure of state ideology is more strongly correlated with state income, both past and present, than are the more error-prone historical measures. Also, the historical measures of ideology become increasingly correlated with income when smaller states are culled.

9. We employ *per capita* income here instead of median income, because only per capita income is available for all six decades of our analysis. For 1990, the measure of per capita income is actually for 1988.

Table 9.7. *Regressing state welfare/education spending on state income and state ideology, 1940-90, for 30 northern states*

Welfare/ education spending	Per capita income	State Ideology			Adjusted R^2
		Prewar	Postwar	Contemporary	
1940	.78***	.26**			.830
	.84***		.07		.776
	.99***			.12	.777
1950	.66***	.32**			.685
	.67***		.32**		.681
	.70***			.13	.600
1960	.76***	.25*			.758
	.76***		.18		.729
	.76***			.13	.709
1970	.79***	.19			.749
	.80***		.10		.721
	.64***			.29*	.749
1980	.56***	.37**			.542
	.57***		.33*		.514
	.35*			.51**	.598
1990	.75***	.22			.666
	.73***		.15		.638
	.39*			.53**	.735

Note: Per capita income is measured for the census year of the spending measure. Coefficients are standardized regression coefficients.
*Significant at .05; **significant at .01; ***significant at .001 level.

ology. Since it contains little error, our measure of contemporary ideology dominates state income as a predictor of 1980 and 1990 welfare/ education spending, although both ideology and income are statistically significant. For all other comparisons, state income is the dominant variable, but the effect of ideology shows through if a timely measure is used. For instance, contemporary state ideology fails to predict earlier spending. Similarly, prewar ideology predicts earlier spending far better than 1980 or 1990 spending. In general, the closer together the ideology and the spending readings are in time, the stronger the ideology "effect." Postwar ideology presents the most disappointing performance, but with a timely significant "effect" for 1950 spending.

These results hint of an underlying dynamic process, with current state ideology affecting spending both now and, at a decaying rate, in the future. Coefficients for prewar and postwar ideology are attenuated, however, by the limited quality of the measures. The one best measure of ideology – the contemporary reading – does predict 1980 and 1990 spending at the expense of state wealth as predicted. One can readily imagine that better ideology measures for other years would also dominate the prediction of liberal spending at the time.

To see the role of ideology come to life when measurement error is abated, we can redo our regressions while restricting the sample to the 12 largest northern states. Alternatively, rather than discard cases entirely, we can "weight" the 30 northern states by their sample sizes. Table 9.8 displays the results for these two regressions. The most timely measure of ideology and state income are entered as predictors of welfare/education spending at our six decade readings.

With states weighted by their sample sizes, the standardized regression coefficients give the statistical edge to ideology over income, even for the historical pre–1980 regressions. When the 12 largest northern states are considered together, unweighted, this edge becomes clearer. For all but one equation, for 1940, the better predictor of state spending is the measure of state ideological sentiment.

The causal connection

Our historical analysis relies on a policy measure that reflects policy somewhat narrowly in terms of liberal spending. Measuring policy in terms of spending has been the typical practice of state policy analyses (e.g., Dye, 1966; Sharkansky, 1968; Hofferbert, 1974). Past studies have rightly marveled at the degree to which spending variables correlate with state wealth. It is no wonder that these earlier studies focused on state economic development as perhaps the leading cause of state policies.

What these earlier studies lacked was any direct measure – no matter how weak – of state public opinion. Suppose earlier authors had rigged up some measure of state ideology from Gallup polls like we have done. Suppose also that they had related this measure to measures of liberal spending as we have, with appropriate statistical controls. A straighforward regression of environmental variables along with a weak public opinion measure, based on all the states, would not have revealed any important role for state ideology in the policy process.

To uncover the rather important role of public opinion in these earlier

Table 9.8. *State ideology sample size and the welfare/education spending regressions, 1940-90*

Welfare/ education spending	30 Northern states, weighted by sample size			12 Largest northern states, unweighted		
	Income	Ideology	Adjusted R^2	Income	Ideology	Adjusted R^2
1940 spending. prewar ideology	.67***	.34***	.529	.68***	.41*	.848
1950 spending, combined pre-, postwar ideo.	.48***	.51***	.786	.48*	.52*	.741
1960 spending, postwar ideology	.64***	.33**	.797	.35	.61*	.775
1970 spending, postwar ideology	.60***	.31*	.693	.39	.56*	.701
1980 spending, contemporary ideology	.11	.67***	.549	.17	.59	.415
1990 spending, contemporary ideology	.27	.60**	.664	-.13	.89*	.583

Note: Per capita income is measured for the census year of the spending measure. Coefficients are standardized regression coefficients.
*Significant at .05; **significant at .01; ***significant at .001 level.

years required that we had a clear idea of what we were looking for. In this chapter, we have found an important role for state ideology, but to do so, we needed to incorporate rather massive sectional changes in ideological attachments and were compelled to respect the mischief of measurement error. Particularly, as we culled southern states and then small states, we found considerable evidence that state opinion mattered for the decades prior to 1980. In staking this historical claim, our path was illuminated by the experience of our search for the contemporary period, which under favorable measurement conditions found clear evidence of a strong state ideology–policy connection. On theoretical grounds, it would seem quite likely that if state ideology mattered for one particular time, it would also matter for others.

In conducting this historical search, one hope was to find some clue to the dynamics of policy change. As we measured it in terms of liberal spending, relative positions of the states remained remarkably stable over the decades – as did their easiest predictor, state income. Although we emphasized the fact of change, state ideology also showed a stable component, once the twists of how southern and border state residents relate to ideological labels were taken into account. Thus, the configuration of the state opinion–policy relationship changes little on a decade-to-decade basis. Still, the data show hints of evolutionary cause and effect. As the South yielded its preoccupation with the politics of racial segregation and began to approximate two-party politics, southern and border states edged toward the democratic practice of enjoying policies that reflect public preferences. Also, we see evidence, clear in outline but dim in specifics, that when states change ideologically, policy change may result in fairly short order. State governments respond to state preferences today more than to preferences in decades past.

Appendix: Historical question wording variations Gallup poll, (1937–64)

Ideology: Party referent

A. If there were only two political parties in this country, one for conservatives and one for liberals, which would you join?

     AIPO37 - 0069

B. If there were only two political parties in this country, one for conservatives and one for liberals, which do you think you would join?

     AIPO38 - 0127

C. If these two new parties (one for conservatives and one for liberals) were formed, which one do you think you would join?

     AIPO37 - 0094

D. Which party (one for conservatives and one for liberals) do you think you would like to join?

     AIPO38 - 0118

E. If the Democratic and Republican parties went out of existence, would you join the Conservative or the Liberal Party?

     AIPO38 - 0132

F. If our political parties were reorganized and there was one for conservatives and the other for liberals, which party do you think you would like to join?

     AIPO48 - 0421

G. Suppose there were only two major parties in the United States, one for liberals and one for conservatives, which would you be most likely to prefer?

     AIPO60 - 0630
     AIPO61 - 0649
     AIPO62 - 0665
     AIPO63 - 0677
     AIPO64 - 0694
     AIPO64 - 0702

State opinion over time

Ideology: Self-identification

A. In politics do you regard yourself as a liberal or conservative?
  AIPO38 - 0109
B. In politics, do you consider yourself a radical, a liberal or a conservative?
  AIPO39 - 0161 (Form A)
C. In politics, do you consider yourself a conservative, a liberal or a radical?
  AIPO39 - 0161 (Form B)
D. Do you consider yourself to be a conservative or a liberal in your political views?
  AIPO46 - 0387
E. Taking everything into account, would you say that, in general, you think yourself as a liberal or as a conservative?
  AIPO55 - 0547
  AIPO57 - 0577

Party identification

A. In politics, as of today, do you consider yourself a Republican, Democrat, Socialist, or Independent?
  AIPO46 - 0387
  AIPO48 - 0421
B. In politics, as of today, do you consider yourself a Republican, Democrat, or Independent?
  AIPO54 - 0527
  AIPO54 - 0541
  AIPO55 - 0547
  AIPO57 - 0577
  AIPO61 - 0649
  AIPO62 - 0665
  AIPO63 - 0677
  AIPO64 - 0694
  AIPO64 - 0702

10

Conclusions: Democracy in the American states

This book has argued that public opinion is the dominant influence on policy making in the American states. In this concluding chapter, we summarize our evidence for strong democratic representation in the states, place our findings in the context of the behavioral literature on democratic politics, and discuss the implications for the understanding of representative democracy.

Our story depends on the distillation of policy questions to a single dimension of ideology, what is commonly called liberalism–conservatism. Ideology – whether one dimension or many – does not neatly account for all government policies or all public preferences or even keep its precise meaning from one decade to the next. But the simplification of policy to one ideological dimension provides powerful leverage for understanding the ideological connection between public preferences and government policy in the U.S. states. Representation in the states works not necessarily in terms of government compliance with specific public demands (although this assertion is largely untested) but rather in terms of public opinion controlling the general ideological direction of state policy.

Our project was set in motion by the availability of state-level samples of ideological preference. Aggregation of opinion from the CBS/NYT surveys provided plausible scores for the states in terms of ideological identification plus the important variable of party identification. Given the sample sizes, these measures are highly reliable from a statistical standpoint. Moreover, for the 1976–88 period for which we collected state opinion data, the ideological orderings of state electorates appear extremely stable. States moved around only slightly on the scale of relative Democratic versus Republican partisanship and hardly at all on ideology. This result conveniently allowed us to pool the full accumulated set of respondents for the 1976–88 period without fear of states changing dramatically over the time period.

The patterns of ideology and partisanship we find in the states are not

Conclusions

simple reflections of the demographics of the states. We find that the states have distinct ideological centers of gravity and patterns of partisan attachments that are not attributable simply to the social and economic characteristics with our respondents. The importance of this finding is that it demonstrates that states, as political communities, do have values and traditions that can be measured only with survey research and are explainable in terms of a shared common political culture. State publics are, in a sense, more than the sum of their demographic parts.

Our crucial concern about state-level ideology is the relationship between state opinion and policy. We constructed a policy index composed of eight indicators of the relative liberalism–conservatism of state policies. We found strong observable correlations of .82 for the full set of states and a remarkable .94 for the 11 largest states for which measurement error is minimal. This result holds up in the face of controls for the socioeconomic variables that the state policy literature had insisted dominate the state policy process. Our evidence shows that the apparent statistical power of state socioeconomic variables is largely an illusion. Socioeconomic variables – wealth, education, urbanism – simply reflect the state public's ideological taste. With ideology taken into account, they make little statistical contribution.

Had political scientists known in the 1960s and 1970s that their measurable socioeconomic variables like state wealth were actually proxies for state ideology, research on comparative state politics might have gone a different direction. In light of our current interpretation, earlier research on the importance of socioeconomic (or "environmental") variables is consistent with our claim that state politics does exactly what it is supposed to do in theory – faithfully translate public preferences into broad patterns of policy outcomes.

Parties and elections are the central conduits for mass influence in our model. Our analysis of state party elites illuminates the policy tension between the centrifugal push by party activists toward their "extreme" ideologies and the centripetal pull toward the center by the more moderate electorate. The ideological orientations of state-level political parties are jointly explained by their two, often conflicting constituencies: party activists and the general electorate.

Party positions affect elections largely via their cumulative influence on the state electorate's party identification. In each state, most voters see the Democrats to their left and the Republicans to their right. Voters respond in Downsian fashion to the parties' proximities to the voters' own ideological preferences. Operationally, when the two parties are too liberal for the average voter, the Republican Party gains identifiers; when the parties are too conservative, the Democrats gain.

State partisanship matters considerably in state politics because it is the dominant cause of the parties' relative strengths in the state legislature. State partisanship influences gubernatorial elections too, but to a far lesser degree. Gubernatorial election outcomes start with the normal vote baseline from state partisanship, but they are strongly influenced by the idiosyncratic issues of the specific campaigns.

It is important to note that state-level party identification is not simply a function of the state electorate's liberalism or conservatism. Instead, state partisanship depends on the relative approximation of the two state party positions to the electorate's mean preference on the ideological continuum. This dependence is revealed by the way state partisanship correlates with state-level voting for president, for which the relevant party positions are nationally fixed rather than variable by state. Where state partisanship is skewed Republican by overly liberal parties, presidential voting is more Democratic than one would expect; where state partisanship is skewed Democratic by overly conservative parties, presidential voting is more Republican than one would expect. State partisanship appears to fully incorporate state ideology as well as state party positions: When party positions and state partisanship are controlled, state ideology shows no additional independent effect on state voting at any level.

A key question is whether certain conditions enhance the degree of democratic representation this book describes. Interestingly, the one identifiable variable that statistically divides states in terms of responsiveness is Daniel Elazar's classification of state political subculture as traditionalistic, individualistic, or moralistic. We find the lowest responsiveness of policy to opinion in the traditionalistic (largely southern) states and the highest responsiveness in the individualistic states, where the policy process appears driven by the parties' willingness to accommodate state opinion over activist ideology. For parties in individualistic states, winning seems to dominate ideology. Moralistic states, on the other hand, show parties driven more by their own ideological concerns than by electoral necessity. In moralistic states, the ideological distances between the parties are greater, and legislators appear more faithful to their party programs.

We also investigated whether representation varies across time. Analysis of a collection of Gallup polls from the 1930s to the present revealed considerable change in state electorates' ideologies over the decades, particularly in the South. The meaning of the liberal–conservative distinction – although never precise – evolves over the years with the issues of national politics and the labels elites use to identify their positions on those issues. Southerners, in particular, changed from being relatively liberal before World War II to now quite conservative. This shift was brought about by the intrusion first of race onto the agenda of U.S. politics and then by the more recent social agenda of concerns such as abortion rights, life styles, and law and order.

The most important aspect of our historical investigation is to show that state policy responsiveness is not unique to the 1970s or 1980s. Stretching back to before World War II – and here we stretched our data resources to the limit – we uncovered ample evidence of the opinion-policy connection in the states. When opinion changes (which is not often or much), policy does seem to follow.

Ultimately, our message about representation in the states is a simple one. At the ballot box, state electorates hold a strong control over the ideological direction of policies in their states. In anticipation of this electoral monitoring, state legislatures and other policymakers take public opinion into account when enacting state policy. These means of control are uncertain in any particular application but accumulate to create a striking correlation between the mean ideological preference of state electorates and the mean ideological tendency of state policy.

THE PUZZLE OF REPRESENTATION

The process we describe places responsibility for ideological direction on the shoulders of state electorates. Somehow, state electorates are up for this task. The puzzle is how they exert their control, given what modern political science knows about the limitations of individual voters. Let us briefly review the evidence regarding ideology and the U.S. voter.

Much of what we know about U.S. voters comes from the unfavorable portrait presented by Campbell, Converse, Miller, and Stokes in *The American Voter* (1960) and subsequent work. In the first detailed study of the presidential voters at the national level, *The American Voter* found that few Americans were motivated by policy issues or used the spatial map of the Left–Right ideological continuum for political guidance. They described a largely nonideological electorate that gave shockingly little attention to the policy issues of the campaign, voting largely as a function of long–ingrained party identifications plus reactions to candidate personalities (Campbell et al., 1960). When they looked for the informational basis for representation in congressional elections, Stokes and Miller (1966) found little there either; voters in congressional elections were woefully ill informed. Their findings of citizen ignorance about the policy positions of their congressional candidates became a benchmark documenting citizen failure to meet the apparent standards expected by democratic theory. Perhaps most devastating of all was the discovery that perhaps a meaningful public opinion did not even exist. In an important and influential paper, Converse (1964) argued that a substantial portion of the public responses to survey questions about the issues of the day are really "nonattitudes." And thinking about politics ideologically – so common among political elites – was nearly absent for the mass public. While Converse's work stirred up considerable controversy, it remains difficult, based on the evidence, to challenge the accuracy of his general portrait of the average citizen as someone with little interest in or information about politics.

Subsequent survey research suggests a greater public facility with the ideological language of liberalism versus conservatism and a greater degree of ideologically motivated voting than *The American Voter* authors were initially willing to credit. But even taking into account the updated evidence, ideology activates no more than a minority even in the most heated of campaigns (see, e.g., Nie, Verba, and Petrocik, 1979; Knight, 1985). And no evidence has surfaced to doubt *The American Voter*'s general portrait of an inattentive electorate. In terms of the strong expectations of democratic theory, the accumulation of evidence from survey research only reinforces the now familiar image of the average voter as inadequate for the task assigned by democratic theory: to serve as the engine of representative democracy.

Our special challenge is to reconcile the limited political capabilities of individual citizens, which we know from survey research, with the strong linkage between state electorates' ideological preferences and the ideological direction of their states' policies. How can voters who are individually uninformed and inactive manage collectively to achieve such levels of policy responsiveness from government? One's initial assumption is likely to be that if most individuals are inattentive, poorly informed, and given to vote on the basis of image and candidate familiarity rather than on issues, then the quality of collective decisions must be similarly impoverished. But this pessimistic conclusion does not follow. The correct answer is that the quality of an electorate's collective decision can be greater than the individual decision processes of the citizens who make up the electorate. Let us examine how this happens.

With his "jury theorem," Condorcet (1785) was the first to articulate the powers of aggregation in the electoral context. When individuals hold disparate beliefs regarding some truth, most individual perceptions must necessarily be incorrect. Yet under plausible conditions, as a group these individuals will arrive at the appropriate answer with remarkable consistency (Feld and Grofman, 1988; Grofman and Owen, 1986; Miller, 1986). They do so because errors cancel out. In this way, the collective political intelligence and attentiveness of an electorate can exceed that which one would infer from knowledge of individuals' survey responses.

One context in which this process can be clearly seen is the public's evaluation of economic performance. Consider the contrast between the

Conclusions

macrolevel and microlevel analysis of economic conditions and voting behavior. At the macrolevel, when they vote or even pass judgment on the president's performance, the citizenry responds rationally and predictably to even relatively slight changes in the economy. On the other hand, the microbases for such clear aggregate patterns are obscure and difficult to find. Perceptions of the economy, generally accurate in the aggregate, are woefully ignorant among individuals (Conover, Feldman, and Knight, 1987).

Consider the contrast between the macrolevel and microlevel analysis of policy representation in Congress. Studies of congressional voters show that individuals are generally vague at best regarding the ideological record of their congressmember or senator. One might infer, then, that where congressional candidates stand ideologically has little bearing on their electoral success. However, as errors cancel at the macrolevel, constituencies' mean perception of representative ideology correlates quite strongly with objective measures of representative ideology, such as the ratings by ideological groups (Erikson, 1981, 1990). The result is that constituency-level congressional elections are often decided by the relative ideological proximity of candidates to constituencies (Erikson and Wright, 1980, 1993).

Impressive also is the evidence from experimental studies of voting under various degrees of voter information (McKelvey and Ordeshook 1986, 1990). Deficiencies in information do very little to affect electoral outcomes. Well-informed and poorly informed experimental electorates appear to make about the same kinds of collective decisions, each approximating the Downsian outcome of selecting the more proximate candidate, where that criterion is applicable.

The lesson is an important one. What we learn about individuals in terms of their lack of political sophistication does not apply fully to electorates. Lack of political concern within the citizenry does not mean politicians can treat electorates as though voters are fools. That many people cannot articulate their detailed issue preferences and cannot report accurately where their elected officials stand on issues does not mean that legislators can do whatever they want in the policy arena. Public opinion as an entity is a more sophisticated, stable, and reasonable force than we could ever guess from looking at the political attitudes and knowledge of individual citizens.

The key is what Converse (1990, 383) termed the "miracle of aggregation." When we aggregate across individual respondents identified by socially heterogeneous characteristics, such as social class, regions, race, religion, or for us, the state of residence, response patterns of the aggregate are more clearly defined and generally better behaved than are their individual-level counterparts. As measured in surveys, one finds considerable noise in the measurement of individual ideology positions or – even harder – perceptions of the ideological positions of political actors or political parties. They contain errors due to genuine individual confusion, idiosyncratic interpretations of the questions, the context of the interview (both in its immediate surroundings and in the larger sociopolitical context of the moment), and other sources. This individual error, which often dominates in analyses of survey data, cancels out in the aggregation process. We may consider any response to a survey being constituted by two parts: the real signal and noise, which is error from such multiple potential sources as those just mentioned. With individual data, the signal-to-noise ratio is frequently very low, so much so that analysts frequently see noise as the dominant feature of the survey response. At the macrolevel, this random noise cancels out so that upon aggregation the signal-to-noise ratio is much more favorable.

The idea is simple but important. Because people have some idea of their interests and some idea of where candidates and the parties stand, as a group they can make much "better" decisions than they do as individuals. Even when many citizens mistakenly vote for the "wrong" candidate (in the sense that with a lot more information and study, they would vote differently), such errors will tend to cancel out so that in the end the full electorate will often behave very much, although not exactly, as it would have had individuals had much better information and were less error prone in their decision making.

We do not want to overstate the powers of aggregation here. It remains entirely possible for politicians to successfully misrepresent themselves to majorities of the electorate. Aggregation will mitigate the problems due to idiosyncratic or random error in voter perceptions and decisions, but it does not lessen the effects of effective and deceptive appeals to voters' values. The only protection here is that elections are periodic and the electorate can therefore change its decisions. Thus, even if occasionally mistaken, public opinion remains important, indeed vital, as long as we can assume that "you cannot fool all the people all the time."

Aggregation gain

In the process we describe, aggregation works to connect state opinion to state policy, with both variables condensed to a point in a single dimension of ideological space. So far, the gain from aggregation is restricted to the signal that comes through when preferences, perceptions, or votes are measured at the group rather than individual level. For the study of representation in the states, we profit from additional aggregation processes as well.

Aggregating over issue preferences. Implicitly, one's net ideological preference is an aggregation over a variety of concerns. When asked whether

Conclusions

they are liberal, moderate, or conservative, respondents must take into account their positions across numerous issues, as well as affective reactions to groups and ideologically known leaders (Conover and Feldman, 1981; Carmines and Kuklinski, 1990). Thus, self-identified ideology is already a summary response, and studies frequently find individual vote choices are more strongly related to this summary measure than to specific issues.

Aggregating over time. We also aggregate over time. If there are temporally fluctuating aspects to ideological self-identification, these would tend to cancel out for our state electorates in our summary measure. The clarity of issue choices in an election does influence the impact of ideology, and this, of course, varies over time and across campaigns (Page, 1978; Nie, Verba, and Petrocik, 1979; Wright and Berkman, 1986). This aggregation over time should help to even out short-term variations in underlying state ideological preferences.

Aggregating over constituencies. Our analysis also entails a tremendous aggregation over constituencies. For a study of dyadic representation (the relationship between the legislator and his or her district), it is most appropriate to sample opinion at the district level. Of course, our respondents are sampled and aggregated to the state level, not at the level of the individual state legislative district. This process squeezes additional noise out of the representational relationship. Certainly, if we could measure the process accurately, we would find that more liberal state legislative districts manage to elect, on average, more liberal state legislators. Such a relationship becomes even stronger when aggregated to the state level, as it has been here, than if we had investigated the same relationship at the district level. The "errors" of representation with some state legislators being too liberal and others somewhat too conservative for their districts should tend to cancel out across a full legislature, so that the whole is more representative than the individual parts.

Aggregation across policy outcomes. Finally, we have aggregated across policies. Our main analysis has examined our composite measure of state policy liberalism, which is made of up eight different state policies. The overall index tends to perform better in our analysis than do the individual components, although each of them bears a modest relationship with state opinion.

It takes these multiple aggregations to obtain the evidence of a strong ideological connection between opinion and policy in the states, plus the evidence of the partisan and electoral behavior that produces it. The argument is not that public opinion always triumphs or anything close to that. We argue instead that when it comes to the general ideological direction of a state's policy making, the ideological preferences of the state electorate is the dominant guiding force. Put another way, the simple logic of democratic electoral politics constrains the ideological tendency of state policy to stay within the fairly narrow channels defined by the state public's specific ideological tastes.

DEMOCRACY AND REPRESENTATION IN THE STATES

Public opinion, as it operates in the political arena, is a collective, not an individual, phenomena. Democratic theorists often write of public opinion as a collective entity – of the "will of the people" or the reactions of "the public" to new political events. With the availability of a wealth of survey data, political scientists, however, have generally addressed questions about public opinion by trying to explain individual opinion formation and change rather than by making "electorates" their units of analysis. An unfortunate by-product of this emphasis on the individual over the aggregate has been the disconnection of the study of mass behavior from the larger body of democratic theory and from the study of political institutions and policy making. Scholars who study the individual citizen often describe the typical voter as unfit for the job prescribed by versions of democratic theory that stress popular control of government. As we have pointed out, the dynamics and properties of collective opinion are fundamentally different from those of individual opinion. For citizens as a group, opinion is better informed, more perceptive, and more stable than for individuals. Moreover, forces that move collective opinion in unmistakable ways at the macrolevel are often but a faint whisper, all but inaudible in the noisy data of individual-level survey responses.

Let us add a caveat here so that we do not overstate our argument. We see public opinion in much the same way as V. O. Key (1961, chap. 21) when he wrote about public preferences forming "opinion dikes" within which activists and elected officials may act. Public opinion, in this perspective, seldom "demands" much, nor does it speak with a clear voice. Rather, it sets the boundaries that rational politicians seek to learn and then heed. Within these dikes, or areas of discretion, many of the more visible aspects of day-to-day political life in the states have their influence. Party and electoral elites work to define agendas and define issues; interest groups work for leverage and favor; and the major presence of the national government with its imposing rules and constraints limits the options and offers opportunities in many policy areas.

We do not assert that policy making in the states is determined by state opinion exclusively or with unerring fidelity. Only the most naive version of democratic theory would argue for such a simple equation between citizen preferences and government action. Our claim is more modest: We assert that public opinion does have a strong influence on general patterns of state policy – the correspondence is strong, but we do not claim any one-to-one fidelity.

Conclusions

In our view, the appropriate message is that even under adverse conditions such as the limited interest and information that the average voter has regarding state politics, public opinion can be observed to influence state policy. This statement is cautiously worded, but it presents an optimistic message. If public opinion matters under adverse conditions, certainly it could influence policy even more if state publics were given greater informational opportunities. We may also speculate that a more informed public would be more cognizant of its political interest. If even weakly informed state publics influence policy, one can imagine the progress in state-level democracy if citizens were more fully capable of performing the task of governing that is assigned them by democratic theory.

References

Abramowitz, Alan I. 1988. "Explaining Senate Elections Outcomes." *American Political Science Review* 82: 385–403.

Aldrich, John H. 1983. "A Downsian Spatial Model with Party Activism." *American Political Science Review* 77: 974–90.

Almond, Gabriel, and Sidney Verba. 1963. *The Civic Culture: Political Attitudes and Democracy in Five Nations.* Princeton, N.J.: Princeton University Press.

Alt, James E. 1985. "Political Parties, World Demand, and Unemployment: Domestic and International Sources of Economic Activity." *American Political Science Review* 79: 1016–40.

Backstrom, Charles H. 1977. "Congress and the Public: How Representative Is One of the Other?" *American Politics Quarterly* 5: 411–35.

Baer, Denise L., and David A. Bositis. 1988. *Elite Cadres and Party Coalitions: Representing the Public in Party Politics.* New York: Greenwood.

Beck, Nathaniel. 1982. "Parties, Administrations, and American Macroeconomic Outcomes." *American Political Science Review* 76: 83–93.

Black, Earl, and Merle Black. 1988. *Politics and Society in the South.* Cambridge, Mass.: Harvard University Press, 1987.

Black, Merle, David M. Kovenock, and William C. Reynolds. 1974. *Political Attitudes in the Nation and the States.* Chapel Hill, N.C.: Institute for Research in the Social Science.

Boles, Janet K. 1979. *The Politics of the Equal Rights Amendment.* New York: Longman.

Brady, David W. 1988. *Critical Elections and Congressional Policymaking.* Stanford, Calif.: Stanford University Press.

Browning, Robert X. 1985. "Presidents, Congress, and Policy Outcomes: U.S. Social Welfare Expenditures, 1949–1977." *American Journal of Political Science* 29: 197–216.

Browning, Robert X., and William R. Shaffer. 1987. "Leaders and Followers in a Strong Party State." *American Politics Quarterly* 15: 87–106.

Bullock, Charles S., and David W. Brady. 1983. "Party, Constituency, and Roll-Call Voting in the U.S. Senate." *Legislative Studies Quarterly* 8: 29–43.

Burnham, Walter Dean. 1970. *Critical Elections and the Mainsprings of American Politics.* New York: Norton.

Burstein, Paul. 1981. "The Sociology of Democratic Politics and Government." In Ralph H. Turner and James F. Short, Jr., eds. *Annual Review of Sociology,* vol. 7, pp. 291–319. Palo Alto, Calif.: Annual Reviews, Inc.

References

Calvert, Randall L. 1985. "Robustness of the Multidimensional Voting Model: Candidate Motivations, Uncertainty and Convergence." *American Journal of Political Science* 29: 69–95.

Cameron, David C. 1978. "The Expansion of the Public Economy: A Comparative Analysis." *American Political Science Review* 72: 1243–61.

Campbell, Angus. 1966. "Surge and Decline: A Study of Electoral Change." In Campbell et al., *Elections and the Political Order,* pp. 40–62. New York: Wiley, 1966.

Campbell, Angus, Philip E. Converse, Warren E. Miller, and Donald E. Stokes. 1960. *The American Voter.* New York: Wiley.

1966. *Elections and the Political Order.* New York: Wiley.

Cantril, Hadley. 1951. *Public Opinion, 1935–46.* Princeton, N.J.: Princeton University Press.

Carmines, Edward G., and James H. Kuklinski. 1990. "Incentives, Opportunities, and the Logic of Public Opinion in American Political Representation." In John A. Ferejohn and James H. Kuklinski (eds.), *Information and Democratic Processes,* pp. 240–68. Urbana: University of Illinois Press.

Carmines, Edward G., and James A. Stimson. 1989. *Issue Evolution: Race and the Transformation of American Politics.* Princeton, N.J.: Princeton University Press.

Carmines, Edward G., and Richard A. Zeller. 1979. *Reliability and Validity Assessment.* Beverly Hills, Calif.: Sage.

Castles, Francis G. 1982. "Politics and Public Policy." In Francis G. Castles (ed.), *The Impact of Parties on Public Expenditures,* pp. 21–96. Beverly Hills, Calif.: Sage.

Clubb, Jerome M., William H. Flanigan, and Nancy H. Zingale. 1980. *Partisan Realignment: Voters, Parties, and Government in American History.* Beverly Hills, Calif.: Sage.

Committee on Political Parties of the American Political Science Association. 1950. "Toward a More Responsible Two-Party System." *American Political Science Review* 44: Supplement.

Condorcet, Marquis de. 1785. *Essai sur l'application de l'analyse a la probabilite des decisions rendues la pluralit des voix.* Paris: Imprimerie Royale.

Conover, Pamela J., and Stanley Feldman. 1981. "The Origins and Meaning of Liberal/Conservative Self-Identifications." *American Journal of Political Science* 25: 617–45.

Conover, Pamela J., Stanley Feldman, and Kathleen Knight. 1987. "The Personal and Political Underpinnings of Economic Forecasts." *American Journal of Political Science* 31: 559–83.

Converse, Jean M., and Howard Schuman. 1984. "The Manner of Inquiry: An Analysis of Survey Question Form Across Organizations and Over Time." In C. F. Turner and E. Martin (eds.), *Surveying Subjective Phenomena.* Vol. 2, pp. 283–316. New York: Russell Sage Foundation.

Converse, Philip E. 1964. "The Nature of Belief Systems Among Mass Publics." In David Apter (ed.), *Ideology and Discontent,* pp. 206–61. New York: Free Press.

1966. "The Concept of the Normal Vote." In Campbell et al., *Elections and the Political Order,* pp. 9–39. New York: Wiley.

1975. "Public Opinion and Voting Behavior." In Fred I. Greenstein and Nelson W. Polsby (eds.), *Handbook of Social Science,* vol. 4., pp. 75–169. Reading, Mass.: Addison-Wesley.

References

1990. "Popular Representation and the Distribution of Information," In John A. Ferejohn and James H. Kuklinski (eds.), *Information and Democratic Processes*, pp. 369–90. Urbana: University of Illinois Press.

Cook, Thomas D., and Donald T. Campbell. 1979. *Quasi-Experimentation: Design and Analysis Issues for Field Settings*. Chicago: Rand McNally.

Cotter, Cornelius, James Gibson, John Bibby, and Robert Huckshorn. 1984. *Party Organizations in American Politics*. New York: Praeger.

Council of State Governments. 1982. *The Book of the States, 1982*. Lexington, Ky.

David, Paul T. 1972. *Party Strength in the American States, 1872–1970*. Charlottesville: University of Virginia Press.

Dawson, Richard E., and James A. Robinson. 1963. "Inter-Party Competition, Economic Variables, and Welfare Policies in the American States." *Journal of Politics* 25: 265–89.

Dennis, Jack. 1978. "Trends in Public Support for the American Party System." In Jeff Fishel (ed.), *Parties and Elections in an Anti-Party Age*. Bloomington: Indiana University Press.

Downs, Anthony. 1957. *An Economic Theory of Democracy*. New York: Harper.

Dye, Thomas R. 1966. *Politics, Economics, and the Public: Political Outcomes in the American States*. Chicago: Rand McNally.

1979. "Politics vs. Economics. The Development of the Literature on Policy Determinism." *Policy Studies Journal* 7: 652–62.

1984. "Party and Policy in the States." *Journal of Politics* 46: 1097–116.

1990. *American Federalism: Competition Among Governments*. Lexington, Mass.: Lexington Books.

Elazar, Daniel. 1966. *American Federalism: A View from the States*. New York: Crowell.

1970. *Cities of the Prairie: The Metropolitan Frontier and American Politics*. New York: Basic.

1972. *American Federalism: A View from the States*. 2d ed. New York: Crowell.

Enelow, James M., and Melvin J. Hinich. 1984. *The Spatial Theory of Voting: An Introduction*. New York: Cambridge University Press.

Erikson, Robert S. 1981. "Measuring Constituency Opinion: The 1978 U.S. Congressional Election Survey." *Legislative Studies Quarterly* 6: 235–46.

1990. "Roll Calls, Reputations, and Representation in the U.S. Senate." *Legislative Studies Quarterly* 15: 623–42.

Erikson, Robert S., and David W. Romero. 1990. "Candidate Equilibrium and the Behavioral Model of the Vote." *American Political Science Review* 84: 1103–26.

Erikson, Robert S., Norman R. Luttbeg, and Kent L. Tedin. 1991. *American Public Opinion: Its Origins, Content and Impact*, 4th ed. New York: Macmillan.

Erikson, Robert S., and Gerald C. Wright, Jr. 1980. "Policy Representation of Constituency Interests." *Political Behavior* 2: 91–106.

1993. "Voters, Candidates and Issues in Congressional Elections." In Lawrence C. Dodd and Bruce I. Oppenheimer (eds.), *Congress Reconsidered*, 5th ed. pp. 91–115. Washington: Congressional Quarterly Press.

Feld, Scott L. and Bernard Grofman. 1988. "Ideological Consistency as a Collective Phenomena." *American Political Science Review* 82: 773–88.

Fenton, John H. 1957. *Politics in the Border States*. New Orleans: Hauser.

1966. *Midwest Politics*. New York: Holt, Rinehart and Winston.

References

Fitzpatrick, Jody L. and Rodney E. Hero. "Political Cultures and Political Characteristics of the American States." *Western Political Quarterly* 41: 145–53.

Frankel, Martin R., and Lester R. Frankel. 1987. "Fifty Years of Survey Sampling in the United States." *Public Opinion Quarterly* 51: S127–S138.

Gallup, George. 1948. *A Guide to Public Opinion Polls.* Princeton, N.J.: Princeton University Press. Revised edition.

Gallup, George (ed.), 1972. *The Gallup Poll: Public Opinion, 1935–1971.* New York: Random House.

Garand, James C. 1985. "Partisan Change and Shifting Expenditure Priorities in the American States, 1945–1978." *American Politics Quarterly* 13: 355–91.

Glenn, Norval D. 1975. "Trend Studies with Available Data: Opportunities and Pitfalls." In J. C. Southwick (ed.), *Survey Data for Trend Analysis: An Index to Repeated Questions in U. S. National Surveys Held by the Roper Public Opinion Research Center,* pp. 16–150. Williamstown, Mass.: Roper.

Glenn, Norval D., and W. Parker Frisbie. 1977. "Trend Studies with Survey Sample and Census Data." *Annual Review of Sociology* 3: 79–104.

Godwin, R. Kenneth, and W. Bruce Shepard. 1976. "Political Process and Public Expenditures: A Re-Examination Based on Theories of Representative Government." *American Political Science Review* 70: 1127–35.

Goodin, Robert E. 1983. "Voting Through the Looking Glass." *American Political Science Review* 77: 420–34.

Gray, Virginia. 1973. "Innovation in the States: A Diffusion Study." *American Political Science Review* 67: 1174–85.

Grofman, Bernard, and Guillermo Owen. 1986. "Condorcet Models: Avenues for Future Research." In Grofman and Owen (eds.), *Information Pooling and Group Decision Making,* pp. 93–102 Greenwich, Conn.: JAI.

Hanson, Russell L. 1983. "The 'Content' of Welfare Policy: The State and Aid to Families with Dependent Children." *Journal of Politics* 45: 771–85.

1984. "Medicaid and the Politics of Redistribution." *American Journal of Political Science* 28: 313–39.

Hayes, Susan W., and Jeff Stonecash. 1981. "The Source of Public Policy: Welfare Policy in the American States." *Policy Studies Journal* 9: 681–98.

Hero, Alfred O., Jr. 1969. "Liberalism–Conservatism Revisited: Foreign vs. Domestic Federal Policies, 1937–1967." *Public Opinion Quarterly* 33: 399–408.

Hibbs, Douglas A. 1977. "Political Parties and Macroeconomic Policy." *American Political Science Review* 71: 1467–87.

1987. *The American Political Economy: Macroeconomic Politics in the United States.* Cambridge, Mass.: Harvard University Press.

Hicks, Alexander, and Duane Swank. 1984. "On the Political Economy of Welfare Expansion." *Comparative Political Studies* 17: 81–119.

Hofferbert, Richard. 1966. "The Relationship Between Public Policy and Some Structural and Environmental Variables." *American Political Science Review* 60: 73–82.

1968. "Socioeconomic Dimensions of the American States: 1890–1960." *Midwest Journal of Political Science* 12: 401–18.

1972. "State and Community Policy Studies: A Review of Comparative Input–Output Analyses." In James A. Robinson (ed.), *Political Science Annual,* vol. 3, pp. 3–72. Indianapolis: Bobbs-Merrill.

1974. *The Study of Public Policy.* Indianapolis: Bobbs-Merrill.

References

Holbrook-Provow, Thomas M. 1987. "National Factors in Gubernatorial Elections." *American Politics Quarterly* 15: 471–83.

Hotelling, Harold. 1929. "Stability in Competition." *The Economics Journal* 39: 41–57.

Huckfeldt, R. Robert. 1979. "Political Participation and the Neighborhood Social Context." *American Journal of Political Science* 23: 579–92.

1984. "Political Loyalties and Social Class Ties: The Mechanisms of Contextual Influence." *American Journal of Political Science* 28: 399–417.

Jackman, Robert W. 1975. *Politics and Social Equality, A Comparative Analysis.* New York: Wiley.

1980. "Socialist Parties and Income Inequality: A Comparative Analysis." *Journal of Politics* 42: 135–49.

Jacob, Herbert, and Michael Lipsky. 1968. "Outputs, Structure, and Power: An Assessment of Changes in the Study of State and Local Politics." *Journal of Politics* 30: 510–38.

Jacobson, Gary C. 1990. *The Electoral Origins of Divided Government.* Boulder, Colo.: Westview.

Jennings, Edward. 1979. "Competition, Constituencies, and Welfare Policies in the American States." *American Political Science Review* 73: 414–29.

Jewell, Malcolm E. 1980. "State Polls." *Comparative State Politics Newsletter* 1: 14–19.

1982. "The Neglected World of State Politics." *Journal of Politics* 44: 638–57.

Jewell, Malcolm E., and David M. Olson. 1988. *Political Parties and Elections in American States.* 3rd ed. Chicago: Dorsey.

Johnson, Douglas W., Paul R. Picard, and Bernard Quinn (eds.). 1974. *Church and Church Membership in the United States.* Washington: Glenmary Research Center.

Jones, Ruth S., and Warren E. Miller. 1984. "State Polls: Promising Data Sources for Political Research." *Journal of Politics* 46: 1182–92.

Joslyn, Richard A. 1980. "Manifestations of Elazar's Political Cultures: State Public Opinion and the Content of Political Campaign Advertising." *Publius: The Journal of Federalism* 10: 37–58.

Kenney, Patrick J. 1983. "The Effect of State Economic Conditions on the Vote for Governor." *Social Science Quarterly* 64: 154–62.

Kenney, Patrick J., and Tom W. Rice. 1983. "Popularity and the Vote: The Gubernatorial Case." *American Politics Quarterly* 11: 237–41.

Key, V. O. 1949. *Southern Politics: In State and Nation.* New York: Knopf.

1961. *Public Opinion and American Democracy.* New York: Knopf.

Kiewiet, D. Roderick, and Mathew D. McCubbins. 1985. "Congressional Appropriations and the Electoral Connection." *Journal of Politics* 47: 59–82.

Kinder, Donald E. 1983. "Diversity and Complexity in American Public Opinion." In Ada W. Finifter (ed.), *Political Science: The State of the Discipline,* pp. 389–25. Washington: American Political Science Association.

Kirkpatrick, Jeanne J. 1976. *The New Presidential Elite.* New York: Russell Sage Foundation.

Kish, Leslie. 1965. *Survey Sampling.* New York: Wiley.

Klingman, David, and William W. Lammers. 1984. "The 'General Policy Liberalism' Factor in American State Politics." *American Journal of Political Science* 28: 598–610.

Knight, Kathleen. 1985. "Ideology and the 1980 Election: Ideological Sophistication Does Matter." *Journal of Politics* 47: 828–53.

References

Kweit, Mary. 1986. "Ideological Congruence Among Party Switchers and Non-switchers: The Case of Party Activists." *American Journal of Political Science* 30: 184–96.

Ladd, Everett Carll, Jr., with Charles D. Hadley, Jr. 1978. *Transformations of the American Party System: Political Coalitions from the New Deal to the 1970s.* New York: Norton. Revised edition.

Lange, Peter, and Geoffrey Garrett. 1985. "The Politics of Growth: Strategic Interaction and Economic Performance in Advanced Industrial Democracies." *Journal of Politics* 47: 792–827.

LeBlanc, Hugh L. 1969. "Voting in State Senates: Party and Constituency Influences." *Midwest Journal of Political Science* 13: 33–57.

Lockard, Duane. 1959. *New England State Politics.* Princeton, N.J.: Princeton University Press.

Lott, John R. Jr., and Michael L. Davis. 1992. "A Critical Review and an Extension of the Political Shirking Literature." *Public Choice* 74: 461–84.

Lowery, David. 1985. "The Keynesian and Political Determinants of Unbalanced Budgets: U.S. Fiscal Policy from Eisenhower to Reagan." *American Journal of Political Science* 29: 428–60.

———. 1987. "The Distribution of Tax Burdens in the American States: The Determination of Fiscal Incidence." *Western Political Quarterly* 40: 137–58.

Lowery, David, and Lee Sigelman. 1982. "Political Culture and State Public Policy: The Missing Link." *Western Political Quarterly* 35: 376–84.

Lowery, David, Virginia Gray, and Gregory Hager. 1989. "Public Opinion and Policy Change in the American States." *American Politics Quarterly* 17: 3–31.

MacKuen, Michael B., Robert S. Erikson, and James A. Stimson. 1992. "Question Wording and Macropartisanship." *American Political Science Review* 86: 475–81.

Magleby, David B. 1984. *Direct Legislation: Voting on Ballot Propositions in the United States.* Baltimore: Johns Hopkins University Press.

Mann, Thomas E. 1978. *Unsafe at any Margin: Interpreting Congressional Elections.* Washington: American Enterprise Institute.

McClosky, Herbert, Paul J. Hoffman, and Rosemary O'Hara. 1960. "Issue Conflict and Consensus Among Party Leaders and Followers." *American Political Science Review* 54: 406–27.

McKelvey, Richard D., and Peter C. Ordeshook. 1986. "Information, Electoral Equilibria, and the Democratic Ideal." *Journal of Politics* 48: 909–37.

———. 1990. "Information and Elections: Retrospective Voting and Rational Expectations." In John A. Ferejohn and James H. Kuklinski (eds.), *Information and Democratic Processes*, 281–312. Urbana: University of Illinois Press.

Miller, Nicholas. 1986. "Information, Electorates, and Democracy: Some Extensions and Interpretations of the Condorcet Jury Theorem." In Bernard Grofman and Guillermo Owen (eds.) *Information Pooling and Group Decision Making*, pp. 173–92. Greenwich, Conn.: JAI.

Miller, Warren E. and M. Kent Jennings. 1986. *Parties in Transition: A Longitudinal Study of Party Elites and Supporters.* New York: Russell Sage Foundation.

Miller, Warren E., and Donald E. Stokes. 1963. "Constituency Influence in Congress." *American Political Science Review* 57: 45–56.

Monroe, Alan. 1979. "Consistency Between Constituency Preferences and National Policy Decisions." *American Politics Quarterly* 7:3–19.

References

Moon, Bruce E., and William J. Dixon. 1985. "Politics, the State, and Basic Human Needs: A Cross-national Study." *American Journal of Political Science* 29: 661–94.

Morehouse, Sarah McCally. 1981. *State Politics, Parties, and Policy.* New York: Holt, Rinehart, and Winston.

Nardulli, Peter. 1990. "Political Subcultures in the American States: An Empirical Examination of Elazar's Formulation." *American Politics Quarterly* 18: 287–315.

Nelson, Douglas, and Eugene Silberberg. 1987. "Ideology and Legislative Shirking." *Econometric Inquiry* 25: 15–25.

Nice, David C. 1983. "Representation in the States: Policymaking and Ideology." *Social Science Quarterly* 64: 404–11.

Nie, Norman H., Sidney Verba, and John R. Petrocik. 1979. *The Changing American Voter.* Cambridge, Mass.: Harvard University Press. Revised edition.

Page, Benjamin I. 1978. *Choices and Echoes in Presidential Elections.* Chicago: University of Chicago Press.

Page, Benjamin I., and Robert Shapiro. 1992. *The Rational Public.* Chicago: University of Chicago Press.

Patterson, Samuel C. 1968. "The Political Cultures of the American States." *Journal of Politics* 30: 187–209.

Patterson, Samuel C., and Gregory A. Caldiera. 1983. "Getting Out the Vote: Participation in Gubernatorial Elections." *American Political Science Review* 77: 675–89.

Peltzman, Sam. 1984. "Constituent Interest and Congressional Voting." *Journal of Law and Economics* 27: 181–210.

Peters, John G., and Susan Welch. 1978. "Political Corruption and Political Culture." *American Politics Quarterly* 6: 345–56.

Phares, Donald. 1980. *Who Pays State and Local Taxes?* Cambridge, Mass.: Oelgeschalager, Gunn, and Hain.

Plotnick, Robert D., and Richard F. Winters. 1985. "A Politico-economic Theory of Income Redistribution." *American Political Science Review* 79: 458–73.

Pool, Ithiel de Sola, Robert P. Abelson, and Samuel Popkin. 1965. *Candidates, Issues, and Strategies.* Cambridge, Mass.: MIT Press.

Poole, Keith T., and Howard Rosenthal. 1984. "The Polarization of American Politics." *Journal of Politics* 46: 1061–79.

Rabinowitz, George, Paul Henry Gurian, and Stuart Elain McDonald. 1984. "The Structure of Presidential Elections and the Process of Realignment, 1944 to 1980." *American Journal of Political Science* 27: 611–35.

Ranney, Austin. 1971. "Parties in State Politics." In Herbert Jacob and Kenneth Vines (eds.), *Politics in the American States.* 2d ed., pp. 82–121. Boston: Little, Brown.

——— 1976. "Parties in State Politics," in Herbert Jacob and Kenneth Vines (eds.), *Politics in the American States.* 3rd ed., pp. 51–92. Boston: Little, Brown.

Ranney, Austin, and Willmore Kendall. 1954. "The American Party System." *American Political Science Review* 48: 477–85.

Rosten, Leo (ed.). 1975. *Religion in America.* New York: Simon and Schuster.

Rotunda, Ronald D. 1986. *The Politics of Language: Liberalism as Word and Symbol.* Iowa City: University of Iowa Press.

Savage, Robert L. 1981. "Looking for Political Subcultures: A Rummage Sale Approach." *Western Political Quarterly* 34: 331–36.

References

Schattsneider, E. E. 1942. *Party Government*. New York: Holt, Rinehart and Winston.

Schiltz, Timothy D., and R. Lee Rainey. 1978. "The Geographical Distribution of Elazar's Political Subcultures Among the American Public: A Research Note." *Western Political Quarterly* 35: 410–15.

Schwarz, John E., and Barton Fenmore. 1977. "Presidential Election Results and Congressional Roll Call Behavior: The Case of 1964, 1968 and 1972." *Legislative Studies Quarterly* 2: 409–22.

Schwarz, John E., Barton Fenmore, and Thomas Volgy. 1980. "Liberal and Conservative Voting in the House of Representatives: A National Model of Representation." *British Journal of Political Science* 10: 317–39.

Seidman, David. 1975. "Simulation of Public Opinion: A Caveat." *Public Opinion Quarterly* 39: 331–42.

Sharkansky, Ira. 1968. *Spending in the American States*. Chicago: Rand McNally. 1969. "The Utility of Elazar's Political Culture." *Polity* 2: 66–83.

Sharkansky, Ira, and Richard I. Hofferbert. 1969. "Dimensions of State Politics, Economics, and Public Policy." *American Political Science Review* 63: 867–79.

Sigelman, Lee, and Roland Smith. 1980. "Consumer Legislation in the American States: An Attempt at Explanation." *Social Science Quarterly* 61: 58–70.

Sinclair, Barbara. 1982. *Congressional Realignment, 1925–1978*. Austin: University of Texas Press.

Smith, Tom W. 1978. "In Search of House Effects: A Comparison of Responses to Various Questions by Different Survey Organizations." *Public Opinion Quarterly* 42: 443–63.

1982. "House Effects and the Reproducibility of Survey Measurements: A Comparison of the 1980 GSS and the 1980 American National Election Study." *Public Opinion Quarterly* 46: 54–68.

1987. "The Art of Asking Questions, 1936–1985." *Public Opinion Quarterly* 51: S95–S108.

Sorauf, Frank J., and Paul Allen Beck. 1988. *Party Politics in America*. 6th ed. Boston: Little, Brown.

Soule, John W., and Wilma E. McGrath. 1975. "A Comparative Study of Presidential Nomination Conventions: The Democrats 1968 and 1972." *American Journal of Political Science* 19: 501–17.

Squire, Peverill. 1989. "Challengers in U.S. Senate Elections." *Legislative Studies Quarterly* 14: 531–47.

Stimson, James A. 1991. *Public Opinion in America: Moods, Cycles, and Swings*. Boulder, Colo.: Westview.

Stipak, Brian, and Carl Hensler. 1982. "Statistical Inference in Contextual Analysis." *American Journal of Political Science* 26: 151–75.

Stokes, Donald E., and Warren E. Miller. 1966. "Party Government and the Salience of Congress." In Campbell et al., *Elections and the Political Order*, pp. 194–216. New York: Wiley.

Sullivan, John L., and Robert E. O'Connor. 1972. "Electoral Choice and Popular Control of Public Policy." *American Political Science Review* 66: 1256–68.

Swansbrough, Robert H., and David M. Brodsky. 1988. *The South's New Politics: Realignment and Dealignment*. Columbia: University of South Carolina Press.

Tindall, George Brown. 1967. *The Emergence of the New South, 1913–1945*. Baton Rouge: Louisiana State University Press.

Tompkins, Mark E. 1984. "The Electoral Fortunes of Gubernatorial Incumbents: 1947–1981." *Journal of Politics* 46: 520–43.

References

Treadway, Jack M. 1985. *Public Policymaking in the States*. New York: Praeger.

Tufte, Edward. 1978. *Political Control of the Economy*. Princeton, N.J.: Princeton University Press.

Turner, Charles F. 1984. "Why Do Surveys Disagree? Some Preliminary Hypotheses and Some Disagreeable Examples." In C. F. Turner and E. Martin (eds.), *Surveying Subjective Phenomena*, vol. 2, pp. 159–214 New York: Russell Sage Foundation.

Uslaner, Eric M. 1978. "Comparative State Policy Formation, Interparty Competition and Malapportionment: A New Look at V. O. Key's Hypothesis." *Journal of Politics* 40: 409–32.

Uslaner, Eric M., and Ronald E. Weber. 1977. *Patterns of Decision Making in State Legislatures*. New York: Praeger.

Van Arnhem, J., M. Corina, and Geurt J. Schotsman. 1982. "Do Parties Affect the Distribution of Income? The Case of Advanced Capitalist Democracies." In Francis D. Castles (ed.), *The Impact of Parties on Public Expenditures*, pp. 283–364. Beverly Hills, Calif.: Sage.

Waksberg, Joseph. 1978. "Sampling Methods for Random Digit Dialing." *Journal of the American Statistical Society* 73: 40–6.

Wald, Kenneth D. 1992. *Religion and Politics in the United States*. 2d ed. Washington: Congressional Quarterly.

Walker. Jack. 1969. "The Diffusion of Innovations among the American States." *American Political Science Review* 63: 880–99.

Wattenberg, Martin P. 1986. *The Decline of American Political Parties: 1952–1984*. Cambridge, Mass.: Harvard University Press.

Weber, Ronald E., Anne H. Hopkins, Michael L. Mezey, and Frank Munger. 1972. "Computer Simulation of State Electorates." *Public Opinion Quarterly* 36: 49–65.

Weber, Ronald E., and William R. Shaffer. 1972. "Public Opinion and American State Policy Making." *Midwest Journal of Political Science* 16: 633–99.

Weissberg, Robert. 1976. *Public Opinion and Popular Government*. Englewood Cliffs, N.J.: Prentice-Hall.

Winters, Richard F. 1976. "Partisan Control and Policy Change." *American Journal of Political Science* 20: 597–636.

Wittman, Donald. 1983. "Candidate Motivation: A Synthesis of Alternatives." *American Political Science Review* 77: 142–57.

———. 1990. "Spatial Strategies when Candidates Have Policy Preferences." In James M. Enelow and Melvin J. Hinich (eds.), *Advances in the Spatial Theory of Voting*. New York: Cambridge University Press.

Wright, Gerald C. 1974. *Electoral Choice in America*. Chapel Hill: Institute for Research in Social Sciences, University of North Carolina.

———. 1976. "Linear Models for Evaluating Conditional Relationships." *American Journal of Political Science* 20: 349–73.

———. 1977. "Contextual Models of Electoral Behavior: The Southern Wallace Vote." *American Political Science Review* 71: 497–508.

———. 1986. "Elections and the Potential for Policy Change in the U.S. House of Representatives." In Gerald C. Wright, Leroy N. Rieselbach and Lawrence C. Dodd (eds.), *Congress and Policy Change*, pp. 94–119. New York: Agathon.

———. 1989. "Policy Voting in the U.S. Senate: Who Is Represented?" *Legislative Studies Quarterly* 14: 465–86.

Wright, Gerald C., and Michael Berkman. 1986. "Candidates and Policy in United States Senate Elections." *American Political Science Review* 80: 567–88.

References

Wright, Gerald C., Robert S. Erikson, and John P. McIver. 1985. "Measuring State Partisanship and Ideology with Survey Data." *Journal of Politics* 47: 469–89.

———. 1987. "Public Opinion and Policy Liberalism in the American States." *American Journal of Political Science* 31: 980–1001.

Index

Index

Index

Shapiro, Robert Y., 2, 5–6
Sharkansky, Ira, 9n, 48, 75n, 151–2, 232, 239
Shepard, W. Bruce, 9
short-term partisan forces, 178–9, 193–8, 208–11
Sigelman, Lee, 9, 75, 151
Silberberg, Eugene, 3n
simulation
    of state gubernatorial election results, 194–7
    of state opinions, 7, 8, 61
    of state presidential election results, 182–94
    of state U.S. senate election results, 197–8
Sinclair, Barbara, 5
size of place, see urbanism
Smith, Roland, 9, 75
Smith, Tom W., 214
socioeconomic variables
    and political attitudes, 9–10, 82–4, 229–31
    and public policy, 8–10, 82–9
Sorauf, Frank J., 115
Soule, John W., 103n
South, the
    conservative policies of, 235–7
    Democratic partisanship of, 217–20
    increasing conservatism of, 224–6
    and representation process, 138, 146–9
spending, state, 232–8
Squire, Peverill, 179
states
    as contextual variables, 47–8, 69
    estimates of state level variables, 15, 16, 40, 54, 67, 78, 105
    as research laboratories, 5–6
Stimson, James A., 5, 214
Stipak, Brian, 62
Stokes, Donald E., 3n, 4–5, 169, 178–179, 247
Stonecash, Jeff, 9, 152
Sullivan, John L., 103n
Swank, Duane, 120
Swansbrough, Robert H., 28

tax policy, 76–7, 85, 90
Tedin, Kent L., 1, 90
Texas, 114
Tindall, George Brown, 224n
Tompkins, Mark E., 179
Treadway, Jack M., 5–6
Tufte, Edward, 120
Turner, Charles F., 214

union membership, 63–4, 70n
urbanism
    and policy liberalism, 82–9
    and political attitudes, 50, 51, 60, 70n, 83–4, 229–31
Uslaner, Eric M., 9, 98, 127
Utah, 41, 62

validity, definitions, 24–5
van Arnhem, J., 120
Verba, Sidney, 152, 248, 252
Vermont, 113
Volgy, Thomas, 5

Waksberg, Joseph, 13, 215
Wald, Kenneth D., 65n
Walker, Jack, 73, 75
Washington, 41
Wattenberg, Martin P., 96
wealth, see income
Weber, Ronald E., 7, 62, 98, 127
Weissberg, Robert, 2
Welch, Susan, 152
welfare, see Aid to Families with Dependent Children, spending, state
West Virginia, 55
Winters, Richard, 3, 8, 9, 121
Wisconsin, 114, 217n
Wittman, Donald, 3, 103n
Woods, Harriet, 199
Wright, Gerald C., 5, 8n, 14, 70, 82n, 98, 103n, 109, 111, 157, 179, 249, 251

Zingale, Nancy H., 5
Zeller, Richard A., 21

Printed in the United States
841100003B